The media's watching ~~Vault.~~ S0-AXB-030
Here's a sampling of our coverage.

"Unflinching, fly-on-the-wall reports... No one gets past company propaganda to the nitty-gritty inside dope better than these guys."
— *Knight-Ridder newspapers*

"Best way to scope out potential employers...Vault.com has sharp insight into corporate culture and hiring practices."
— *Yahoo! Internet Life*

"Vault.com has become a de facto Internet outsourcer of the corporate grapevine."
— *Fortune*

"For those hoping to climb the ladder of success, [Vault.com's] insights are priceless."
— *Money.com*

"Another killer app for the Internet."
— *New York Times*

"If only the company profiles on the top sites would list the 'real' information... Sites such as Vault.com do this, featuring insights and commentary from employees and industry analysts."
— *The Washington Post*

"A rich repository of information about the world of work."
— *Houston Chronicle*

VAULT
> the insider career network™

challenging

From left to right:

– Sylvia Bass, VP, Rewards Business Development,
  Consumer Card Services

– Bruce Shelton, Manager of Corporate Card Marketing
  American Express Establishment Services

– Tareef Shawa, VP, Business Development, Global Travel

– Rachel Sha, Director
  American Express U.S. Risk Management

What happens when great thinkers and doers from a variety of backgrounds come together? Typically, success is what happens. Winning in today's business world requires an intrinsic understanding of the unique needs and goals of very diverse customers in widespread markets. At American Express, the connection between the *diversity of our workforce* and our overall performance quality is clearly valued. We know it's *the link that enables us to drive competitive advantages* in the financial services industry.

For us, hiring *talented, dedicated go-getters* makes the measura difference. We seek people who thrive on questioning tradition approaches and redefining accepted standards. Here, the sta quo is always up for debate, and our team members are encouraged to share their *distinct perspectives and ideas* to help us reach our goal of becoming the world's most respec service brand.

A multi-billion dollar leader with diversified, global busine operations, including travel, corporate and credit services a well as banking, insurance and accounting practices, *Americ Express is a happening place for ambitious people seekin exciting challenges!* To learn more about our dynamic company and our progressive initiatives in support of our diverse workforce, visit us at:

diversified financial services opportunities
around the corner
& around the world

www.americanexpress.com/jobs

American Express is an equal opportunity employer

VAULT GUIDE TO
THE TOP 50
FINANCE
EMPLOYERS

VAULT GUIDE TO
THE TOP 50 FINANCE EMPLOYERS

CHRIS PRIOR AND DEREK LOOSVELT

Library of Congress CIP Data is available.

ISBN 1-58131-164-8

Printed in the United States of America

ACKNOWLEDGEMENTS

Vault would like to acknowledge the assistance and support of Matt Doull, Ahmad Al-Khaled, Lee Black, Eric Ober, Hollinger Ventures, Tekbanc, New York City Investment Fund, American Lawyer Media, Globix, Hoover's, Glenn Fischer, Mark Fernandez, Ravi Mhatre, Carter Weiss, Ken Cron, Ed Somekh, Isidore Mayrock, Zahi Khouri, Sana Sabbagh and other Vault investors. Many thanks to our loving families and friends.

This book could not have been written without the extraordinary efforts of Suzanne Baran, Hans H. Chen, Jayne Feld, Anita Kapadia, Hal Levey, Marcy Lerner, Tom Lott, Brook Moshan, Rob Schipano, Ed Shen, Elizabeth Silver, Tyya N. Turner and Jake Wallace. Thanks also to Hussam Hamadeh, Samer Hamadeh, Todd Kuhlman, Mark Oldman, Kristy Sisko and Dan Stanco.

Special thanks to all of the recruiting coordinators and corporate communications representatives who helped with the book. We appreciate your patience with our repeated requests and tight deadlines.

The Vault Guide to the *Top 50 Finance Employers* is dedicated to the finance professionals who took time out of their busy schedules to be interviewed or complete our survey

who benefits most

from your hard work?

That's the question that makes many people consider working for themselves. The freedoms of self-employment offer great choices that affect the quality of your life and the lives of others. You choose with whom you want to work and the level of success to which you aspire. With hard work, your income can be a reflection of your energy, commitment and drive—not someone else's expectations.

With 145 years of industry experience, Northwestern Mutual understands the importance of its Financial Representatives making the right self-employment choices—because success begins with choosing the path that's right for you.

Take the online Self-Employment Screen and explore the opportunities that are most suitable to your personality. Log on to http://careers.nmfn.com and explore "Begin Now."

Send resume to:
resume@northwesternmutual.com

Northwestern Mutual
FINANCIAL NETWORK®

Are you there yet?®

www.nmfn.com

THE VAULT PRESTIGE RANKINGS   5

OVERVIEW OF FINANCE INDUSTRIES   15

THE JOBS   31

Investment Banking

Investment Management

Commercial Banking

THE VAULT TOP 50   73

WORTH MENTIONING   301

FINANCE RECRUITERS DIRECTORY   309

APPENDIX   317

Applying for Business school?

Taking the **GMAT*** ?

Short on time to prepare?
Want more than "tricks?"

Manhattan GMAT*

The new standard in GMAT test-prep.
Designed for students applying to top schools -
who need top scores on the test.

· Nine-week advanced course with free homework help
· Private/custom instruction and online tutoring

150 West 25th Street, 10th floor

Join the experts at NYC's only test
prep firm dedicated solely to the
GMAT.

For more information or to register,
call **212-721-7400**
or visit **www.manhattangmat.com**

*GMAT is a registered trademark of the Graduate Management Admissions Council.

Introduction

It's been a hectic year for the finance industry. Since the last edition of this guide was published at the end of last summer, the industry has suffered attacks from within and without. The terrorist attacks of September 11, 2001, affected many finance firms directly, and the economic slump that followed hit the securities industry hard. The accounting industry was turned upside down by the Enron scandal. The energy trader's collapse in late 2001 was blamed in part on misleading financial statements that were approved by one of the accounting industry's leaders, Arthur Andersen. Finally, Wall Street firms are under investigation for reports issued by their research analysts. Regulators and law-enforcement agencies have charged that analysts' recommendations were influenced by potential investment-banking revenues, rather than the prospects of the companies there were covering.

Still, job seekers are expected to continue seeking work at finance firms. The Bureau of Labor Statistics predicts that the accounting field will see 10 to 20 percent job growth by 2010; the securities industry will grow by more than 20 percent. Both estimates are equal to or greater than the estimated job growth of the general economy.

Why the interest in finance jobs? For one thing, the finance industry is relatively stable. Finance firms aren't immune to layoffs (something 2001 made abundantly clear), but there are many sectors that are less cyclical than the general economy, making a job there less susceptible to an economic slump. Simple demographic trends point to increased demand for some of the services offered by finance companies. For example, the percentage of the population nearing or at the retirement age (traditionally between 65-70 years old) means that more Americans will be in the market for retirement products. That means more brokerage accounts, more 401(k)s and more IRAs — and, of course, more people to manage them.

But the greatest lure of the industry is its generous compensation. In commercial banking, entry-level jobs pay base salaries that start at $45,000 — a pretty good haul, by most standards. In investment banking, college graduates at large firms can pull down $55,000 to $65,000 in base salary, plus thousands in signing and relocation bonuses, plus yearly bonuses equal to approximately 60 to 70 percent of the base salary. All together, first-year analysts (as they're called) at Wall Street firms can make between $75,000 and $90,000. Asset management, another stable and lucrative field, isn't too shabby, either. Junior-level employees at investment management firms can pull down $40,000-$50,000 per year. Accounting firms seem to be the laggard, with base pay starting as low as $29,000. However, salaries in that industry can still grow quickly, and partners at a large firm average more than $200,000 in compensation per year.

Last year's *Guide* focused on the investment banking, asset management and commercial banking industries, as the demand for those was the greatest within the finance world. However, the Andersen/Enron case has put the spotlight on accounting, so this *Guide* will include that once-boring, now-hot field. Basically, investment banking is the business of raising money for companies through public markets. Commercial banking is the loaning of money to businesses. Investment management involves handling money and investments for both institutions and individuals. Accounting is defined as the recording, summary and reporting of relevant financial information for use by insiders and outsiders. More simply, accountants maintain financial records for use by company management, investors and potential investors.

If this is all a little confusing, don't worry. What follows is a basic guide to those industries — what they do, what separates them from the others, what it means to work in those industries — as well as trends that affect the finance industry in general. You'll also know who the players are in each industry, what their employees think about the firms and what it's like to work at these companies. You'll also find the Vault Top 50, which lists the 50 most prestigious finance firms according to Vault's independent survey of finance professionals.

A Guide to this Guide

All of our profiles follow the same basic format. Here's a guide to each entry.

Firm facts

• **Departments:** A listing of the firm's major divisions.

• **The Stats:** A listing of basic information about the firm, usually information that is available to the general public. This includes the firm's leadership (generally, the person responsible for day-to-day operations, but it can include the chairman and relevant department heads), employer type (e.g., public, private, government or non-profit), ticker symbol and exchange (if public), 2001 revenues and net income (usually only for public companies; we do have some numbers for private companies, but they're usually estimates from third-party sources. In some cases, the firm has confirmed that information.), number of employees and number of offices.

• **Key Competitors:** A listing of the firm's rivals. Size, business lines, geography and reputation are taken into account when evaluating rivals. We tried to limit every firm to four competitors at the most.

• **Uppers and Downers:** The best and worst things, respectively, about working at the firm. Uppers and downers are taken from the opinions of insiders based on our surveys and interviews.

• **Employment Contact:** The person (or people) that the firm identifies as its contact(s) for submitting resumes or employment inquiries. We've supplied as much information as possible, including names, titles, mailing addresses, phone or fax numbers, e-mail addresses and web sites. Since companies process resumes differently, the amount of information may vary. For example, some firms ask that all employment-related inquiries be sent to a central processing office while other firms mandate that all job applications be submitted through the company web site. We provided as much information as possible and have attempted to verify the information with the firms.

• **The Buzz:** When conducting our prestige survey, we asked respondents to include comments about the firms they were rating. We collected a sampling of these comments in The Buzz. We tried to include quotes that represented the common outside perceptions of a given firm. The quotes may not always reflect what insiders say in our surveys and interviews, but we think The Buzz is a way of gauging outside opinion of a company.

The profiles

There are two types of profiles in this book. Firms ranked in the Top 25 received longer, more in-depth profiles. Firms 26-50 are shorter but similar to the Top 25 profiles. There's also a short "Worth Mentioning" section that has three companies that didn't make our rankings but are still worthy of inclusion and study. TD Securities and Federated Investors are worthy competitors in their respective industries; Arthur Andersen is worth mentioning for obvious reasons. Virtually all profiles are divided into three sections: The Scoop, Getting Hired and Our Survey Says; (some profiles have only Scoop and Getting Hired sections).

- **The Scoop:** The company's history, a description of the business, recent clients or deals and other significant developments.

- **Getting Hired:** An overview of the company's hiring process, including a description of campus recruiting procedures, the number of interviews, the types of people that you meet (e.g., peers vs. supervisors), the kinds of questions asked and other tips on getting hired.

- **Our Survey Says:** Quotes from surveys and interviews done with employees or recent employees at the company. Includes information on culture, pay, hours, training, diversity, offices, dress code and other things significant to job-seekers.

THE VAULT PRESTIGE RANKINGS

**Deloitte
& Touche**

be there

METHODOLOGY

In a year that's seen so many changes, it seems fitting that Vault's finance career guide should be radically different, as well. Last year's edition of this book rated 25 finance firms in three industries: investment banking, investment management and commercial banking. This guide — the *Vault Guide to the Top 50 Finance Employers* — has (obviously) expanded to rank 50 companies. Also, we've thrown accounting firms in the mix.

Accounting was added for several reasons. First, the skills required are similar to those in the other finance industries, and recruiters in the field often target the same audience as for the other sectors. More importantly, accounting has been a hot field, largely due to the role of accounting firms in corporate bankruptcy and fraud cases. Anecdotal evidence suggests that more people are taking an interest in the field, both as a possible vocation and as a key aspect of the corporate world.

Vault invited 62 companies in these fields to participate in our survey. Firms were asked to distribute the survey, which was done online, to relevant employees. The survey consisted of questions about life within the firm and a prestige rating. Participants were asked to rate companies with which they were familiar on a scale of 1-10, with 10 being the most prestigious. They were not allowed to rate their own employer.

Seven companies — CIBC World Markets, Houlihan Lokey Howard & Zukin, Jefferies & Company, Lehman Brothers, Salomon Smith Barney, TD Securities and UBS Warburg — agreed to participate. All surveys were completely anonymous. For those companies that refused our request, Vault sought contacts at the firm through other sources. Those finance professional took the same survey as the employees at firms that participated.

All told, 330 finance professionals filled out Vault's 2002 finance employee survey from February 2002 through May 2002. Vault averaged the prestige scores for each firm and ranked them in order, with the highest average score being our No. 1 firm. That firm, for the second year in a row, was investment bank Goldman Sachs. New York-based Goldman received a score of 8.905, almost a half a point more than competitor Morgan Stanley (8.434), which also came in second last year.

Seven out of the top 10 companies are considered investment banks (that is, most of their business falls under traditional investment banking functions).

One, J.P. Morgan Chase, is considered a hybrid as it also has significant operations in commercial banking. Two of the top 10 are investment managers. For the top 50 as a whole, 24 companies are considered investment banks, 15 are investment managers, six are commercial banks, four are accounting firms and one is a hybrid. The highest-ranking investment manager is Fidelity Investments at No. 6 with a 7.195 prestige score. The highest-ranking accounting firm is Deloitte & Touche at No. 20 (5.783). Citigroup, the highest-rated commercial bank, is No. 12 (6.323). Profiles of all firms begin on page 73.

Note on Robertson Stephens: Investment bank Robertson Stephens, formerly a division of FleetBoston Financial, was rated No. 31 in our initial survey with a score of 4.943. In the spring of 2002 FleetBoston announced plans to sell or spin off Robertson Stephens, once a leading investment bank for the technology industry. However, FleetBoston could find no takers and the market made a public offering unrealistic. FleetBoston reportedly reached a tentative agreement to sell Robertson Stephens to its management in early July, but that deal fell through. The bank decided to close Robertson Stephens in mid-July, just a few weeks before the *Vault Guide to the Top 50 Finance Employers* went to press. Since Robertson Stephens had ceased to exist, we removed Robertson Stephens from our rankings and have no profile of the firm in this Guide. Firm No. 31 (ironically, FleetBoston, with a score of 4.844) and all firms below scored lower than Robertson Stephens.

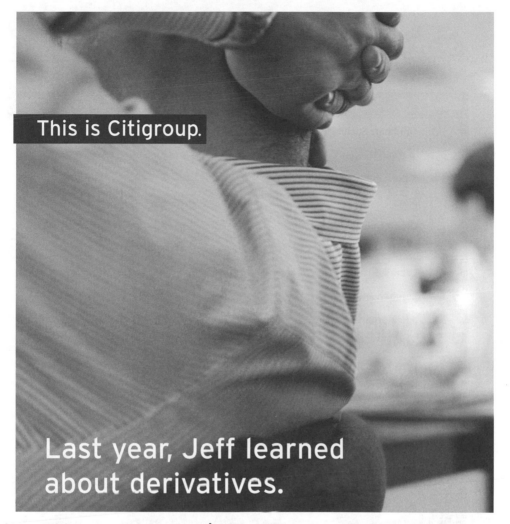

This is Citigroup.

Last year, Jeff learned
about derivatives.

This year, he traded $200 Million worth of them.

During a course in investments, something "clicked"–Jeff knew he wanted to
become a derivatives trader. A year later, he was helping to conduct some of
the biggest trades in the world. Jeff believes this could have only happened
at Citigroup. With a revolutionary business model that is quickly changing the
industry, Citigroup recruits ambitious, highly talented people and allows them
to find their own path to their potential. To find out more, come to one of our
on-campus presentations or have a look online. Who knows? It could be one of
the best investments you'll ever make. **Citigroup.com**

citigroup

Salomon Smith Barney & Citibank

The Vault 50 • 2003[†]

[The 50 most prestigious finance employers]

RANK	FIRM	SCORE	2002 RANK	HEADQUARTERS
1	Goldman Sachs	8.905	1	New York, NY
2	Morgan Stanley	8.435	2	New York, NY
3	Salomon Smith Barney	7.582	7	New York, NY
4	Merrill Lynch	7.364	4	New York, NY
5	Credit Suisse First Boston	7.324	3	New York, NY*
6	Fidelity Investments	7.195	6	Boston, MA
7	Lazard	7.132	10	New York, NY*
8	Lehman Brothers	6.881	11	New York, NY
9	J.P. Morgan Chase	6.827	5	New York, NY
10	Janus Capital	6.371	9	Denver, CO
11	UBS Warburg	6.333	18	New York, NY*
12	Citigroup	6.323	15	New York, NY
13	Deutsche Bank	6.263	16	New York, NY*
14	Putnam Investments	6.191	8	Boston, MA
15	BlackRock	6.184	NR	New York, NY
16	Vanguard Group	6.100	12	Malvern, PA
17	Pequot Capital Management	6.027	13	Westport, CT
18	Bear Stearns	5.965	25	New York, NY
19	Dresdner Kleinwort Wasserstein	5.857	NR	New York, NY
20	Deloitte & Touche	5.783	NR**	New York, NY
21	Ernst & Young	5.583	NR**	New York, NY
22	T. Rowe Price	5.561	14	Baltimore, MD
23	PricewaterhouseCoopers	5.496	NR**	New York, NY
24	Gabelli Asset Management	5.460	21	Rye, NY
25	Thomas Weisel Partners	5.344	23	San Francisco, CA

*U.S. Headquarters
**Accounting firms were not rated in the 2001 survey
† Vault rankings span two calendar years; they are dated as the second of these years. For example, our 2003 rankings are based on surveys completed in summer 2002 and apply to the 2002-2003 academic year.

RANK	FIRM	SCORE	2002 RANK	HEADQUARTERS
26	Alliance Capital Management	5.330	20	New York, NY
27	KPMG	5.304	NR**	New York, NY
28	CIBC World Markets	5.089	NR	New York, NY
29	Allen & Company	5.068	NR	New York, NY
30	SG Cowen	4.973	NR	New York, NY
31	FleetBoston Financial	4.844	NR	Boston, MA
32	Banc of America Securities	4.833	NR	New York, NY
33	Houlihan Lokey Howard & Zukin	4.699	NR	Los Angeles, CA
34	Charles Schwab	4.685	19	San Francisco, CA
35	Bank of America	4.661	NR	Charlotte, NC
36	WR Hambrecht + Co.	4.539	NR	San Francisco, CA
37	TIAA-CREF	4.485	NR	New York, NY
38	CalPERS	4.463	17	Sacramento, CA
39	Legg Mason	4.440	NR	Baltimore, MD
40	U.S. Bancorp Piper Jaffray	4.408	NR	Minneapolis, MN
41	Broadview International	4.370	NR	Fort Lee, NJ
42	American Century Investments	4.342	NR	Kansas City, MO
43	Franklin Resources	4.339	24	San Mateo, CA
44	The Capital Group Companies	4.318	NR	Los Angeles, CA
45	Jefferies & Company	4.256	NR	New York, NY
46	Wachovia	4.217	NR	Charlotte, NC
47	Peter J. Solomon Company	4.147	NR	New York, NY
48	Wells Fargo	4.138	NR	San Francisco, CA
49	SoundView Technology Group	4.066	NR	Old Greenwich, CT
50	The Bank of New York	4.001	NR	New York, NY

Industry Rankings

Below are charts detailing the placement of the top firms from each industry in the Top 50.

Investment Banking

RANK	FIRM	SCORE	OVERALL RANK
1	Goldman Sachs	8.905	1
2	Morgan Stanley	8.435	2
3	Salomon Smith Barney	7.582	3
4	Merrill Lynch	7.364	4
5	Credit Suisse First Boston	7.324	5
6	Lazard	7.132	7
7	Lehman Brothers	6.881	8
8	J.P. Morgan Chase	6.827	9
9	UBS Warburg	6.333	11
10	Deutsche Bank	6.263	13

Investment banks dominated the Top 50 and the Top 25. In fact, we didn't have to go beyond 13 to find the Top 10 investment banks in our survey.

Investment Management

RANK	FIRM	SCORE	OVERALL RANK
1	Fidelity Investments	7.195	6
2	Janus Capital	6.371	10
3	Putnam Investments	6.191	14
4	BlackRock	6.184	15
5	Vanguard Group	6.100	16
6	Pequot Capital Management	6.027	17
7	T. Rowe Price	5.561	22
8	Gabelli Asset Management	5.460	24
9	Alliance Capital Management	5.330	26
10	Charles Schwab	4.685	34

Though not as dominant as investment banking, investment management firms posted a strong showing in our Top 50 ranking. Eight firms were in the Top 25.

Commercial Banking

RANK	FIRM	SCORE	OVERALL RANK
1	Citigroup	6.323	12
2	FleetBoston Financial	4.844	31
3	Bank of America	4.661	35
4	Wachovia	4.217	46
5	Wells Fargo	4.138	48

Commercial banks posted a weaker showing. Only six firms in this sector made the Top 50. Here are the Top 5 commercial banks.

Accounting

RANK	FIRM	SCORE	OVERALL RANK
1	Deloitte & Touche	5.783	20
2	Ernst & Young	5.583	21
3	PricewaterhouseCoopers	5.496	23
4	KPMG	5.304	26

It was a rough year for accounting. An industry that is normally anonymous got a ton of publicity in 2001-2002, most of it bad. Whereas observers once spoke of the Big Five, thanks to the demise of Arthur Andersen, soon it will be the Big Four. Andersen was No. 59 in our survey of 61 firms, and it wouldn't have even made the top five in its field. Chicago-based Grant Thornton edged Andersen in our survey, taken before Andersen was convicted of obstruction of justice.

OVERVIEW OF THE FINANCE INDUSTRY

Too busy
signing on the dotted line
to sign off on your
new ski chalet?

A dramatically enhanced version of **TheDeal.com** is appearing on the desktops and laptops of leading dealmakers everywhere. The redesigned TheDeal.com offers a new and improved set of information tools, freeing up time for the financiers, executives, attorneys and advisers at America's top firms and corporations to get on with the business of deals. The expanded M&A, private equity, bankruptcy coverage and other critical areas present the most complete and concise source of analysis and data for today's demanding dealmakers.

Deal Extra, our premium edition of columns and commentary, is now available. For just $89* for a full year's subscription–that's only 35 cents a day–you'll receive unlimited access to insightful deal analysis, TheDeal.com's archives and special reports. Join now and lock in this low price during the launch of Deal Extra.

TOO BUSY TO GO TO YOUR CLUB?
SAVE TIME BY JOINING.

The Year in Review

September 11, 2001

In the most devastating terrorist attack in the nation's history, over 3,000 people died on September 11, 2001, when hijacked commercial airliners were crashed in New York, Washington, D.C., and Somerset County, Pa. Two of the planes, hijacked out of Boston, were flown into the two towers of the World Trade Center. Within 90 minutes, both towers collapsed, causing a final death toll of 2,823. A third plane crashed into the Pentagon, killing 189 people. A fourth plane crashed in a field southeast of Pittsburgh, killing all 44 passengers and crew.

While the victims of the attacks came from all walks of life, the finance industry was especially hard hit. Cantor Fitzgerald, one of the world's largest and most influential bond brokerages, had offices on several floors near the top of the north tower of the World Trade Center. The firm's death toll was staggering — 658 of the firm's 960 employees located in the building died in the attacks. Boutique investment bank Keefe, Bruyette & Woods lost 67 employees, mostly traders and analysts who worked in the firm's offices in the south tower. All told, over 1,500 of the people killed in the attacks worked in the finance industry.

Besides the catastrophic human toll, the attacks had severe economic consequences. On September 17, 2001, the first day of trading after the attacks, the Dow Jones Industrial Average fell 7.12 percent — a steep decline, but only the fourteenth-largest single-day percentage loss on record. Again, finance firms were disproportionately affected. Falling stock markets are bad for investment banking and investment management firms, which make their money off the fluctuations of the market. Additionally, many insurance companies had large exposure to the financial losses in the attacks. The economy was already in the middle of a mild recession, and many predicted it would get worse. Expecting a deep recession, many companies, including finance firms, tightened their belts in the fall and winter of 2001, and production fell while layoffs rose. However, the recession did not become as severe as many had feared. Still, looming over the finance industry — indeed, the whole world — is the political uncertainty that followed the attacks.

How the mighty have fallen

It's not easy to fall from grace as fast as Enron and Arthur Andersen did. But both firms, once among the most respected in their industries, are teetering at the brink of extinction, their reputations ruined, in a spectacular collapse that may lead to broad changes in corporate governance and accounting standards.

Houston, Texas-based Enron was once a high-flying energy trader, near the top of the Fortune 500. The company's stock was one of the top performers of the late 1990s, and was owned by institutional and individual investors. Naturally, while the stock was soaring, everyone was happy. The first hint of trouble came in August 2001, when CEO Jeffery Skilling resigned, citing personal reasons. Kenneth Lay, the company's chairman, took over for Skilling. Two months after Skilling's departure, the firm announced a $618 million loss for the third quarter and a $1.2 billion reduction in shareholder's equity. The sudden reversal of fortune caught the attention of the Securities and Exchange Commission and other regulators. In November 2001, Enron restated its earnings for the previous five years, wiping out approximately $586 million in earnings. The company's shares plummeted and more questions about Enron's business began to surface. In early December, Enron formally filed for bankruptcy.

The sudden collapse of Enron can largely be blamed on its reliance on off-balance sheet partnerships that took on debts and investments. The partnerships, often named after characters or other references to the "Star Wars" movie franchise, allowed the company to keep liabilities off its balance sheet. While Enron claimed the partnerships were not a part of Enron, company executives were often named as key executives of the partnerships, and debts were often guaranteed by Enron stock. In short, the relationship between Enron and the partnerships was much closer than the company initially disclosed, and Enron was directly responsible for any losses or liabilities from the partnerships. The losses should have been recorded on Enron's financial statements for years, which would have reduced the company's profits and, presumably, investor enthusiasm for the company's stock.

So how did Enron manage to slip these illegal partnerships past investors, analysts and regulators? It helped (a lot) that its auditor, Arthur Andersen, gave Enron's financial statements a clean bill of health. The Chicago-based accounting firm had been Enron's auditor since the company was formed in

1985 by the merger of two Texas energy firms. It continued as Enron's accountant and approved the partnerships even though some on the audit team had misgivings about the company's practices. Some observers felt Andersen stuck with Enron because of the large fees — $52 million in 2000 — that Enron generated for Andersen. Complicating matters was the fact that some of the fees were for consulting services. The possible conflict of interest in offering auditing and consulting work to the same client had been an issue in the professional services industry for years.

When questions about Enron's business began to surface, investigators began to subpoena Andersen's records related to the audit. Andersen later admitted that some records had been intentionally destroyed — even after they were subpoenaed. The admission put Andersen on the spot. The Department of Justice began an obstruction of justice investigation. Andersen tried to negotiate a settlement with the DOJ, but none could be reached. In March 2002, the DOJ unsealed an indictment against Arthur Andersen alleging one count of obstructing justice in trying to destroy its Enron records. After more unsuccessful negotiations, the firm's obstruction of justice trial began in Houston in May 2002.

The firm claimed that the document destruction cited in the document was isolated, confined to its Houston office. It implicated David Duncan, the partner in charge of the Enron account, who was let go by the firm in January 2002. The firm said Duncan initiated the document destruction without the consent of the firm's senior partners. Duncan, who pled guilty to obstruction in exchange for his testimony, claimed the shredding was done in keeping with the firm's document-retention policy and with the knowledge of firm lawyers. The jury disagreed, and in early June 2002 Arthur Andersen was found guilty of obstruction of justice. Unless the verdict is overturned on appeal, Andersen will exit the auditing business in August 2002.

The final effects of the Andersen case have yet to be revealed. It's possible that Andersen, despite the damage to its reputation and the lost clients, affiliates and partners, can still hang on as a player in the professional services field. However, it's also possible that the firm could fold entirely or be bought out by a competitor after the firm's legal woes are resolved. Another scenario: a restructured Andersen is relegated to a lesser role in the accounting field.

Whatever happens to Andersen, the accounting field has already been affected by the Enron mess. After the fall of Enron, pressure on professional services firms to separate their accounting and consulting practices increased. PricewaterhouseCoopers and Deloitte & Touche, the two Big Five firms that hadn't already done so, agreed in early 2002 to split the two units and avoid potential conflicts of interest.

The larger issue is that of accounting oversight. Accounting firms have historically been self-policing, with little government regulation. There were some calls to end that autonomy and monitor the way accounting firms do business and how they audit public companies' financial statements. It's likely that some kind of reform will be mandated.

Analyze this

The Enron collapse was one incident of several that reduced investors' confidence in the financial markets. Other accounting scandals of lesser magnitude (like Global Crossing and Worldcom, to name a few) shook investor confidence. The uneasiness spread beyond the accounting field. In April 2002, New York State Attorney General Eliot Spitzer announced an investigation into the research practices at bulge bracket firm Merrill Lynch, alleging that research analysts allowed potential investment-banking fees to influence the rating given to companies covered by the firm. Spitzer cited e-mails written by member of the firm's Internet research group that were seized during the investigation. Stocks being touted by the company were panned in the e-mail; Spitzer cited examples where Merrill Lynch employees called certain stocks "junk" and "crap." Though Merrill insisted the e-mails were taken out of context, the firm later agreed to a $100 million settlement, saying that the cost of litigation and damage to the firm's reputation would be greater. The firm also made changes to its research group, removing links between investment-banking fees and analyst compensation, disclosing investment-banking relationships in research reports and installing a compliance monitor to oversee the research department.

The investigation hasn't stopped at Merrill, though. Salomon Smith Barney and its star telecom analyst, Jack Grubman, faced a similar probe. At issue is Grubman's relationship with Global Crossing, the telecom company that restated its earnings after questions about its accounting. Spitzer alleged that Grubman was too close to Global Crossing to be objective, even going so far as to advise the firm on potential transactions. Spitzer is looking into whether

Grubman's compensation was tied to his role as adviser instead of his work as an analyst. While Salomon Smith Barney has denied wrongdoing, it voluntarily adopted the reforms agreed to by Merrill Lynch.

Other firms, and other states, have become involved in the probe. Spitzer and other state attorneys general have split up the investment-banking industry, with states agreeing to limit their probes only to certain firms. While the final financial cost is difficult to predict, it's likely that other firms will adopt practices similar to Merrill Lynch's in order to fend off potential probes by state and federal authorities.

What's What?
Industry Overviews

Investment Banking

Investment banking is the business of raising money for companies. Companies need capital in order to grow their business; they turn to investment banks to sell securities to investors — either public or private — to raise this capital. These securities come in the form of stocks or bonds.

Generally, an investment bank is comprised of the following areas:

Corporate finance

The bread and butter of a traditional investment bank, corporate finance generally performs two different functions: 1) mergers and acquisitions advisory and 2) underwriting. On the mergers and acquisitions (M&A) advising side of corporate finance, bankers assist in negotiating and structuring a merger between two companies. If, for example, a company wants to buy another firm, then an investment bank will help finalize the purchase price, structure the deal and generally ensure a smooth transaction. The underwriting function within corporate finance involves raising capital for a client. In the investment-banking world, capital can be raised by selling either stocks or bonds to investors.

Sales

Sales is another core component of the investment bank. Salespeople take the form of: 1) the classic retail broker, 2) the institutional salesperson or 3) the private client service representative. Brokers develop relationships with individual investors and sell stocks and stock advice to the average Joe. Institutional salespeople develop business relationships with large institutional investors. Institutional investors are those who manage large groups of assets, like pension funds or mutual funds. Private Client Service (PCS) representatives lie somewhere between retail brokers and institutional salespeople, providing brokerage and money management services for extremely wealthy individuals. Salespeople make money through commissions on trades made through their firms.

Trading

Traders also provide a vital role for the investment bank. Traders facilitate the buying and selling of stock, bonds or other securities, either by carrying an inventory of securities for sale or by executing a given trade for a client. Traders deal with transactions large and small and provide liquidity (the ability to buy and sell securities) for the market. (This is often called making a market.) Traders make money by purchasing securities and selling them at a slightly higher price. This price differential is called the "bid-ask spread."

Research

Research analysts follow stocks and bonds and make recommendations on whether to buy, sell or hold those securities. Stock analysts (known as equity analysts) typically focus on one industry and will cover up to 20 companies' stocks at any given time. Some research analysts work on the fixed-income side and will cover a particular segment, such as high-yield bonds or U.S. Treasury bonds. Salespeople within the I-bank utilize research published by analysts to convince their clients to buy or sell securities through their firm. Corporate finance bankers rely on research analysts to be experts in the industry in which they are working. Reputable research analysts can generate substantial corporate finance business and substantial trading activity and thus are an integral part of any investment bank.

Syndicate

The hub of the investment-banking wheel, syndicate provides a vital link between salespeople and corporate finance. Syndicate exists to facilitate the placing of securities in a public offering, a knock-down, drag-out affair between and among buyers of offerings and the investment banks managing the process. In a corporate or municipal debt deal, syndicate also determines the allocation of bonds.

Investment Management

Investment management, also known as asset management, is a straightforward business. A client entrusts his money to an asset manager, who then invests it to meet the client's objectives. Still, outside of the relatively small circle of asset managers, the profession is little understood.

Asset managers have many potential career paths ahead of them. Asset managers who work for mutual funds, for example, manage money for retail clients, while asset managers at investment banks often invest money for institutional investors, like companies or municipalities. Asset managers can also work for hedge funds, which combine outside capital with capital contributed by the partners of the fund and invest the money (using complex and sometimes risky techniques) with the goal of receiving extraordinary gains.

Insiders say that investment management is a misunderstood field. "So many people think it's investment banking; they think it's capital markets," says Michael Weinstock, a recruiter with Manhattan-based Advisors Search Group. Essentially, says Weinstock, "The industry is built around people who would like to have their money managed, whether it's for pension funds, 401(k) plans, endowments, foundations, high-worth individuals, families or trusts." Investment management relies on customers who feel comfortable "giving money to a professional and saying, 'You're on the pulse of the market. Watch my money for me. Manage it for me.' [Investment managers] have the autonomy to do this without clearing every trade with our clients."

Buy side versus sell side

To manage the assets under their purview, investment managers buy stocks, bonds and other financial products from salespeople at investment banks, who are on what is called the "sell side." Because sell-siders earn commissions on every trade they facilitate, they provide research and ideas to the buy side — along with perks like prime seats to sporting events, sold-out concerts and expensive dinners at fancy restaurants — in hopes of making their securities look especially appealing. "In general, if the sell-side person is with you, there's no limit on what he can spend," says an insider at Lazard, an international investment bank and money manager.

Back on the "buy side," asset management firms build their business around supporting the people who manage portfolios, including analysts, administrative support staff and marketers who drum up the business and educate clients about their investments.

Although asset management firms exist virtually everywhere there's money to invest, New York and Boston are buy-side centers. The largest firms employ several hundred professionals to manage total assets upwards of hundreds of billions of dollars, covering both institutional and individual clients. Smaller shops may employ three or four professionals to handle $300 to $800 million in institutional money. Firms serving high-wealth clients use about the same number of people to manage slightly less money. Major firms also have roots in Los Angeles, San Francisco and Chicago. Other cities considered up-and-coming include Baltimore, Minneapolis, Atlanta, Denver, Dallas, Fort Worth and San Diego.

Commercial Banking

"Neither a borrower nor a lender be," Polonius advises Laertes in *Hamlet*. Good thing commercial banks haven't taken Shakespearean bromides to heart. (It didn't get Polonius anywhere, either.) Commercial banks, unlike investment banks, generally act as lenders, putting forth their own money to support businesses as opposed to investment advisors who rely on other folks — buyers of stocks and bonds — to pony up cash. This distinction, enshrined by fundamental banking laws in place since the 1930s, has led to noticeable cultural differences (exaggerated by stereotype) between commercial and investment bankers.

Commercial bankers (deservedly or not) have a reputation for being less aggressive, more risk-averse and simply not as mean as investment bankers. Commercial bankers also don't command the eye-popping salaries and elite prestige that I-bankers receive.

There is a basis for the stereotype. Commercial banks carefully screen borrowers because the banks are investing huge sums of their own money in companies that must remain healthy enough to make regular loan payments for decades. Investment bankers, on the other hand, can make their fortunes in one day by skimming off some of the money raised in a stock offering or invested into an acquisition. While a borrower's subsequent business decline can damage a commercial bank's bottom line, a stock that plummets after an offering has no effect on the investment bank that managed its IPO.

We'll take your money

Commercial bankers make money by their legal charter to take deposits from businesses and consumers. To gain the confidence of these depositors, commercial banks offer government-sponsored guarantees on these deposits on amounts up to $100,000. But to get FDIC guarantees, commercial banks must follow a myriad of regulations (and hire regulators to manage them). Many of these guidelines were set up in the Glass-Steagall Act of 1933, which was meant to separate the activities of commercial and investment banks. Glass-Steagall included a restriction on the sale of stocks and bonds (investment banks, which could not take deposits, were exempt from banking laws and free to offer more speculative securities offerings). Deregulation — especially the Financial Services Modernization Act of 1999 — and consolidation in the banking industry over the past decade have weakened these traditional barriers.

The lending train

The typical commercial banking process is fairly straightforward. The lending cycle starts with consumers depositing savings or businesses depositing sales proceeds at the bank. The bank, in turn, puts aside a relatively small portion of the money for withdrawals and to pay for possible loan defaults. The bank then loans the rest of the money to companies in need of capital to pay for, say, a new factory or an overseas venture. A commercial bank's customers can range from the dry cleaner on the corner to a multinational conglomerate. For very large clients, several commercial banks may band together to issue "syndicated loans" of truly staggering size.

Commercial banks lend money at interest rates that are largely determined by the Federal Reserve Board (currently governed by the bespectacled Alan Greenspan). Along with lending money that they have on deposit from clients, commercial banks lend out money that they have received from the Fed. The Fed loans out money to commercial banks, that in turn lend it to bank customers in a variety of forms — standard loans, mortgages, and so on. Besides its ability to set a baseline interest rate for all loans, the Fed also uses its lending power to equalize the economy. To prevent inflation, the Fed raises the interest rate it charges for the money it loans to banks, slowing down the circulation of money and the growth of the economy. To encourage economic growth, the Fed will lower the interest rate it charges banks.

Making money by moving money

Take a moment to consider how a bank makes its money. Commercial banks in the U.S. earn 5 to 14 percent interest on most of their loans. As commercial banks typically only pay depositors 1 percent — if anything — on checking accounts and 2 to 3 percent on savings accounts, they make a tremendous amount of money in the difference between the cost of their funds (1 percent for checking account deposits) and the return on the funds they loan (5 to 14 percent).

Accounting

Is accounting the new hot field? It wasn't too long ago that question would have been a joke, at best. Accounting has always been thought of as a dry, dull profession, practiced by skilled but boring bean counters obsessed with making the numbers line up. Then came Enron. The Houston, Texas-based energy firm collapsed in late 2001, losing hundreds of millions of dollars for investors. While there were many factors that led to the Enron crisis, one was the work of Arthur Andersen, the accounting firm that audited Enron's financial statements as required under United States securities law. Suddenly, accounting was the talk of the business world, and interest in the field by lay people and job seekers skyrocketed.

So, what exactly is accounting, and why do we need it? Put simply, accounting is a system by which economic information is identified, recorded, summarized and reported for the use of decision makers. This system feeds back information to organizations and individuals, who use the data to reshape their environment. More specifically, publicly reported accounting numbers influence the distribution of scarce resources. The economic effects of reported accounting numbers directly affect the transfer of resources among entities and individuals. It aids in decision making by showing when and where money has been spent and commitments have been made, by evaluating performance, and by indicating the financial implications of choosing one strategy over another. It also helps predict the future consequences of decisions and highlights current weaknesses and opportunities. As such, accounting can be considered the language of business.

Accounting can be defined in three ways: one, as a service activity (provides quantitative financial information that helps decision making regarding the use of resources in business and non-business entities); two, as a descriptive/analytical discipline (identifies events and transactions that characterize economic activity and describe the financial condition and operating results of a specific economic entity); and three, as an information system (collects and communicates economic information about a business entity to a wide variety of persons). All three of these definitions are underscored by the key qualitative characteristics of accounting: relevance, timeliness, reliability, consistency and comparability.

Financial accounting

Financial accounting addresses the needs of decision makers external to the organization. These decision makers can include credit and equity investors, suppliers, lenders, government agencies and regulatory bodies, special interest groups, labor unions, consumer groups and the general public. The financial accounting process culminates in the preparation of financial reports relative to the enterprise as a whole that help answer the following questions about a firm's financial success: What is the financial position of the firm on a given day? How well did the firm do during a given period?

Accountants address these questions via financial reporting by preparing the three primary financial statements: balance sheet, income statement and statement of cash flows. The balance sheet shows the position of the firm on a given day, most commonly the last day of a quarter or year; as such, it is commonly referred to as an entity's financial "snapshot." The income statement and statement of cash flows show cumulative performance over time, most commonly an entire quarter or full year.

Management accounting

Managerial accounting is the field of accounting that serves internal decision makers, such as top executives, college deans, hospital administrators and people at other management levels within an organization. It involves the identification, measurement, accumulation, analysis, preparation, interpretation and communication of financial information. Decision makers use the information to plan, evaluate and control within an organization and to assure appropriate use of, and accountability for, its resources.

THE JOBS

Investment Banking

By far, investment banking careers are the most coveted in the finance industry. What is it that investment bankers do? Employees in the industry's four groups — corporate finance, sales and trading, research, and syndicate — have very different roles.

Corporate Finance

Stuffy bankers?

The stereotype of the corporate finance department is stuffy, arrogant, white, male MBAs who frequent golf courses and talk on cell-phones incessantly. While this stereotype isn't completely true, corporate finance remains the most white-shoe department in the typical investment bank. The atmosphere in corporate finance is, unlike that in sales and trading, often quiet and reserved. Junior bankers sit separated by cubicles, quietly crunching numbers hour after hour after hour.

Depending on the firm, corporate finance can also be a tough place to work, with unforgiving bankers and extremely high expectations of performance. Stories of analyst abuse abound, and some bankers come down hard on new analysts to scare and intimidate them. The lifestyle for corporate finance professionals can be a killer. In fact, many corporate finance workers find that they literally dedicate their lives to the job. It is not uncommon for analysts and associates to pull back-to-back all-nighters; many say that their personal relationships suffer. Fortunately, these long hours pay remarkable dividends in the form of six-figure salaries and huge year-end bonuses.

Bankers tend to be highly intelligent, motivated and confident. Money is important to corporate bankers, and many work in the field in the hopes of retiring early.

The deal team

Investment bankers generally work in deal teams that, depending on the size of a deal, vary somewhat in makeup. Because titles and roles really do not change between underwriting and M&A, we have included both in this explanation. In fact, at most smaller firms, underwriting and transaction advisory functions are not separated, and bankers typically pitch whatever business they can scout out within their industry sector.

Analysts

Analysts are the grunts in the corporate finance world. They often toil endlessly with little thanks, relatively low pay (when calculated on an hourly basis) and barely enough free time to sleep four hours a night. Typically hired directly out of top undergraduate universities, this crop of bright, highly motivated kids does the financial modeling and basic entry-level duties associated with any corporate finance deal.

Modeling every night until 2 a.m. and not having much of a social life proves to be unbearable for some analysts, and after two years, many analysts leave the industry. Unfortunately, employers recognize the transient nature of analysts and work them to the bone. The unfortunate analyst who screws up or talks back too much may find himself subject to particular torture. Such disfavored analysts are seldom called to work on live transactions, and do menial work or just put together pitchbooks all the time.

Location has a big influence on first-year analyst pay. In New York City, pay for first-year analysts often reaches $45,000 to $60,000 per year, with an annual bonus of approximately $30,000. While this seems to be a lot for a 22-year-old with an undergrad degree, it's not a great deal if you consider that analysts routinely work more than 80 hours a week. There are some (albeit slight) advantages to this grueling schedule: Analysts often get free dinner while working late, and the lack of free time to spend money means most analysts can save a fair amount.

At regional firms, pay typically is 20 percent less than that of their New York counterparts. At the same time, regional analysts often work shorter hours and live in areas where the cost of living is much lower. Be wary, however, of the occasional small regional firm that pays at the low end of the scale but still demands New York City hours. While the salary generally doesn't increase much for second-year analysts, the bonus can double for those second-years with demonstrated high performance. At this level, bonuses depend mostly on an analyst's contribution, attitude and work ethic, not the overall performance of the company.

Associates

Much like analysts, associates work very hard, up to 100 hours a week and rarely less than 80. Associates stress over pitchbooks and models all night long and become true experts in financial modeling on Excel. These tasks aren't entirely unlike the typical responsibilities of the analyst. Unlike analysts, however, associates gain exposure to clients more quickly. Most importantly, they're not quite at the bottom of the totem pole. Associates quickly learn to play quarterback and hand off menial modeling work and research projects to analysts.

Associates, who typically come straight from top MBA programs, usually only have a summer's worth of experience in corporate finance. They must learn the business (almost) from the beginning. The overall level of business sophistication an MBA possesses, however, makes a tremendous difference, and associates quickly earn the luxury of more complicated work and better bonuses.

Associates are much better paid than analysts. They typically start in the $80,000 range, and bonuses normally hit $25,000 in the first six months. (At most firms, associates start in August and get what's called a "stub bonus" in January.) Newly minted MBAs benefit from signing bonuses and forgivable loans as well, especially on Wall Street. These can add up to another $25,000 to $30,000, depending on the firm, providing total compensation of up to $130,000.

Vice presidents

Upon attaining the position of vice president, those in corporate finance enter the realm of real bankers. The lifestyle becomes much more manageable once the associate moves up to VP. On the plus side, weekends free up, all-nighters drop off and the general level of responsibility increases — VPs are the ones telling analysts to stay late on Friday nights. In the office, VPs manage the financial modeling/pitchbook production process in the office. On the negative side, the wear and tear of traveling that accompanies banker responsibilities can be difficult.

As a VP, one begins to handle client relationships and thus spends much more time on the road than analysts or associates. You can look forward to being on the road at least three to four days per week, usually visiting clients and potential clients. Don't forget about closing dinners (to celebrate completed deals), industry conferences (to drum up potential business and build a solid network within an industry) and, of course, roadshows. VPs are perfect candidates to baby-sit company management on roadshows.

The formula for paying bankers varies dramatically from firm to firm. Some adhere to rigid formulas based on how much business a banker brings in, while others pay based on a subjective allocation of corporate finance profits. No matter how compensation is structured, however, when business is slow, bonuses taper off dramatically. For most bankers, typical salaries may range from $100,000 to $200,000 per year, but bonuses can be significantly greater. Total packages for VPs on Wall Street often hit over the $500,000 level in the first year — and pay can skyrocket from there.

Directors/Managing directors

Directors and managing directors are the major players in corporate finance. Typically, MDs work their own hours, deal with clients at the highest level and disappear whenever a drafting session of a prospectus takes place, leaving this grueling work to others. MDs mostly develop and cultivate relationships with various companies in order to generate corporate finance business for the firm. MDs typically focus on one industry, develop relationships with the management teams of companies in the industry and visit these companies on a regular basis. These visits are aptly called sales calls.

Top bankers at the MD level might be pulling in bonuses of up to $1 million or more a year, but slow markets (and hence slow business) can cut that number dramatically. It is important to realize that for the most part, MDs act as relationship managers, and are essentially paid on commission. For top performers, compensation can be almost inconceivable. Superstar bankers have signed compensation deals worth tens of millions of dollars for a few years' committment.

Sales and Trading

The war zone

If you've ever been to an investment banking trading floor, you've witnessed the chaos. There's usually a lot of swearing, yelling and shouting: a pressure cooker of stress. Sometimes the floor is a quiet rumble of activity, but when the market takes a nosedive, panic ensues and the volume kicks up a notch. Traders must rely on their market instincts, and salespeople yell for bids when the market tumbles. Deciding what to buy or sell, and at what price to buy and sell, isn't easy when there's millions of dollars at stake.

However, salespeople and traders work much more reasonable hours than research analysts or corporate finance bankers. Rarely does a salesperson or trader venture into the office on a Saturday or Sunday, making the trading floor completely devoid of life on weekends.

The players

The players in the trading game depend on the firm. There are no hard and fast rules regarding whether or not one needs an MBA. The degree itself, though less applicable directly to the trading position, tends to matter beyond the trader level. Managers (heads of desks) and higher-ups are often selected from the MBA ranks.

Generally, regional I-banks hire clerks and/or trading assistants (non-MBAs) who are sometimes able to advance to a full-fledged trading job within a few years. Other banks, like Merrill Lynch and others on Wall Street, hire analysts and associates just as they do in investment banking. Thus a trading analyst on Wall Street does a stint of two or three years before going back to business school, and the associate position begins after one earns his or her MBA. The ultimate job in trading is to become a full-fledged trader or a manager of a trading desk. Here we break out the early positions into those more common at regional I-banks and those more common on Wall Street.

Entry-level positions

Regional Frameworks — Traditional Programs

Clerks: The bottom rung of the ladder in trading in regional firms, clerks generally balance the books, tracking a desk or a particular trader's buy and sell transactions throughout the day. A starting point for an undergrad aiming to move up to an assistant trader role, clerks gain exposure to the trading floor environment, the traders themselves and the markets. However, clerks take messages, make copies, get coffee and are hardly respected by traders. And at bigger firms, this position can be a dead-end job: clerks may remain in these roles indefinitely, while new MBAs move into full-time trading positions or top undergrads move into real analyst jobs.

Trading Assistants: Typically filled by recent graduates of undergraduate universities, the trading assistant position is more involved in trades than the clerk position. Trading assistants move beyond staring at the computer and balancing the books to become more involved with the actual traders. Backing up accounts, relaying messages and reports to and from the floor of the NYSE and actually speaking with some accounts occasionally — these responsibilities bring trading assistants much closer to understanding how the whole biz works. Depending on the firm, some undergrads move immediately into a trading assistant position with the hope of moving into a full-time trading job.

Clerks and trading assistants at some firms are hired with the possibility of upward advancement, though promoting non-MBAs to full-time trading jobs is becoming more uncommon, even at regional firms.

Wall Street Analyst and Associate Programs

Analysts: Similar to corporate finance analysts, trading analysts at Wall Street firms typically are smart undergraduates with the desire to either become a trader or learn about the trading environment. Quantitative skills are a must for analysts, as much of their time is spent dealing with books of trades and numbers. The ability to crunch numbers in a short time is especially important on the fixed-income side. Traders often demand bond price or yield calculations with only a moment's notice, and analysts must be able to produce. After a two- to three-year stint, analysts move on to business school or go to another firm, although promotion to the associate level is much more common in trading than it is in corporate finance. Salaries mirror those paid to corporate finance analysts.

Associates: Trading associates, typically recent business school graduates, begin in either rotational programs or are hired directly onto a desk. Rotations can last anywhere from a month to a year, and are designed both to educate new MBAs on various desks and to ensure a good fit prior to placement. As in other areas of investment banks, new MBAs begin at around $80,000 in salary with about $25,000 bonus at major Wall Street banks. Second-year associate compensation also tracks closely to that of the second-year corporate finance associate. Associates move to full-fledged trading positions generally in about two to three years, but can move more quickly if they perform well and there are openings (turnover) on the desk.

Full-fledged trading positions

Block trader: These are the folks you see sitting on a desk with dozens of phone lines ringing simultaneously and four or more computer monitors blinking, with orders coming in like machine-gun fire. Typically, traders deal in active, mature markets, such as government securities, stocks, currencies and corporate bonds. Sometimes hailing from top MBA programs, and sometimes tough guys who worked their way up from the mailroom, traders historically are hired based on work ethic, attitude and street-smarts.

Sales-trader: Sales-traders essentially operate in a dual role as both salesperson and block trader. While block traders deal with huge trades and often massive inventories of stocks or bonds, sales-traders act somewhat as a go-between for salespeople and block traders and trade somewhat smaller blocks of securities. In contrast to the pure block trader, the sales-trader actually initiates calls to clients, pitches investment ideas and gives market commentary. The sales-trader keeps abreast of market conditions and research commentaries, but unlike the salesperson, does not need to know the ins and outs of every company when pitching products to clients. Salespeople must be well-versed in the companies they are pitching to clients, whereas sales-traders typically cover the highlights and the big picture. When specific questions arise, a sales-trader will often refer a client to the research analyst.

Structured product trader: At some of the biggest Wall Street firms, structured product traders deal with derivatives, a.k.a. structured products. (Derivatives are complex securities that derive their value from, or have their value contingent on, the value of other assets like stocks, bonds, commodity prices or market index values.) Because of their complexity, derivatives typically require substantial time to price and structure and so foster an environment entirely different than that encountered by a block trader who deals with heavy trading flows and intense on-the-spot pressure. Note, however, that common stock options (calls and puts) and even Treasury options trade much like any other liquid security. The pricing is fairly transparent, the securities standardized and the volume high. Low-volume, complex derivatives, such as interest rate swaps, structured repurchase agreements and credit derivatives require pricing and typically more legwork prior to trading.

Note that in trading, job titles can range from associate to VP to managing director. But the roles of a trader change little. The difference is that MDs typically manage the desks, spending their time dealing with desk issues, risk management issues and personnel issues.

Sales: the basics

Sales is a core area of any investment bank, comprising the vast majority of people and the relationships that account for a substantial portion of any investment bank's revenues. This section illustrates the divisions seen in sales today at most investment banks. Note, however, that many firms, such as Goldman Sachs, identify themselves as institutionally focused I-banks and do not even have a retail sales distribution network. Goldman does, however, maintain a solid presence in providing brokerage services to the vastly wealthy through a division called private client services (PCS for short).

Retail brokers: Some firms call them account executives and some call them financial advisors or financial consultants. Regardless of the official designations, they are still referring to your classic retail broker. The broker's job involves managing the account portfolios for individual investors — usually called retail investors. Brokers charge a commission on any stock trade and also give advice to their clients regarding stocks to buy or sell and when to buy or sell them. To get into the business, retail brokers must have an undergraduate degree and demonstrated sales skills. The Series 7 and Series 63 examinations are also required before selling commences. Having connections to people with money offers a tremendous advantage for a broker just starting out.

The players in sales

For many, institutional sales offers the best of all worlds: great pay, fewer hours than in corporate finance or research, less stress than in trading and a nice blend of travel and office work. As with traders, the hours typically follow the market, with a few tacked on at the end of the day after the market closes. Another plus for talented salespeople is that they develop relationships with key money managers. On the downside, many institutional salespeople complain that many buy-siders disregard their calls, that compensation can vary according to performance and that constantly entertaining clients can prove exhausting.

Sales assistant: This position is most often a dead-end job. It is extremely difficult to move into institutional sales without an MBA, so sales assistants take on a primarily clerical role on the desk. Handling the phones, administrative duties, message taking, letter writing — there's nothing glamorous about being an assistant.

Associates: The newly hired MBA is called an associate or sales associate. Like analogous associates in other investment banking departments, a sales associate spends a year or so in the role learning the ropes and establishing himself. Associates typically spend one to two months rotating through various desks, ensuring a solid fit between the desk and the new associate. Once the rotations end, the associate is placed on a desk and the business of building client relationships begins.

Most sales associates out of business school pull in the standard package on Wall Street: $80,000 base, plus bonuses of $25,000 in the first six months. Pay escalation in the first year depends on the bonus, which often ranges from 50 percent of salary to 90 percent of salary. Beyond that, compensation packages depend on the firm — most pay packages are based on commissions generated for the firm.

Salesperson: The associate moves into a full-fledged salesperson role extremely quickly. Within a few months on a desk, the associate begins to handle "B" accounts and gradually manages them exclusively. A salesperson's ultimate goal is the account at a huge money manager, such as Fidelity or Putnam, that trades in huge volumes on a daily basis. Therefore, a salesperson slowly moves up the account chain, yielding B accounts to younger salespeople and taking on bigger and better "A" accounts. Good salespeople make anywhere from $250,000 to beyond $1 million per year in total compensation.

Salespeople usually focus by region. For example, an institutional equity salesperson will cover all of the buy-side firms in one small region or city like New England, San Francisco or Chicago. Many salespeople cover New York, as the sheer number of money managers in the city makes for a tremendous volume of work. Salespeople work on specific desks on the trading floor next to traders. Because so much of their work overlaps, sales and trading truly go hand-in-hand.

Private client services

The private client services (PCS) job can be exhilarating, exhausting and frustrating — all at once. As a PCS representative, your job is to bring in individual accounts with at least $2 million to $3 million in assets. This involves incessantly pounding the pavement and reading the tape (market news) to find clients, followed by advising them on how to manage their wealth. PCS is a highly entrepreneurial environment. Building the book is all that matters, and managers don't care how a PCS representative spends his or her time, whether on the road, in the office or at parties — the goal is to bring in the cash. Culture-wise, therefore, one typically finds a spirited, entrepreneurial group of people, working their own hours and talking on the phone for the better part of the day. It is not uncommon for PCS pros to leave the office early on Fridays with a golf bag slung over one shoulder for a game with clients or with a few bigshots with money to invest (read: potential clients).

The growth in PCS

Just a few years ago, PCS was considered a small, unimportant aspect of investment banking. PCS guys were essentially brokers, always bothering other departments for leads and not as sophisticated as their counterparts in corporate finance or institutional sales and trading. Times have changed, however. Today, spurred by the tremendous stock market wealth that has been created over the past few years, PCS is a rapidly growing part of virtually every investment bank. While in the past, many banks essentially had no PCS division, or simply hired a few star retail brokers to be PCS representatives, Wall Street is recruiting heavily on MBA campuses today, looking for good PCS talent.

Research

If you have a brokerage account, you have likely been given research on stocks that you asked about or own. The intermediaries between companies and the buy side, corporate finance and sales and trading, research analysts form the hub of investment banks.

To the outsider, it seems that research analysts spend their time in a quiet room poring over numbers, calling companies and writing research reports. The truth is an entirely different story, involving quite a bit of selling on the phone and on the road. Analysts produce research ideas, hand them to associates and assistants and then man the phone talking to buy-side stock/bond pickers, company managers and internal salespeople. They become the managers of research reports and the experts on their industries to the outside world. Thus, while the lifestyle of the research analyst would initially appear to resemble that of a statistician, it often comes closer to that of a diplomat or salesperson.

The players

Research assistants: The bottom-level number crunchers in research, research assistants generally begin with no industry or market expertise. They come from solid undergraduate schools and performed well in school, but initially perform mundane research tasks, such as digging up information and editing/formatting reports. Research assistants also take over the spreadsheet modeling functions required by the analyst. Travel is limited for the budding research assistant, as it usually does not make sense financially to send anyone other than the research analyst to meetings with company officials or money managers.

Research associates: Burdened with numbers and deadlines, the research associate often feels like a cross between a statistician and a corporate finance analyst. Long hours, weekends in the office and number-crunching sum up the routine of the associate. However, compared to analyst and associate analogues in corporate finance, the research associate works fewer hours, often makes it home at a reasonable hour and works less on the weekend. Unfortunately, the associate is required to be present and accounted for at 7:30 a.m., when most morning meetings take place.

Mirroring the corporate finance analyst and associate positions, research associates can be bright, motivated kids directly out of top undergraduate universities; at firms dedicated to hiring MBAs in research, the research associate role is the entry-level position once an MBA has been earned.

A talented research associate can earn much in the way of responsibility. For example, the research associate may field phone calls from smaller "B" accounts (i.e., smaller money managers) and companies less important to the analyst. (The analyst handles the relationships with the biggest buy siders, best clients and top salespeople.) When it comes to writing reports, some analysts give free reign to associates. Also, research associates focus on one industry and typically work for only one full-fledged research analyst. This structure helps research associates delve deeper into the aspects of one industry group and enables them to work closely with a senior-level research analyst.

To start, research assistants/associates out of undergrad typically get paid similarly to the corporate finance analyst right out of college. After one or two years, the compensation varies dramatically, depending on performance and the success of the analysts in the industry group, as well as the associate's contribution. For the first-year MBA research associate, the compensation is similar to I-banking associates: $80,000 salaries with $30,000 signing bonuses, plus a $30,000 year-end bonus, are typical.

Research analysts: The research analyst, especially in equity, is truly a guru. Analysts follow industries, recommend stocks to buy and sell and convince salespeople and buysiders why a given company is a good investment. The path to a research analyst position is either through solid industry experience or the research assistant/associate path.

Research analysts combine the in-depth knowledge of stock pickers with the sales skills required to sell their opinions to buysiders and brokers. Analysts spend considerable time talking to investors, salespeople and traders either discussing buy and sell ideas or industry and company trends and news. Analysts also are called on to defend their rating of a particular company. Research analysts travel regularly, meeting with investors and money managers, management at the companies they cover or people influential in the industry.

Compensation packages for research analysts run the gamut. An analyst's compensation is determined by a number of factors, including the accuracy of his or her predictions, the trading activity within the firm of stock under coverage and, in some cases, corporate finance business of companies in their industry. (Companies such as Merrill Lynch and Salomon Smith Barney, under pressure from investigations and lawsuits, have stopped the practice of including corporate finance revenues in analyst compensation.) Also important is the analyst's reputation in the industry. An analyst that is selected as an "All American" (i.e., tops in their industry) by *Institutional Investor* can demand million-dollar packages; in bull markets, famous analysts can demand even more.

Syndicate

What does the syndicate department at an investment bank do? Syndicate usually sits on the trading floor, but syndicate employees don't trade securities or sell them to clients. Neither do they bring in clients for corporate finance. What syndicate does is provide a vital role in placing stock or bond offerings with buy-siders, and truly aim to find the right offering price that satisfies the company, the salespeople, the investors and the corporate finance bankers working the deal.

Syndicate and public offerings

In any public offering, syndicate gets involved once the prospectus is filed with the SEC. At that point, syndicate associates begin to contact other investment banks interested in being underwriters in the deal. Before we continue with our discussion of the syndicate's role, we should first understand the difference between managers and underwriters and how fees earned through security offerings are allocated.

Managers

The managers of an IPO get involved from the beginning. These are the I-banks attending all the meetings and generally slaving away to complete the deal. Managers get paid a substantial portion of the total fee — called underwriting discounts and commissions on the cover of a prospectus, and known in the industry as the spread. In an IPO, the spread is usually 7 percent, unless the deal is huge, which often means that the offering company can negotiate a slightly lower rate. For a follow-on offering, typical fees start at 5 percent and decrease again as the deal-size increases.

Deals typically have between two and five managers. To further complicate matters, these managers are also often called managing underwriters, as all managers are underwriters, but not all underwriters are managers. Confused? Keep reading.

Underwriters

The underwriters on the deal are so called because they are the ones assuming liability, though they usually have no shares of stock to sell in the deal. They are not necessarily the I-banks that work intimately on the deal; most underwriters do nothing more than accept any potential liability for lawsuits against the underwriting group.

Underwriters are selected by the lead manager in conjunction with the company. This role is often called participating in the syndicate. In a prospectus, you can always find a section entitled "Underwriting" that lists the underwriting group. Anywhere from 10 to 30 investment banks typically make up the underwriting group in any securities offering.

In the underwriting section, listed next to each participant is a number of shares. While underwriting sections list quite a few investment banks and shares next to each bank, it is important to realize that these banks do not sell shares. Neither do they have anything to do with how the shares in the deal are allocated to investors. They merely assume the percentage of liability indicated by the percentage of deal shares listed in the prospectus. To take on such liability, underwriters are paid a small fee, depending on their level of underwriting involvement (i.e., the number of shares next to their name). The managers in the deal will account for the liability of approximately 50 percent to 70 percent of the shares, while the underwriters account for the rest.

Maintaining the book

So what's syndicate's role in all of this? In short, they act as the go between for their own bank and outside entities. Syndicate professionals put together the underwriting group for deals their banks manage, make sure their bank is included in the underwriting process of deals it is not managing, allocate stock to buy-side firms indicating interest in a deal and determine the price for an offering.

The bank lead managing a deal is responsible for maintaining the book, which is a listing of all investors who have indicated an interest in the deal. Potential investors place orders either for a specified number of shares at any price or for a specified number of shares up to a specific price. The orders start to come together during the roadshow, but a significant number of orders don't come in until a day or two before the pricing of a deal. Thus, a manager often doesn't know until the last minute if they can sell a deal.

Syndicate also attempts to gauge a potential investor's true interest in a deal. The day before an offering is priced, syndicate at a lead manager makes last-minute calls to potential buyers to feel out their interest in the deal. It's important to the manager that investors are interested in holding the stocks/bonds for the long term. Those money managers who don't have long term interest are called flippers; they hope to sell the security shortly after opening for a quick profit. Institutional money managers who buy into a deal just to sell their shares on the first day only cause the stock to immediately trade down when it debuts on the market.

Pricing and allocation

How does syndicate price a stock? Simple — by supply and demand. There are a fixed number of shares or bonds in a public deal available, and buyers indicate exactly how many shares they wish to purcase and what price they are willing to pay. The problem is that virtually every deal is oversubscribed, i.e., there are more shares demanded than available for sale. Therefore, syndicate must determine how many shares to allocate to each buyer. To add to the headache, because investors know that every successful deal is oversubscribed, they inflate their actual share indications. So, a 10 percent order may in fact mean that the money manager actually wants something like 2 percent or 3 percent of the deal. The irony, then, is that any money manager who actually got as many shares as she asked for would immediately cancel her order, realizing that the deal was a "dog."

In the end, the combination of syndicate's experience with investors and instincts about buyers tells them how many shares to give to each buy-sider. Syndicate tries to avoid flippers, but can never entirely do so.

After the book is set, syndicate calls the offering company to report the details. This pricing call, as it is known, occurs immediately after the roadshow ends and the day before the stock begins trading in the market. Pricing calls sometimes results in yelling and swearing from the management teams of companies going public. Remember that in IPOs, the call tells the company's executives what their firm is worth — reactions sometimes border on the extreme. If a deal is not hot (and many are not), then the given price may be disappointing to the company. "How can my company not be the greatest thing since sliced bread?" CEOs often wonder.

Because of this tension over the offering price, senior syndicate professionals must be able to handle difficult and delicate situations. But it's not just company management that must be handled with care. During a deal, syndicate must also deal with the salesforce, other underwriters and buy-siders. Similar to the research analyst, the syndicate professional often finds that diplomacy is one of the most critical elements to success. Successful syndicate pros can read between the lines and figure out the real intentions of buy-siders (are they flippers or are they committed to the offering, do they really want 10 percent of the offering, etc.). Also, good syndicate associates are proficient at schmoozing with other investment banks and garnering underwriting business (when the syndicate department is not representing the manager).

Who works in syndicate?

As for the players in syndicate, some have MBAs and some don't. Some worked their way up, and some were hired directly into an associate syndicate position. The payoffs in syndicate can be excellent for top dogs, however, as the most advanced pros often deal directly with clients (management teams doing an offering), handle pricing calls and talk to the biggest investors. They essentially become salespeople themselves, touting the firm, their expertise in placing stock or bonds and their track record. Occasionally, syndicate MDs will attend an important deal pitch to potential clients, especially if he or she is a good talker. At the same time, some syndicate professionals move into sales or other areas, often in order to get away from the endless politicking involved with working in the syndicate department.

Beginners in the syndicate department help put together the book, schedule roadshow meetings and work their way up to dealing with investors, other I-banks and internal sales. Because syndicate requires far fewer people than other areas in the bank, fewer job openings are to be found. Rarely does a firm recruit on college campuses for syndicate jobs — instead, firms generally hire from within the industry or from within the firm.

Investment Management

Overview

Investment management aspirants must have keen analytical and math skills — and a passion for the news. Specifically, you'd better love to read *The Wall Street Journal* and business publications like *Barron's* and *Forbes*. The field has typically been a hard one to break into. Once you're in, however, opportunities for advancement and financial gain abound. Some firms will rarely consider someone for the career track from outside the top MBA programs, while at other firms, insiders say having an MBA "is not a huge advantage." One potential job-snaring credential: Investment management professionals are increasingly sitting for the "intensive" three-part exam called the Chartered Financial Analyst (CFA) Program, a globally recognized standard for measuring the competence and integrity of financial analysts.

Sane salaries, saner hours

"This is not an industry that jumps up and wows people fresh out of school with some outrageous salary," says Michael Weinstock, who specializes in recruiting for investment management firms. "[Investment management firms] are very conservative. They tend to start people at an okay salary — nothing to really go out and buy beers for the world."

Salaries range between $35,000 to $40,000 for someone right out of a bachelor's degree program. Some top firms pay $50,000 base and a small bonus, others report. Someone out of an MBA program can expect to make a base salary in the "high five figures," insiders say. However, if a firm values you, your salary could double or triple in a few years time.

Although entry-level employees start at lower salaries than their counterparts in investment banking, insiders say it's a worthwhile trade-off. Typically, they don't work as many long and tortured hours as their I-banking brethren.

For experienced investment managers, the financial picture becomes rosier. Senior asset managers are generally paid based upon the amount of money they manage. The average salary for professionals with 10 or more years of experience is $200,000, according to the Association for Investment Management and Research (AIMR), a non-profit association based in

Charlottesville, Va., composed of 45,000 financial analysts, portfolio managers and other investment professionals worldwide. The AIMR based its findings on 1999 compensation data from more than 8,500 members in the United States and Canada.

Top performers, including the highest-level portfolio managers, analysts and marketers, pull in salaries ranging between $1 million and $3 million. The rewards can also be exceptional for high-risk managers of hedge funds, which are private pools of capital usually limited to wealthy investors.

In this chapter we will provide an overview of the roles and lifestyles of the positions in investment management and paths to upper management positions.

How to break in

As the bull market fueled the popularity of mutual funds over the last few years, freshly minted MBAs were able to score high-paying investment analyst and portfolio management positions. This is a relatively new trend, as investment management is an industry that values experience (read: the more gray hair, the better). Another reason new blood is welcomed: More investment banks have been growing their asset management businesses and thus need new employees.

Investment management is largely protected against the volatility of the market, unlike investment banking. Many lines of business for investment banks are very sensitive to the economy in general. For example, underwriting of IPOs and other equity issues declines in times of recession. In asset management, firms make money based on a percentage of the entire amount they handle, whether they make or lose money for the client.

Despite the increasing number of available investment management positions, it's still relatively hard to break into the business. Traditionally, someone fresh out of college would work for a few years as a financial analyst in big-money corporations, such as a General Electric, to gain experience, says Donald Tuttle, vice president of special projects at the AIMR and a former college business professor. "You learn to evaluate your own corporation, how a corporation should be financed, how to try to keep costs down," Tuttle says. "Then, after acquiring three or four years of experience in a job like that, you go back to school at a top-line MBA program. You will have a lot of opportunities either on the buy side or sell side."

Investment Management and the CFA

If you're interested in asset management, taking the CFA may be a wise career move. Although it's all take-at-home studying, many insiders say it covers "every intricate aspect" of money management. Nearly 36,000 professionals are CFAs. Approximately 60,000 people sit for one part of the six-hour, graduate-level exam worldwide every June. The exams get progressively harder from level one to level three — and only about 50 percent of people pass level one each year.

"It's typically the benchmark most money management firms use to separate the men from the boys and the ladies from the girls," says one investment manager. "You're telling your firm that you're destined to do bigger, better things. And you're, in a very nice and nonchalant way, telling the firm 'I'm hoping that you're going to come across for me, upgrade me and promote me, or otherwise I'm going to take my CFA designation and shop it to a competitor.'"

The exams, which are taken over at least three years, test ethical and professional standards, securities analysis and investment valuation, financial accounting, quantitative analysis, economics, asset allocation and portfolio management, among other subjects. The exams use problems, cases, essays, multiple-choice and "item-set" questions. It costs $250 to register to enter the CFA and $250 or $300 to take exams, depending on the level.

Besides working in the field for at least three years and passing all three exams, professionals must commit to abide by the AIMR code of ethics and standards of professional conduct to gain their title.

Career Path

Recent college graduates typically enter the industry as investment research assistants or portfolio manager assistants. Each position offers a great opportunity to work directly with senior analysts and portfolio mangers, and learn the nuances and fundamentals of the business. Investment research assistants' duties include maintaining investment models, gathering industry and company information and helping devise company and industry recommendations. Portfolio manager assistants screen for potential investments, monitor portfolio characteristics and assist in client relations.

Most people spend two to three years in these positions and then return to business school. There are a few instances when assistants are promoted into the position of investment research associate (this is rare and tends to occur at the smaller investment management firms).

Another, less traveled route for recent college graduates is to join a firm's marketing or sales department as a marketing or sales associate. Marketing associates assist in creating portfolio review presentations and in developing promotional presentations for potential new clients. Sales associates assist in answering request for proposals (RFPs) issued by institutions seeking to hire new investment managers. Furthermore, they assist senior client servicing officials in maintaining and expanding client relationships.

Marketing and sales have become an increasingly critical role in the investment management industry. This path is an outstanding alternative for those interested in the industry, but not driven by investing money. Alternatively, the role of marketing or sales associate can serve as an entry point into the industry and a springboard to a switch to the investment side.

Recent MBA graduates, or those with considerable investment experience, typically enter the industry as an investment research associate. They are usually assigned a small industry to cover, providing them an opportunity to get their feet wet.

Investment research associates are counted on to provide insight and investment recommendations to portfolio managers. The typical day includes listening to company management conference calls, attending industry conferences, building investment models, developing industry trends and benchmarking a company's progress to its peers.

Success as an associate analyst will lead to advancement to larger industries and can lead to a portfolio manager position.

The portfolio manager path

There really isn't a clear-cut track to becoming a portfolio manager, insiders say. In most cases, it's more like an apprentice situation. After a few years in research, administration or some sort of portfolio support job, one is given a portion of a fund to manage. The amount of assets you manage grows as you gain experience.

Vault spoke to one veteran portfolio manager at The Bank of New York who had a circuitous career path. He was a liberal arts major in college who took no business courses outside of economics. He started working on the client side at a firm in 1991, mostly because jobs were scarce in Boston at that time. "I didn't like the job itself, but I liked the industry," he admits. His next job was as a portfolio assistant at a major commercial bank in New York. His role was to review trust accounts to make sure investments complied with the strict rules of the Prudent Investor Act, which governs how trusts are to be managed. He gradually started managing small books of business using the firm's guidelines and advice from more experienced managers to learn the trade. At the same time, he started studying for the three-part CFA exam.

Today, he is managing a book of business (industry jargon for a stable of clients) worth about $600 million for about 80 high-wealth clients. In his job, he knows his clients personally. He likes this kind of money managing better than his previous experiences with mutual fund investment, which were more about "meeting numbers." "This tends to be very relationship-oriented," he says. "If you had to compare what we do to another profession, it's the family doctor. We develop the same kind of rapport and relationship."

Knowing clients personally in some ways makes the job more stressful, he says. "You really are the one on the line, the one deciding 'I want to buy this stock and not that stock.'" Strong ethics and a sense of responsibility are necessary, he says, because the ramifications are great. "This is people's retirement money. That's a tremendous responsibility."

Another advantage, he says, are the hours. He says he works an average of 65 or 70 hours a week, but some slow weeks end after 45 hours. "Decembers tend to be bad because you are figuring out taxes," he says. Then again, "there have been times when I've gone home at 4 p.m., which is something I distinctly value." He usually arrives at the work early and can leave when the markets close, but some portfolio managers come in just before the 8:30 a.m. meeting and leave around 7 p.m.

There's flexibility, he says, because he gets to schedule client meetings around his life. Client relationships take up about 35 to 40 percent of his time. He crosses the country to visit clients about 10 percent of the time, and sometimes they meet him in Manhattan. Otherwise, he's doing investment research, which sometimes entails attending conferences held by sell-side research firms where he might learn, for example, how "a company plans to use the proceeds of a second public offering to acquire another firm."

Sometimes, he says, clients are surprised when they meet him because they realize how young he is. Age discrimination goes both ways, he says. Some people seek him out because they think a younger manager is going to have a better understanding of technology. Others don't want someone without 30 years of experience touching their money. "I get comments all the time like, 'Hmmm, how long have you been doing this?'" he says. "They're trying to benchmark me in some way without necessarily asking about my age. I find I can address it simply by doing my job well."

Commercial Banking

Credit Analyst

Credit analysts examine the credit-worthiness of potential borrowers by studying business models, industry characteristics and sources of cash flow drivers. They also study a firm's profitability, capital structure, leverage, liquidity and management of existing capital. Finally, they consider the financial risk of a loan. Once they've done that, credit analysts will write credit reports that the bank uses in its internal credit approval process and will continue to act as contacts between their departments and their clients, other banks and other departments within the bank.

"You're at a disadvantage when you're an analyst because you very rarely get to meet the client, and it makes it much more difficult to do your job because you have to go by the numbers and the numbers don't always tell the whole story," says one commercial banker who started her career as a credit analyst with Bank of America.

But at the same time, credit analysts say that they're receiving the training they need to progress in commercial banking or other aspects of finance. Young credit analysts typically must undergo bank-sponsored training programs that last anywhere from a year to 18 months. Part of the time, beginning commercial bankers spend time in the classroom, reading case studies and learning about commercial credit, accounting and corporate finance. Trainees may also be required to perform basic research on prospective borrowers. After the training, these bankers may rotate through different areas of the bank, such as a branch office or private banking operation. Their training ends when they are chosen to fill a full-time opening.

"With the experience and skills I've gained as a credit analyst, I believe that I have many options," says one young analyst. "Credit training allows you to understand businesses and companies, rather than just financial products. In the long term I may enter one of the following fields: corporate finance (company side), venture capital, investment banking, money management or equity research."

Credit analysts say, "The money's pretty decent when compared to other people" in their age group (credit analysts are typically in their early 20s), though they complain the "lifestyle sucks."

Day in the life of a credit analyst

8:30 a.m. — 9:00 a.m.: Arrive at work and check mail and messages. "There's constant phone contact with clients and co-workers from 9:00 a.m. until 5:00 p.m.," says one analyst.

9:00 a.m. — 9:30 a.m.: Speak to vice presidents about new loan deal. One analyst calls this one of the "fun parts" of the job. "It's great exposure, and you get a great sense of business — as opposed to just finance."

9:30 a.m. — 10:00 a.m.: Gather information — financial statements, SEC filings and news releases — on new deal .

10:00 a.m. — 1:00 p.m.: Perform "brain work" on gathered information. This includes: 1) understanding the company's business model, industry characteristics and main cash flow drivers; 2) analyzing the company's profitability, capital structure, leverage, liquidity and working capital management and 3) assess operating risk, financial risk and other credit risks.

1:00 p.m. — 2:00 p.m.: Lunch or gym.

2:00 p.m. — 5:00 p.m.: Work on financial projections.

5:00 p.m. — 7:00 p.m.: Work on credit memo report.

7:00 p.m. — 8:00 p.m.: Dinner at the cafeteria "while complaining to co-workers about all the work that was just dumped on me."

8:00 p.m. — 10:45 p.m.: Resume working on credit memo report.

10:45 p.m. — 11:00 p.m.: "Check basketball or baseball scores" and take a car home.

Loan Officer

Loan officers are the workhorses of the commercial banking industry. They structure loans, watch over them for the continued health of the borrower and bring in new customers and new depositors. Working with the credit reports prepared by analysts or based on their own research, loan officers draft the terms of a loan, balancing the need to keep borrowers happy against the bank's need to remain profitable and solvent.

To rustle up new business, commercial loan officers might call up businesses and ask them about their business goals and capital needs. Tax attorneys, accountants and other professional service providers can refer new business, as can existing borrowers. Similarly, mortgage loan officers build relationships with commercial developers and real estate agencies, which might then turn to the loan officer for financing.

Alyssa Lange is vice president and senior relationship manager at City National Bank, a $10 billion (in terms of assets) regional bank headquartered in Beverly Hills, Calif. Lange manages a $90 million portfolio spread out over 12 commercial borrowers, including a fuel broker, a consumer goods importer and a barbecue manufacturer. To encourage new business, Lange is also responsible for meeting any consumer credit needs of the executives of these 12 borrowers. This could include mortgages, personal credit cards or auto loans. To accomplish that goal, Lange works with her colleagues in the private banking and investment departments of her bank.

"I do what it takes to make everybody happy on the business side, as well as for the executives, to make their lives less burdensome," Lange said. "I just let them know what they've got, and if there's ever a time when they need anything, they know they can call me."

Lange structures her own loans, but she typically secures the sign-off from the senior loan officer for the region and one other bank official. The bank's senior loan committee may also review larger loans, those more than $7.5 million. Her biggest deals usually require the sign-off of the chief credit officer of the bank.

"During the process, if you're proposing on a new borrower, you always have credit administrators — if it's in their authority — look over the deal as it's proceeding, so no one's caught off guard," Lange said.

Lange spent three years with Bank of America as a credit analyst, but says she's much happier now that she gets to meet the executives to whom she loans money. Those meetings make credit evaluations much easier, Lange said.

"You just become much more familiar with the operation when you've gone out and met them and talked to them," Lange said. "You're much more apt and able if you're talking about their business to ask questions. Something might come up and you'll say, 'I had no idea this was part of your business strategy.'"

Loan officers are also responsible for building up their portfolio with new clients.

"Sometimes I see things in the newspaper, a developer's name or an organization, and think they might be worthwhile calling on," said one assistant vice president at a small regional bank in New Jersey. "We do something here called blitzes. We go out and canvas areas where we have our branches. I may meet prospective clients that way."

Loan Review Officer/Loan Work-Out Officer

Loan review and loan workout officers ensure that terms set by loan officers meet both the bank's policies and banking regulations and work with troubled creditors to resolve outstanding loan payments.

Loan review officers scrutinize loans structured by more junior loan officers for the proper authorization, repayment schedules and procedures. For example, a bank might require loans to real estate developers to contain terms on how much rent the developers must charge. Loan review officers must make sure this policy is followed and included in the terms of a specific loan.

Ronald Yancis is now a vice president for quality control at Central Progressive Bank, a regional bank located in Hammond, La.,about 40 miles east of Baton Rouge. He has spent the past 30 years as a loan review officer and loan workout officer, working with everyone from oilmen to shopkeepers.

After graduating from the University of Mississippi, Yancis earned an MBA in 1969. He began teaching finance at a junior college in northern Mississippi, working in the summers with the Comptroller of the Currency in Memphis. That turned into a full-time job as "an unofficial bank examiner" until 1980, when he joined the First National Bank of Jefferson Parish in Louisiana.

Part of Yancis' job today involves loan administration and compliance. "I make sure loans were done by the proper officers, that those people had the authority to prepare those loans," Yancis said. "Now with banking, there's a lot more turnover than you used to see. They're beginning to compress managerial experience. These guys have finance experience, but it's all from college. They'll bring in these deals and try and put them together and not put them together right."

Yancis emphasized that loan officers and loan review officers must maintain a close watch on their borrowers over the life of the loan.

"After five years, we'll look over the financial statement," Yancis said. "If it's a fixed-rate loan, then we might raise rates. If a borrower is struggling, we'll raise the rate. It never goes away. If you get a financial statement this year, you'll want a financial statement next year, to make sure the company is doing well."

For companies that can't make their payments or might even default on a loan, Yancis' experience as a work-out officer comes to the fore. Working with a struggling company, Yancis will try to "work out" a way for the borrower to make his payments. In the early 1980s, when the oil business began drying up in Texas, Yancis was placed in charge of an effort to recoup a multi-million dollar loan from a wildcat oil driller whose wells had run dry. With an additional $250,000 from the bank, Yancis assembled a syndicate of oil speculators and begged a Dallas oilman to move his rig to some undrilled wells the borrower still owned.

"Here's what I'll do," Yancis told the Dallas oilman, "I ain't got the money to pay you, but I've asked a handful of investors to come together. If you put your rig in and hit oil, you'll be one of the first investors to get paid." Yancis said the oilman agreed. "It cost $600,000 just to move the rig, but he did it on a handshake. We hit, and we did that eight more times. With what was coming out, in the long run, the bank wound up getting its money."

Day in the life of an assistant vice president in commercial lending

9:00 a.m.: I arrive at work and start typing a commitment letter that outlines the terms of a loan between the bank and a new borrower. This is a new loan for an existing client, a heating and air conditioning contractor, who is expanding his business. This takes most of the morning, since the letter must conform exactly to the proposal I worked up earlier.

12:00 p.m.: I begin working on a term sheet, or letter of intent, between the bank and a potential client. The term sheet outlines terms for lending money. I'm reviewing some things and I'm looking to see if this is something that meets our lending criteria.

1:00 p.m.: Lunch at the bank's lunchroom, where I catch up on the news. I read the local paper and try to glance through *The Wall Street Journal*. I get a copy from my boss.

2:00 p.m.: Finish letter of intent.

3:00 p.m.: Prepare a memo on loan closing and review a second loan package.

6:00 p.m.: Drive home. "Sometimes, I'll take work home, review loan packages at night or write proposals," says one source. "If I'm out of the office during the day, I can't do this stuff during normal hours, and I don't want to be in the office at all hours during the night, so I'll just bring it home."

Accounting

Overview

The "accounting firm" label might now be something of a misnomer as traditional accounting organizations have developed a number of services beyond the traditional audit and tax functions. Most large firms, including the Big Five, call themselves "professional services" firms. In addition to traditional tax and accounting, these firms often supply other services, including corporate finance and mergers and acquisitions advice, management consulting, personal financial planning and legal services. Post-Enron, this diversification has come under fire as some industry observers feel that firms are reluctant to offer fair, critical audits for fear of losing out on contracts for more lucrative services. Regulators have been pressuring the firms to address this conflict, and most of the Big Five have taken steps to separate audit and consulting divisions.

Segmentation of accounting careers

While there are many ways to classify accountants, the most common division is between public and private accountants. Public accountants mainly deal with financial accounting and private accountants can deal with both financial and management accounting.

Public accountants receive a fee for services provided to individuals, businesses and governments. Public accounting firms vary greatly in size and the type of services provided. Most public accounting firms provide some combination of auditing, tax and management consulting services. There are small organizations, which mainly provide tax or bookkeeping services for smaller firms that do not have an internal accounting department. The majority of larger firms' clients have an internal accounting department. The larger firms handle audits of public companies, which are required by securities law.

Most accountants start their careers at a public accounting firm, gaining valuable experience and training, and from move to private accounting. For example, public accountants are well positioned to become a chief financial officer of an organization.

Private accountants work for businesses, the government or non-profit agencies. Most corporations have an internal accounting group that prepares the financial information (both tax and audit) for the public accountants, tracks company performance for internal evaluation, and works with management on issues related to acquisitions, international transactions, and any other operational issue that arise in the running the company. An accountant within a corporation is generally an internal auditor or a management accountant, though there are other roles that private accountants can fill.

Government accountants can work at the federal, state or local level. Many government organizations have large accounting departments to analyze the performance and allocation of their funds. The Department of Defense, the General Accounting Office, the Internal Revenue Service, and the Securities Exchange Commission typically hire large numbers of accountants for services and evaluations within the organization. Employees at the Internal Revenue Service typically review individual and corporate tax returns. The SEC hires experienced accountants to evaluate filings made by public companies. These employees will ensure that firms are complying with the regulations of the SEC.

Non-profit organizations are formed with a specific purpose, typically religious, charitable, educational, literary or scientific in nature. These organizations are usually exempt from federal taxation. Non-profit accounting is similar to for-profit accounting; both require an understanding of the guidelines for Generally Accepted Accounting Principles (GAAP). In addition to knowing GAAP, non-profit accountants must understand the Financial Accounting Standards Bureau (FASB) standards written specifically for these companies, as well as the tax regulations specific to non-profit organizations. The accounting group in these organizations is typically smaller than those of for-profit companies, so an employee in a non-profit may be responsible for more than one area of accounting (e.g., financial statements and tax issues).

Quality of life

Compared to the frenetic world of investment banking, accounting is a pretty relaxed environment for its workers. However, there are periods of high stress. While accountants generally put in eight to 10 hour days, there are certain busy periods that can keep accountants anchored to the desk for 12-

hour days. For tax accountants, the weeks before tax filing deadline (March 15, April 15, September 15 and October 15) can increase workload. For public accountants, January through April is a busy time, while government accounts are under the gun in July and August.

Entry-level salaries for public accountants ranged from $29,000-$40,000 in 2000, with partners making between $180,000 to $260,000. The starting salary for a government accountant fresh out of school was $22,000. Those with a little experience or a master's degree started at $33,000.

Career Path

Public accounting

Public accounting (both audit and tax) generally entails a fairly rigid, hierarchical career path:

Audit

• **Staff Auditor (year 1-3):** Staff auditors perform the meat of an audit, engaging in the often mentioned "ticking and tying" activities (i.e., analyzing and verifying the information contained in the myriad ledgers and statements provided by the client). They work with the client to obtain information and determine the validity and accuracy of the accounting records. It is the staff accountant's responsibility to investigate specific accounts and to identify, resolve and document any material issues. Staff auditors will often start to direct small audits (and will be referred to as the "acting senior" on the engagement) in their second year.

• **Senior Auditor (year 3-6):** Audit seniors are the glue that holds the audit together. They supervise the audit fieldwork of staff auditors and review their work to ensure the audit is thorough and properly documented. They are also responsible for resolving any accounting issues as they arise. Seniors identify and document audit risks, create and manage client relationships, administer budget issues and ensure that the audit manager and partner are adequately informed of all relevant items. Specific senior auditor activities could include client meetings, partner and manager meetings, research on the relevant accounting standards and conversations with company headquarters.

• **Audit Manager (year 6+):** The manager is ultimately responsible for managing client relationships. Although both the senior and staff auditors will be at the audit site each day during the audit, the manager will typically visit the audit site once a week (maybe more depending upon the status and time remaining to completion for the audit). The manager will perform a high-level review of all the audit work after the senior is satisfied with the thoroughness and resolution of all issues. The manager supervises, trains and evaluates seniors and staff. They are also responsible for audit program approval, personnel scheduling, financial statement disclosure/footnote approval, day-to-day client relationships and final determination of billings for engagements.

• **Partner/Senior Partner:**   Partners are responsible for overall client relationship and business development activities. The partner will sign the audit opinion and is responsible for the overall audit and coordination for the concurring partner review and any correspondence with headquarters. The partner will review and concur on all major accounting issues. The partner may visit the client site once on small audit engagements, if at all. The partner may be the only audit team member that attends audit committee meetings. Only 2 percent of persons entering CPA firms will reach the partner level. Partners typically purchase equity in the firm and share in all profits. Virtually all partners are CPAs.

Tax

• **Tax Staff (year 1-3):**   Like their audit counterparts, tax staff personnel perform the meat of the tax work. They prepare tax returns, research tax issues and counsel clients on tax matters under the supervision of a tax senior and/or tax manager. Generally, tax staff do not have as much direct client contact as their audit counterparts. Tax staff personnel go through a significant amount of learning and training until they get up to speed on basic aspects of income tax reporting, compliance and analysis.

• **Tax Senior (year 3-6):** Tax seniors prepare and review tax returns, research tax issues, offer suggestions for tax planning, manage tax staff and study the Internal Revenue Code and other applicable tax laws for potential client tax savings. They may also work with audit personnel in the preparation of tax items included in financial statement disclosure. This level also requires a significant amount of learning and training, as the tax senior is expected to apply an increased technical tax comfort level to his or her client engagements in preparation for the manager level.

• **Tax Manager (year 6+):** Unlike audit, where staff and seniors have the most extensive exposure to the client, client contact in tax engagements is generally the domain of the tax manager. Tax managers direct and review tax seniors and tax staff personnel; approve corporate tax returns prepared by tax staff; perform tax planning and research unusual tax matters; handle day-to-day client relationship issues; plan engagement billings and other administrative duties. They may also review tax items included in financial statement disclosure. Tax managers are expected to have a strong grasp of the technical tax issues applicable to their specific industry or tax function (e.g., state and local, international). Many tax managers (and partners) are referred to as "Codeheads" for their ability to recite on command the exact Internal Revenue Code section applicable to a given tax issue. They are also expected to begin developing their marketing skills in preparation for the business development responsibilities of the partner level.

• **Tax Partner/Senior Partner:** Similar to their audit counterparts, tax partners are responsible for overall client relationship and business development activities. Tax partners often become experts in a specific industry or tax function.

The CPA exam

The Uniform Certified Public Accountants Exam (CPA) was first administered in 1917. The Board of Examiners of the American Institute of Certified Public Accountants (AICPA) writes and administers the exam. It is designed to assess a candidate's knowledge of four key areas:

• Business Law and Professional Responsibilities (LPR) — CPA's professional responsibilities and the legal implications of business transactions, particularly as they relate to accounting and auditing.

• Auditing (AUDIT) — Generally-accepted auditing standards and procedures.

• Accounting and Reporting — Taxation, Managerial, and Governmental and Not-for-Profit Organizations (ARE) — Federal taxation, managerial accounting, and accounting for governmental and not-for-profit organizations.

• Financial Accounting and Reporting (FARE) — Generally-accepted accounting principles for business enterprises.

The exam is difficult. Historically, approximately 10 percent pass all four parts on the first try. Approximately 50 percent of the people who are sitting for the exam have taken the exam before. It is given twice a year, in May and November, usually the Wednesday and Thursday of the first full week of the month. The two-day exam lasts over 15 and a half hours.

It's held from 9 a.m. to 6 p.m. on Wednesday and 8:30 a.m. to 6 p.m. on Thursday.

Most CPA veterans recommend that you begin studying for the test soon after you graduate. While accounting firms will hire people who haven't yet passed the exam, it's expected that you'll take the exam the first time it's offered after your start date. While firms are generally patient with those who fail a part of the test (allowing them time to re-take the test), you can't get promoted to manager without passing the test.

Non-public accounting

Management accountants often start as cost accountants, junior internal auditors, or trainees for other accounting positions. As they advance in their organizations, they may advance to accounting manager, controller, chief cost accountant, budget director, or manager of internal auditing. Some also become treasurers, financial vice presidents, chief financial officers or corporate presidents. Many senior executives have a background in accounting, internal auditing or finance.

Financial accounting and reporting

- **Staff accountant (1-3 years):** Financial accounting and reporting staff work under the direction of a senior accountant performing detailed work assignments in one or several of the following areas: receivables, payroll, payables, property, general ledger and financial statements

- **Senior accountant (3-6 years):** Senior accountants supervise the work of staff accountants and are responsible for special reports and financial analysis.

- **Accounting manager (6+ years):** Accounting managers assist the controller and are often responsible for one of the functional areas such as financial accounting or budgetary planning and control. They direct the work of personnel involved in detailed accounting entries, internal financial reporting and financial statements.

Internal audit

- **Staff internal auditors (1-3 years):** Internal audit staff work under the direction of seniors and managers in conducting compliance audits and test internal controls and information systems.

- **Senior internal auditors (3-6 years):** Internal audit seniors supervise the testing of internal control and accounting information systems. They often conduct statistical samples of document approval, perform tests to uncover defalcations and perform operational audits for profit improvement recommendations.

- **Internal audit managers (6+ years):** Internal audit managers direct the staff responsible for systematically sampling the adequacy and reliability of internal control systems. They make recommendations for changes as needed, ensure that company policies and procedures are followed and establish the proper techniques to discover and prevent fraud.

Executive level

- **Controller:** The controller functions as the chief accounting executive responsible for organizing, directing and controlling the work of the accounting personnel in collecting financial data for internal and external use. As a member of top management, the controller helps develop forecasts for projects, measures the actual performance against operating standards and interprets the results of operations for all levels of management.

- **Chief Financial Officer:** The CFO advises the president of the organization with respect to financial reporting, financial stability and liquidity, and financial growth. The CFO directs and supervises the work of the controller, treasurer and,sometimes, the internal auditing manager. Other duties include maintenance of relationships with stockholders, financial institutions and the investment community. The CFO contributes to the overall organization planning, policy development and implementation.

THE VAULT 50:
1-25

Goldman Sachs

85 Broad Street
New York, NY 10004
Phone: (212) 902-1000
www.gs.com

DEPARTMENTS

Equities • Finance • Fixed Income,
Currency and Commodities •
Investment Banking • Investment
Management • Investment Research •
Legal, Compliance and Management
Controls • Merchant Banking • Risk
Management

THE STATS

Chairman and CEO:
Henry M. Paulson, Jr.
Employer Type: Public Company
Ticker Symbol: GS (NYSE)
2001 Revenues: $31.1 billion
2001 Net Income: $2.3 billion
No. of Employees: 23,490
No. of Offices: 43

KEY COMPETITORS

Credit Suisse First Boston
J.P. Morgan Chase
Merrill Lynch
Morgan Stanley
Salomon Smith Barney

THE BUZZ
WHAT EMPLOYEES AT OTHER FIRMS ARE SAYING

- "There is no substitute"
- "Not as good as they think"
- "Still the best"
- "Full of themselves"

UPPERS

- Good training program
- Prestigious brand name
- Talented co-workers

DOWNERS

- Bureaucracy
- Grueling hours
- Nerdy co-workers

EMPLOYMENT CONTACT

For information regarding
employment and the application
process, visit www.gs.com.

THE SCOOP

Cultivating culture

Founded in 1869 by Marcus Goldman, a European immigrant, Goldman Sachs is one of the nation's oldest and most prestigious investment-banking firms. Goldman has created a reputation among both employees and outsiders that the firm is the pinnacle of investment-banking success. By insisting the firm is paramount, and individual egos a distant second, Goldman Sachs achieved unparalleled success among American I-banks in prompting high-flying corporate whiz kids to bow to the overall interests of the firm. Goldman is also legendary for its secrecy. The firm rarely lets the media see what's going on behind the scenes. Even former employees tend not to speak to the press — perhaps a result of the legal clauses that Goldman reportedly inserts in every employee's contract, requiring that he or she never speak publicly about even the smallest detail of office life.

A long road to going public

Contributing to Goldman's mystique for years was its status as a major Wall Street private partnership. In 1998, however, the firm's partners voted to change this status and offer stock to the public. That IPO was shelved amid concerns about the state of the market. The firm finally went public in May 1999. Within one year of its IPO, Goldman's stock gained 141 percent, outperforming nearly all of Goldman's competitors.

Rising revenues

Goldman Sachs continued its dominance of the investment-banking league tables in 2001, coming in first in IPO underwriting and M&A advisory. The firm completed 15 deals worth $12.8 billion, compared to 47 deals that raised $15.5 billion in the prior year. (Not bad, considering there were only 86 IPOs in 2001.) It led new issues of $3.5 billion for Newark, N.J., insurer Prudential Financial, $2.1 billion for asset-management and insurance concern Principal Financial Group, and $2 billion for Indianapolis health insurer Anthem.

Goldman's M&A advisory revenue comprised 20 percent of overall investment-banking revenue for 2001. The Wall Street Goliath took the top spot in global M&A, advising on $473.1 billion worth of deals in 2001, a 34 percent market share. Goldman advised Washington Mutual on its $5.0 billion purchase of Dime Bancorp (announced in June 2001), Hewlett-Packard on its purchase of Compaq Computer (announced in August 2001) and AT&T Broadband on its $72 billion sale to Comcast (announced in December 2001).

They want your money

Money management is Goldman's new golden ticket. The firm saw years of trying to build an investment management unit pay off in 2001. The group's managed assets and revenues are ahead while the firm's profits have decreased slightly. With inflows of $67 billion, assets under management climbed 19 percent over the past year to $351 billion, largely due to a stream of cash into its money management arm during the market decline. Healthier fund performance didn't hurt, either. The unit reported record net revenues of $1.47 billion for 2001, an increase of 10 percent from the previous year. Many fund companies struggled with declines in revenue of 2 to 4 percent.

Goldman's move up the asset management ladder didn't come without a few changes. In July 2001, John P. McNulty, head of Goldman Sachs' Investment Management Division, retired and was replaced by Philip Murphy and Peter Kraus, the two heads of its Private Wealth Management Division. McNulty, a 22-year veteran, bolstered the group's assets under management from $50 billion in 1995.

Goldman moved into other markets besides asset management since going public. In January 2001, the company acquired Benjamin Jacobson & Sons, a specialist firm on the floor of the New York Stock Exchange, for $250 million in stock and cash. The firm then acquired the specialist assets of TFM Investment Group, an options specialist firm, in December 2001. Its assets will be incorporated into those of SLK-Hull Derivatives, LLC (SHD), a partnership formed by Goldman Sachs through the combination of Spear, Leeds & Kellogg and The Hull Group's option trading businesses to reinforce SHD's leading position in the U.S. options markets.

Layoffs, pre- and post-September 11

Goldman Sachs was not immune to the weak economy of early 2001 and certainly not to the industry-wide post-September 11 slump. Though the firm never officially announced any cuts, there were reportedly several rounds of layoffs in 2001. The firm reportedly cut 12 percent of its worldwide investment-banking staff in May 2001, and it was said to have cut between 300 and 400 more investment bankers after September. However, the firm stepped up its hiring in other areas, keeping total headcount about even. In March 2002, *The Wall Street Journal* reported that Goldman might look to cut 4 to 6 percent of its global work force by the end of 2002.

Early bird gets busted

The firm's reputation was smudged by reports of an insider trading investigation. According to published reports, the SEC is investigating Goldman for profiting from the Treasury Department's plans to discontinue the 30-year bond. Apparently, Pete Davis, a longtime bond industry consultant, called Goldman and other clients about 20 minutes before it became public that the government would stop selling 30-year bonds. Some traders reported that Goldman began snapping up bonds and futures contracts in the 20 minutes before the public became aware of the news. The firm has acknowledged that it received a call from Davis but denied any wrongdoing. The probe is pending.

GETTING HIRED

Old firm, new tricks

Despite consistently hiring the cream of the crop, Goldman changed its hiring process for the 2002 recruiting season. All groups will start recruits off with a 30-minute, two-on-one interview with professional staff (i.e., investment bankers, traders, asset managers, etc.). At the end of the day, the interviewers will meet to review the candidates and determine who merits a second look. Previously, Goldman had been famous for a fairly grueling process, with most candidates reporting at least three rounds of interviews. One source had a mix of fit and technical questions, but got the impression he was being graded on more than his answers. "It didn't matter if I got the questions wrong, but they wanted to see how I thought and how I reacted under pressure. The worst thing to do is to come across as arrogant." Naturally, making a good impression on everyone is important. Says one insider, "Goldman is a very, very consensus-driven place. I think in the full-time hiring process, you could literally meet a total of 25 people."

Goldman veterans say that the firm emphasizes fit more than most banks. "They stress over and over again that anybody graduating from a top MBA program can do what they want them to do," says one source. "But they can't change their personality or make them pleasant to work with. They really put a lot of effort into the personality part." One hire reports receiving "rapid-fire personal questions: 'Why did you go to that school?' 'How were your grades?' 'How were you perceived by your peers?' 'Your professors?'" Personality and GPA aside, one insider says, "You don't have to be a finance expert, but you have to be special in some way. It helps if you were the best at something." Interviewers say they look for "people with smart personalities who aren't afraid to work hard. We especially don't want big egos around the place, so we try and find out how you will be able to work with someone you don't like too much personally."

For summer associates "trying out" for full-time positions, contacts say, "there's very strong attention paid to how well people work together." A current Goldman banker and former summer associate advises those trying to make the cut: "A summer internship is the best way to land a full-time job." It's not a given, though. "It's known on the Street and in business schools that Goldman gives a lot fewer offers to summer associates" than competitors do, says one insider.

OUR SURVEY SAYS

A golden god

Goldman Sachs' workplace is legendary for an "intense, hard-working and competitive" ethic where "success is taken for granted." While the rest of the world may exalt Goldman employees as "arrogant" and "snobby," insiders themselves note that the firm "cuts their egos down to size." Goldman Sachs makes it clear from the beginning that "individual personalities are insignificant" and that "the firm comes first, second and last." One employee says Goldman the culture is "strong and well defined, emphasizing clients, reputation and employees — in that order." Another insider even likens the firm to "the God we are all meant to bow to." Says one source, "I've seen some people from top schools who came across as a bit arrogant, and they were very unwelcome [at Goldman]." One vice president remarks that Goldman employees certainly "take pride in the company's reputation, in preserving the brand." Of course, "culture is a function of the people in charge," says one M&A associate. The people in that group "are very arrogant because they know they're in the elite group in the investment-banking division and, by extension, the whole firm. Everyone who works there knows it."

New hires take some time to get used to the careful scrutiny to which they are subjected, and employees sometimes feel that they "are under constant surveillance." At the same time, analysts and associates praise their fellow employees for being "extremely intelligent and perceptive." One banker admits his colleagues are "incredibly smart," but says, "there's a lot of nerds" at the firm. Nerdy or not, employees are "prepared to make the sacrifices that have to be made for the team to succeed." Reports one associate: "Teamwork is a word that's clichéd and overused, and I sort of cringe when I hear it elsewhere, but in some sense that's really what the firm prides itself on." And teamwork, which is "definitely rewarded," does play out in everyday office life at Goldman. "If you need to talk to someone, they're not going to stop everything they're doing to talk to you, but they'll say, 'Come back at the end of the day.' Even senior people are very accessible," reports one contact. "There's a hierarchy, but there's open access to all levels," echoes another.

However, working as part of a team of Goldman employees "can also be challenging, because you have to hold up your end, and there's always pressure to measure up to your co-workers' high standards." Some insiders also feel that Goldman's emphasis on teamwork comes at a cost. "Individuality and creativity usually are considered much less important than being a good team player," says one contact. Even the most enthusiastic confess that "occasionally the stress of work can get to be too much, and you come close to cracking." One associate says, "One must conform, which feels quite oppressive at times." The associate adds, "The day to day environment can be quite unpleasant." Another contact says that the culture cannot only cramp individual style but might be limiting the firm as a whole. The source explains, "Because of the corporate culture and the goody two-shoes image, [the firm is] less inclined to take risks."

Long on hours, short on salary?

Goldman employees "definitely work, on average, longer hours than people at other firms." Certainly, this comes as no surprise. As one of the top investment banks, employees are guaranteed a hefty workload. After all, one of the most commonly asked questions in a Goldman interview is, "How will you cope with working 90-hour weeks, or longer, for three years?" One associate complains that the hours are "long" and "unnecessary." He goes on to say, "While it is somewhat due to the nature of the business, my biggest complaint is they don't hire enough junior people." Another source has a different complaint for unnecessary hours. "While face time shouldn't be required, it most definitely is."

Workload definitely increases the further down the Goldman chain you are. "For the first few years, analysts usually work between 80 and 110 hours a week" and generally come into the office "at least six days a week, though you're usually there every day of the week." Working until 10 at night is virtually a daily affair, and "all-nighters are pretty frequent" as project deadlines draw near. Even those employees who say that they love working for Goldman concede that the hours "just get a bit too much at times." Summer associates should beware of too few hours. In down times, there often aren't enough deals to go around, meaning some employees are left without meaningful work. "If you're stuck without a project it reflects upon you," warns one former summer worker. "They [might] only have six weeks to judge you instead of 12. It's really key to make sure that you're in a department where you get work."

New hires should find comfort in the fact that "the hours loosen up as you get promoted." Vice presidents rarely work all day on weekends; they reportedly usually "just drop in for a couple of hours on Saturday mornings, tell the analysts and associates what to do, and then leave." But, would-be capital markets employees beware: According to one of the division's associates, who reports not having to work many weekends, "As more and more people from the investment-banking division are fired, we're having to do more of their work, including modeling and pitching, which is increasing our hours."

Longer hours plus a prestigious brand name doesn't exactly add up to higher compensation. "Goldman tends to underpay in the short term and overpay in the long term," says one vice president. Another insider says the firm "generally pays in-line and fair relative to the competition." The contact adds, though, that Goldman has "above average benefits, including additional investment opportunities with private equity and hedge funds." A London source also calls compensation "fair," saying the firm "keeps near the industry average."

Teaching their children well

Goldman certainly trains its employees well. Maybe too well. One insider calls the firm's training "very thorough," but says it's often a problem. "A lot of firms try to pick off our employees after they go through training." If Goldman employees don't get hired away after going through the firm's training program, which one insider says, "has to be the best in the industry," additional educational opportunities also exist. "Goldman's emphasis on employees results in many opportunities to take classes, and we're definitely strong in this area," says a New York employee. Some say that the training program reinforces the Goldman culture and the distaste for doing things differently. In M&A, for example, don't expect to develop your own models. "[At] Goldman you never, ever use your own models," says one M&A associate. "You're always using a template," one of the five or six the firm uses for all deals.

Close, but nice, quarters

Goldman Sachs' New York headquarters is split into two main locations. Goldman's investment-banking business and administrative functions are housed at 85 Broad Street in downtown Manhattan. The sales and trading business is located across the street at One New York Plaza. (The firm also has a few smaller offices in New York.) Goldman's offices are described as "modern" and "beautiful," and the lobbies and hallways are lined with "expensive artwork by renowned artists such as Jasper Johns." Goldman's overseas offices aren't devoid of amenities, either. One U.K.-based banker calls the new fitness center in the London office "fantastic."

All analysts and associates are assigned their own cubicles, and sources complain that working in cubicles eventually "gets tiresome" because they afford little privacy. One analyst notes, "Everyone can listen in on all of your personal phone calls." Junior employees are particularly irked that "senior people can tell whether you're working or slacking off." A former associate recalls, "You can't even read the paper at your desk without the whole floor knowing, so a lot of people take papers to the bathroom and read them in the stalls." However, as employees ascend the corporate hierarchy, the amount of privacy increases considerably. Vice presidents get their own "nice but small" offices, and managing directors have the luxury of large corner offices.

No problems going public

Many industry observers wondered if Goldman's IPO would disturb the mystique and hush-hush culture of the private partnership. Insiders say that post-IPO, the mystique is safe and sound. Explains one associate, "The people who were partners [now managing directors] still control the majority of the firm. The power structure remains the same." One source says the IPO has changed compensation: "Before people would be paid in all cash — now a good portion of your comp will be in stock." That source also notes that the firm has "become more bureaucratic since going public."

Morgan Stanley

1585 Broadway
New York, NY 10036
Phone: (212) 761-4000
www.morganstanley.com

DEPARTMENTS

Asset Management (Individual,
Institutional) • Credit Services •
Securities (Institutional and Retail
Sales and Trading, Investment
Banking, Research)

THE STATS

Chairman and CEO: Philip J. Purcell
Employer Type: Public Company
Ticker Symbol: MWD (NYSE)
2001 Revenues: $43.7 billion
2001 Net Income: $3.5 billion
No. of Employees: 58,540
No. of Offices: 700+

KEY COMPETITORS

Credit Suisse First Boston
Goldman Sachs
Merrill Lynch
Salomon Smith Barney

UPPERS

- Meaningful 360-degree review
  process keeps senior bankers in line
- Rotation system means exposure
  to different products, industry
  groups
- Unquestioned prestige

DOWNERS

- Beeper requirement keeps you on
  a short leash
- Bureaucracy
- Tough hours

EMPLOYMENT CONTACT

Firm-wide Recruiting
Morgan Stanley
1221 Avenue of the Americas
44th Floor
New York, NY 10020
Fax: (212) 762-9242
www.morganstanley.com/careers

THE BUZZ
WHAT EMPLOYEES AT OTHER FIRMS ARE SAYING

- "Gold standard investment bank"
- "Disorganized at the moment"
- "The folks to beat"
- "Declining due to Mack's
  departure"

THE SCOOP

Brokerage behemoth

Morgan Stanley is unquestionably one of the premier bulge-bracket investment banks. The firm reported more than $3.4 billion in I-banking revenues in 2001 and is ranked in the top 10 of every significant league table. The firm's trading operations are even more lucrative; the unit garnered $5.5 billion in revenues in 2001. In addition to its securities businesses, Morgan Stanley offers asset management and research services. Morgan Stanley is one of the largest retail securities firms in the U.S. with 14,000 financial advisers and client assets of more than $570 billion (as of May 31, 2002). Additionally, the firm owns Discover Card, the third-largest credit card company. While the firm's reputation within the I-banking world is fairly spectacular, it might suffer from a second-fiddle complex in its competition with fellow bulge-bracket firm Goldman Sachs. Morgan Stanley usually trails just behind industry leader Goldman in most league tables, including lucrative businesses such as equity underwriting and M&A advisory.

The firm has been feted in the business press recently. Morgan Stanley's European operations are known to be employee friendly. The firm was singled out by *Fortune* as one of the "10 Great Companies in Europe" in the magazine's annual "Best Companies to Work For" list. The U.K.'s *Sunday Times* lauded Morgan Stanley as one of its "100 Best Companies to Work For" for 2002; the firm came in at No. 21. *Fortune* also cited two Morgan Stanley executives as among the "50 Most Powerful Black Executives" in July 2002. William Lewis, head of banking, was No. 13 while Carla Harris, head of equity private placement, was No. 48. Morgan Stanley was the only financial services firm with more than one executive on the list.

Dodging Glass-Steagall

Morgan Stanley Dean Witter (as it was once known) was created in 1997 by the merger of Morgan Stanley and Dean Witter, Discover & Co. Dean Witter was founded in 1924 in San Francisco. Milestones include the firm's IPO in 1972, its 1978 merger with New York-based securities firm Reynolds & Co. (at the time, the largest securities industry merger), its purchase by Sears Roebuck in 1981, the 1986 launch of Discover Card and the 1992 spin-off of the Dean Witter, Discover Group.

Morgan Stanley traces its roots to the former securities operations of J.P. Morgan. In 1933, after the passage of the Glass-Steagall Act, which prohibited firms from operating both commercial and investment-banking businesses, two J.P. Morgan partners (Howard Stanley and Harry Morgan, son of J.P. Morgan) and several other employees split from the bank and formed Morgan Stanley. The new firm was created to concentrate on the securities business, while J.P. Morgan remained a commercial bank. Great moments in Morgan Stanley history include its admission to the New York Stock Exchange in 1941 and its 1986 IPO.

Money mogul

Allowing for the economic slump that pinched revenues across the industry, the year 2001 was an industrious one for Morgan Stanley. The firm came in second in completed M&A deals globally, advising on 305 deals worth $627 billion, and third in announced deals, advising on 313 transactions worth $461 billion, according to Thomson Financial Securities Data. Morgan Stanley's 2001 engagments include AMR Corp.'s acquisition of Trans World Airlines worth $1.3 billion (the deal was announced in January 2001 and approved in April 2001), General Electric's $5.3 billion purchase of Heller Financial (announced in July 2001) and Comcast Corp.'s $72 billion acquisition of AT&T Broadband (announced in December 2001 and pending regulatory approval). Morgan Stanley was the top M&A adviser to insurers in 2001, thanks to the firm's advisory role in AIG's $23.4 billion unsolicited bid to buy American General Corp. The firm continued its roll into 2002. In May 2002, Morgan Stanley advised Wendy's on its $275 million acquisition of the Mexican fast food chain Baja Fresh and also advised PricewaterhouseCoopers and PwC Consulting on the $3.5 billion sale of its consulting unit to IBM in July 2002.

Morgan Stanley is also an underwriting heavyweight. In 2001 the firm was a bookrunner on 15 IPOs worldwide, including three of the largest deals of the year: the $5.8 billion IPO for wireless phone provider Orange and the $2.3 billion KPMG Consulting IPO, both completed in February and the $4.1 billion Agere Systems offering in March. In the first half of 2002, Morgan Stanley was a joint bookrunner on a $1.1 billion IPO for cigarette maker Loews Corp., a sole bookrunner on the $497 million IPO for oil refiner Premcor, and a joint lead manager on ExpressJet's $480 million IPO. Additionally, in April 2002, Morgan lead managed JetBlue's $182 million IPO, one of the hottest offerings of early 2002. In the secondary market, Morgan Stanley was one of the largest underwriters of secondary equity offerings, with 36 deals priced globally in 2001. Among the heavy hitters was the $3.3 billion Sprint follow-on offering, the $2.2 billion ADR offering for KT Corp., the $2.2 billion STMicroelectronics secondary offering and the $1.5 billion accelerated bookbuilt offering for Aegon. The firm also has its hands in big debt deals. In 2002

Morgan Stanley lead-managed four of the five largest corporate debt offerings, including a $6 billion global note offering for AOL TimeWarner, a $6 billion global note transaction for General Electric and a $6 billion extendible monthly securities offering, also for G.E. In addition, Morgan Stanley executed a $5.5 billion senior note deal for Weyerhaeuser to fund its acquisition of Willamette.

New business cards for everyone

Mergers can present brand-name complications. Three-and-a-half years after the marriage of investment career bank Morgan Stanley and retail brokerage Dean Witter, the firm announced in April 2001 it would drop Dean Witter from its marketing moniker, though it kept Dean Witter in its legal name. The firm broke that last Dean Witter tie in June 2002, making the company's legal name just plain Morgan Stanley.

Mack daddy

Meanwhile, Morgan Stanley was busy on another front, dropping its president, John Mack. Mack, the former president and COO of Morgan Stanley, resigned in March 2001. Mack joined Morgan Stanley in 1972 in the firm's bond department. He was named a managing director of the firm in 1979 and president in 1993. His aggressive cost-cutting and firm management style earned him the moniker "Mack the Knife" on Wall Street. *The Wall Street Journal* reported Mack's departure was the result of a power struggle with CEO Phillip Purcell. All looks lovey-dovey, though. Purcell praised Mack, saying, "No one has done more than Mack to make Morgan Stanley Dean Witter the world's leading financial services firm." Mack later caught on as the head of Credit Suisse First Boston.

The death of the Internet?

Like most full-service investment banks, Morgan Stanley embraced the rush to online trading in the late 1990s. The firm repackaged its Discover Brokerage unit as Morgan Stanley Online in November 1999, after months of saying most of its clients wouldn't be interested in online trading. Like many other Internet fads, online trading fizzled when the stock market struggled in 2000 and 2001. As a result, many investors who tried to go it alone fled back to more traditional relationships with brokers and financial advisors. Sensing that personal relationships were becoming more important, Morgan Stanley sold its online accounts to the Bank of Montreal's Harrisdirect unit for $107 million in May 2002. The sale only affected accounts that were solely online; customers who did at least part of their business with Morgan

Stanley brokers stayed with the firm. (This was the Bank of Montreal's second online acquisition from a bulge-bracket firm in three months. Harrisdirect is the latest incarnation of CSFBdirect, acquired in February 2002.)

MS hit hard by WTC attacks

Morgan Stanley was one of the firms hardest hit by the September 11 terrorist attacks on the World Trade Center. The firm had approximately 3,700 employees on 20 floors of the south tower; 13 employees died in the attack. The incident made the firm reevaluate its plans to move some operations to 745 Seventh Avenue, just around the corner from its Times Square headquarters. The space could have housed about 20 percent of the 3,700 employees who worked at the World Trade Center. Company management was reluctant to keep so many employees in one place, fearing that another attack or catastrophic event could cripple the firm. As a result, the company sold the new office space to Lehman Brothers, which also had some of its offices destroyed in the attacks. After some deliberation about where to house displaced New York City employees, Morgan Stanley purchased Texaco's former world headquarters, a 725,000-square-foot office building in Westchester County, N.Y.

The September 11 attacks had other repercussions for Morgan Stanley. In late September of 2001, Morgan Stanley announced cuts of approximately 200 jobs in its investment-banking division. (The firm had cut 1,500 jobs across several divisions in early 2001.) In November 2001, Morgan Stanley reportedly told employees their salaries — base pay only, not bonuses — would be frozen for the next year.

See you in court

Morgan Stanley is no stranger to the occasional scandal. The firm has been battling a sex-discrimination complaint filed by the Equal Employment Opportunity Commission (EEOC) on behalf of Allison Schieffelin, a former convertible bond saleswoman. Schieffelin complained she was underpaid, excluded from client outings and withheld a promotion based on her sex. She originally filed a complaint with the EEOC in 1998; in June 2000, the agency ruled that Schieffelin had grounds for a complaint and forced Morgan Stanley to settle the case. Things took a turn for the worse in October 2000 when Morgan Stanley fired Schieffelin in what the EEOC said was a retaliatory move for her discrimination claim. Morgan Stanley claimed that Schieffelin was dismissed for insubordination — specifically, for an argument in which Schieffelin allegedly stuck her finger in her boss's face and verbally attacked her. The case is still pending.

The firm was glad to see at least one case come to an end recently. A class-action suit filed against Morgan Stanley and star analyst Mary Meeker, who was once called the "Queen of the Internet," was dismissed in August 2001. Amazon and eBay shareholders claimed that Meeker's analysis of the two companies was flawed and biased. The suit was quickly blown out of court. A federal judge dismissed the case, saying the complaint was "hopelessly redundant, argumentative and [contains] much irrelevancy and inflammatory material."

That's heavy, man

In response to the industry-wide criticism of conflicts of interest affecting research analysts, Morgan Stanley instituted a new stock-rating system in March 2002. The new rating system replaced four old ratings — "strong buy," "outperform," "neutral" and "underperform" — with three new ones — "overweight," "equal-weight" and "underweight." Under the new system, analysts rate stocks against each other and the industry, so, in theory, analysts should dole out more of the lowest ratings than before. Previously, 1 percent of the stocks that Morgan covered received the lowest rating (underperform); on the opening day of the new system, Morgan gave 22 percent of the stocks it covers a rating of "underweight," the new lowest moniker.

GETTING HIRED

Wide variety of interviews

Morgan Stanley's interviews are, according to some current employees, "quite formal, even for the investment banking industry." Given its reputation and the weak employment market, the firm can afford to be selective. One contact in the strategic investment division reports that the firm "screened over 500 resumes and interviewed over 100 candidates for two positions" in the most recent recruiting cycle. Technical questions are common; one business school student interviewing for a trading job reports that for his final round he was asked to sit in a chair while a senior director peppered him with questions. "All he did was pace around and throw questions at me — if I was wrong he'd correct me, and then just go to the next one. I remember thinking, 'God, I'm glad I know some of this stuff.' It was a lot of macroeconomics: inflation, interest rates, currencies." Says that contact: "They had me interview with pretty senior people, the head of all treasury trading, and the second in charge of all fixed income." Some recent associate-level hires report undergoing more than one callback round during the business school recruiting process. "I had three more rounds, all in New York [after the on-campus round]," reports one contact.

Recruits for investment banking tell a different story. One associate reports a far less grueling interview process. "It's all in who you meet here," that source explains. "Since it's such a large place, you are going to meet people with very different interviewing styles — I also think that if they have confidence in your technical skills and coursework, then you won't hit many technical questions at all." One former M&A banker agrees. "I wasn't given quantitative questions, because I had a financial background," he says, adding, "Questions were more about fit — why them, what was I looking for, what did I want to get out of the job — as opposed to asking me about discounted cash flows." However, the banker admits, "If I didn't have the background, they would have asked me quantitative questions."

An investment-banking contact reports that at his business school, Morgan Stanley holds only two rounds (one on-campus and one at an office) for both summer and full-time associate hires. "They make very quick decisions," reports that contact. "That's the difference between Goldman and Morgan Stanley." That insider reports that there was one two-on-one interview ("good cop, bad cop"), though "other people had one-on-ones." The second round was all one-on-ones for this contact. During the second round, a Super Saturday-like format, recruits can expect to meet "mostly with managing directors," according to a former employee. If you're lucky enough to land a summer internship, you've got it made. "A large percentage of my summer class got offers to return full-time," reports one banker. The firm's web site, www.morganstanley.com, has an extensive careers section that includes an online application.

OUR SURVEY SAYS

Don't be caught without your white shoes

As one of Wall Street's preeminent "white shoe" firms, Morgan Stanley cultivates an "extremely professional environment" geared toward the "bright, motivated individuals who fill the halls." Insiders say that "everyone seems to have an MBA from a top business school" and state that "no other firm matches Morgan Stanley in terms of education and attitude." One former banker says the firm was "a great place to learn how to work in an intense environment with smart people." Another banker agrees, saying one of the best parts aspects of life at Morgan is "working with hard charging aggressive people who like what they're doing." However, not everyone appreciates this atmosphere. One former analyst calls the people at Morgan Stanley his "biggest disappointment." He explains, "They are boorish, aggressive and elitist — even more so than the rest of Wall Street."

Sources say the firm cultivates a conformist culture. "If you don't fit in, you stand out a lot," observes one banker. "You kind of have to walk the walk and talk the talk." Another insider complains of Morgan Stanley's "extremely rigid organization" and "heavy-handed culture." That insider says the firm "takes pride in 'the Morgan Stanley way.' They have this attitude of, 'This is how we've always done things, and this is how we'll continue to do things.'" Even so, that insider does concede that the bank puts "a lot of time and effort into developing people." Another source echoes this, noting that in her experience, the firm is a "very non-hierarchical meritocracy that fosters creativity and learning." Further supporting the view of Morgan as a meritocracy, a former banker in New York says Morgan "treats people fair and even-handed and makes every effort to make the rules of the game clear: 'If you hit this, you'll get this.' They kept politics to a minimum." The contact does admit, "At the end of the day, you might be able to climb up a rung or two on politics." However, he says, "Mostly, you move up if you perform." Overall, most assert that at Morgan Stanley the "focus is on producing good work."

Investment-banking associates at Morgan are offered a generalist program with three rotations through industry or product groups. These rotations last four months each. Comparing Morgan Stanley to its chief competitor, Goldman Sachs, one insider comments, "There's an incredible amount of mobility when compared to Goldman. You spend your first year as a total generalist and then after two years, if you want, you can switch groups." Another insider brags, "I have a wide latitude to choose my own projects and thus have very interesting projects to do." A former employee says Morgan is a "looser place to work and more individual oriented than Goldman, which is incredibly uptight." He does warn that the house of Morgan isn't what it used to be. "A lot of the senior people who were culture carriers are gone. [Former co-CEO John] Mack was one of the last tangible ties to the old partnership days. Now, there's a lot of new people in there, and it's a less special place as a result."

No suits, but plenty of good apples

The firm, like its Wall Street counterparts, embraced a full-time business casual dress policy in the late 1990s. The firm also issued a brochure highlighting the major do's and don'ts for dressing appropriately at work. Some don'ts: shirts without collars or open-toed shoes. Some do's: khakis and polo shirts in the summer. "Lots of people really push the casual dress envelope," reports one insider. "The pendulum has swung so far that people give you good-humored flack if you wear a suit for a borderline reason," such as interviewing MBA candidates.

Morgan Stanley provides a slew of other perks, including tuition reimbursement, subsidized health club memberships, laptops, car service, meal allowances on nights and weekends and other standard investment banking perks. In addition, insiders say the firm sponsors "lavish" company outings and parties. One source says, "I feel like this firm really cares about making people feel like they are working for a top-notch organization." For the health-conscious, the firm reportedly offers free fruit on every investment-banking floor.

Always on call

One of the famed aspects of Morgan Stanley's culture is that bankers are required to wear beepers, which other banks enjoy pointing out as a Morgan shortcoming during recruiting season. "Depending on how you think about that, [omnipresent beepers are] a good thing or a bad thing," reveals one associate. "The bad thing is, everyone's got access to your number. But the good side is that if you ever want to take a two-hour lunch, you can, because they can page you. If anyone ever complains that you weren't in the office, you can just say 'Why didn't you page me?'" Another source says that having to be on call is "useful to go through. You learn a lot. You learn to prioritize your time." However, he, like many Morgan insiders, has beeper horror stories. "One time," explains the contact, "I was all settled in at home to watch the NCAA men's basketball championship game when I got beeped. I had to go back into the office and missed the game." (Much to his chagrin, he missed a classic. The University of Connecticut, nine point underdogs, beat Duke University 77-74 in one of the biggest upsets in NCAA tournament history.)

360-degree evaluations

Morgan Stanley is also famed for its innovative evaluation system. The 360-degree review evaluation process takes place once a year, but most analysts are reviewed mid-year as well. "So everyone you work with, you put on your list, and that list goes to the HR department," explains one insider. "The HR department sends an evaluation form to everyone you work with. [Morgan Stanley] takes this very seriously. Everyone you work with will give you a formal evaluation. All the evaluations are collected, and a VP or managing director who's in your group is assigned to collate all the information and pull together what the overall evaluation should be."

"You not only get feedback from people above you, but you give them evaluations. The downward evaluations are named, upward are anonymous," says one former analyst. "So if your associate is being a total pain in the ass, you slam [him or her] in the reviews. They take very seriously the opinions of the junior people when evaluating for bonuses, so associates go out of the way to be helpful." "I'd say that is a very unique thing about Morgan," says one banker, who points out that the Morgan Stanley evaluation model was actually a case study at his business school.

Neither time nor money is on your side

The hours at Morgan Stanley can be quite onerous — analysts should be prepared for 100-hour workweeks. Making matters worse, some insiders complain the firm is nowhere near the top of the pay scale. "While I'm happy with my salary, they're notorious for paying below other firms," says one contact, who adds, "The attitude seems to be that you should work there because of the firm's prestige and reputation for excellence, not necessarily for the money." A former employee has a slightly different view, saying Morgan pays "in-line" with the industry. He adds, "They try to be competitive but don't want to be at the very top. They just don't want to run ahead of the pack."

Salomon Smith Barney

388 Greenwich Street
New York, NY 10013
Phone: (212) 816-6000
www.salomonsmithbarney.com

DEPARTMENTS

Equities • Fixed Income • Foreign
Exchange • Global Relationship
Bank • Investment Banking • Public
Finance • Research • Sales and
Trading

THE STATS

Chairman and CEO:
Michael Carpenter
Employer Type:
Subsidiary of Citigroup
2001 Revenues: $27.4 billion
2001 Net Income: $2.6 billion
No. of Employees: 43,890
No. of Offices: 500+

KEY COMPETITORS

Credit Suisse First Boston
Goldman Sachs
J.P. Morgan Chase
Merrill Lynch
Morgan Stanley

THE BUZZ
WHAT EMPLOYEES AT OTHER FIRMS ARE SAYING

- "Knocking on the door of the
  Big Two"
- "Inhumane and too big"
- "The folks to beat"
- "Integrating all the disparate
  pieces of its empire"

UPPERS

- Excellent training program
- Prestigious firm on its way up the
  league tables
- Respectful, bright and friendly
  co-workers

DOWNERS

- Huge firm equals lots of
  bureaucracy
- Long hours
- Pays less than competitors

EMPLOYMENT CONTACT

Investment Banking Recruiting
Caitlin McLaughlin
Director, MBA Recruiting
Kate Schwab
Vice President, Undergraduate
Sales and Trading Recruiting
Cynthia Bohan
Director, MBA Recruiting
Susan Glendon
Director, Undergraduate Recruiting
Equity Research Recruiting
Megan Tencza
Assistant Vice President, Recruiting
**Structured Corporate
Finance/Relationship Management**
Megan Tencza
Assistant Vice President, MBA
Melanie Rose
Undergraduate Recruiting

Salomon Smith Barney
388 Greenwich Street
New York, NY 10013
Fax: (212) 793-9086

THE SCOOP

Throngs of Salomon mergers

Salomon Smith Barney, now the investment-banking arm of Citigroup, has a long history of mergers. The firm traces its roots back to 1873, when trader Charles Barney founded a securities firm in Philadelphia. In 1892 Edward Smith started his brokerage business, also in the City of Brotherly Love. The two firms eventually combined to form Smith Barney, which was acquired by Primerica, a financial services firm run by Sanford "Sandy" Weill, in 1987. Primerica was sold to Hartford-based insurance giant Travelers Group in 1993. In December 1997, Travelers bought Salomon Brothers for more than $9 billion, and merged Salomon Brothers with Smith Barney to create Salomon Smith Barney. Travelers then merged with Citicorp, the New York-based commercial bank, creating the merged entity Citigroup in October 1998.

Salomon Smith Barney provides the full range of financial advisory, research and capital raising services to corporations, governments and individuals. The firm has about 12,100 financial consultants in more than 510 offices across the United States, servicing approximately 7.3 million client accounts with $977 billion in assets. Salomon Smith Barney's global investment-banking operations provide a full range of capital market services, including the underwriting and distribution of debt and equity securities for United States and foreign corporations.

Becoming a giant

Initial results from the Citicorp/Travelers merger were excellent, and analysts raved about the company's future. *Euromoney* named Salomon Smith Barney "Most Improved Investment Bank" in July 1999. In October 1999, Citigroup was able to lure former Treasury Secretary Robert Rubin to the firm, making him chair of the executive committee and part of the chairman's office. After his appointment, rumors surfaced that Rubin was under consideration for the CEO post at Citigroup and the position of chairman of the Federal Reserve. Those rumors were later extinguished as Rubin denied interest in the CEO position and Alan Greenspan was reappointed Fed chairman.

The lone fly in the Citigroup ointment was a complex managment structure that reportedly led to a power struggle between Weill and Reed, at the time co-chairmen and co-CEOs. Reed retired in February 2000, saying he sought the tranquility of life outside corporate America. In April 2000, however, *The Wall Street Journal* published a far different account, reporting that Reed and Weill had clashed over a number of issues, including the bank's Internet strategy, and that some senior managers found the presence of two CEOs disruptive. Citigroup's board of directors debated the issue for several hours in February 2000. At one point, Reed rejected a compromise that would have made him non-executive chairman and left Weill as CEO. After that, the board asked Reed to retire.

Adept with debt

Salomon Smith Barney is a perennial leader in underwriting fixed income offerings and providing liquidity in those markets. In 2001 SSB held on to the top spot in total fixed income offerings, underwriting debt totaling $186 billion, according to Thomson Financial Securities Data. The total constituted a big jump from the $108 billion worth of debt that SSB underwrote in 2000, when the firm was the only bank to break the $100 billion mark. Capitalizing on its fixed income prowess, SSB was also the top underwriter in 2001 of global debt and equity combined, breaking Merrill Lynch's 11-year reign in the category. SSB handled $486 billion in debt and equity issues, garnering the firm a 12 percent share of the worldwide $4 trillion market. "These bragging rights are actually a tangible marketing item," money manager Michael Holland of Holland Balanced Fund told *The Wall Street Journal*. Holland added, "When the king is dethroned, you can bet the new king is going to be making a lot of commotion about that."

SSB also unseated Goldman Sachs in 2001, knocking the bank from its pedestal in the category of disclosed fees from total global debt and equity issues. SSB racked up $2.4 billion in disclosed fees during the year, leaping from its fourth place finish in 2000, when it banked $2 billion in fees. During its monumental 2001, SSB co-lead managed numerous billion dollar plus debt offerings, including AT&T's $10 billion issuance in November, Ford Motor's $9.4 billion issuance in October, and Lucent Technologies' $1.9 billion issuance in August. Without breaking stride, before the 2002 first quarter was finished, SSB already had its hand in a bunch more billion dollar debt deals, including issuances for Mararthon Oil, Sprint and Walt Disney. SSB's recent equity underwriting engagements include Kraft Foods' whopping $8.7 billion IPO in June 2001, Willis Group Holdings' $270 million IPO also in June 2001, tobacco maker Loews Corp.'s $980 million IPO in February 2002 and Travelers' $4 billion IPO in March 2002.

SSB's M&A operation is not too shabby, either. In 2001 the firm was the fourth-ranked M&A adviser, handling $482 billion of business, according to Thomson

Financial. The firm's biggest deals for the year included advising Tyco International on its $10.2 billion acquisition of The CIT Group, USX Corp. on its $9.8 billion purchase of USX Marathon Group and Compaq Computer on its $24.9 billion sale to Hewlett Packard in September 2001.

Making the cut

Salomon Smith Barney was not immune to the layoffs sweeping the industry. In April 2001, SSB's parent Citigroup announced it was cutting several hundred jobs in its 60,000 employee corporate and investment banking operations. "Most of the jobs are in operations and technology, many the result of ongoing integration," a Citigroup spokeswoman told CNNfN. "We've had four mergers in three years, and clearly the layoffs also reflect current market conditions." The spokeswoman would not specify exact numbers, but said less than one percent of the staff would be laid off.

Feeling the heat

SSB was one of several targets of a recent investigation into alleged conflicts of interest among Wall Street firms' research analysts and their investment bankers. The investigation was launched by New York State Attorney General Eliot Spitzer. He first looked into allegations that SSB competitor Merrill Lynch allowed investment-banking fees to influence research coverage. The probe soon expanded to other Wall Street firms. In April 2002, SSB confirmed in an internal memo (obtained by *The New York Times*) that Spitzer had subpoenaed the firm to turnover all related communications between the firm's investment-banking group and its telecommunications research team. The memo also stated that SSB was to turnover all information about how the research team was compensated. In May 2002, Merrill agreed to a settlement with Spitzer. The firm agreed to pay a $100 million fine, set up a committee to oversee its research, separate analysts' compensation from investment-banking fees and disclose any fees in research reports. Salomon Smith Barney adopted similar changes shortly afterwards, minus the $100 million payout.

It remains to be seen whether SSB's early adoption will spare the firm further scrutiny. Spitzer and other observers are focusing on Jack Grubman, the firm's star telecom analyst. Some charge that Grubman, who reportedly made $20 million per year during the bull market, had too cozy a relationship with some of the telecom companies he covered. Grubman had significant influence on firms like Global Crossing and WorldCom — once darlings of an industry that led the stock market plunge in 2001 and 2002. While Grubman's hands-on analysis was applauded during the good times, some raised questions about conflicts of interest when telecom stocks began tanking.

The firm was sucked into another probe in June 2002. The SEC began looking into both SSB's and Citigroup's dealings with Adelphia Communications, the Coudersport, Pa.-based cable provider that had an Enron-like collapse in early 2002. At issue were loans granted from Citigroup to the Rigas family, the clan that founded Adelphia. The loans, totaling $3.1 billion, were given to a partnership owned by the Rigas family and secured by Adelphia Communications. Adelphia didn't disclose that information to the public, even during the disclosure phase of two stock offerings in January and November 2001. Salomon Smith Barney, which led both offerings, made no mention of the loans in its due diligence reports, which has drawn the focus of investigators, especially since the loans were from SSB's parent.

Salary CAP

Some former SSB brokers have taken issue with the firm's Capital Accumulation Plan (CAP). The 400 ex-brokers filed a lawsuit in 2001 against SSB and Citigroup, charging that the company illegally retained money they put into the deferred compensation plan after the brokers left Salomon Smith Barney. The CAP plan allows qualified employees to invest between 5 percent and 25 percent of their salary in Citigroup stock at a 25 percent discount. Some employees also receive part of their bonus in Citigroup stock, which also goes into the CAP fund. The plan vests in two or three years, but all of the money put into the program — both employee and company contributions — is retained by the company if the employee leaves before full vesting. (Most deferred compensation plans allow employees to keep their contributions no matter how long they stay at the firm.) The plaintiffs say that policy is an unlawful retention of their wages; the firm claims the policy is lawful and in keeping with the intentions of the plan. The suit is still pending.

The bank that dare not speak its name

Though rich in history, the Salomon Smith Barney name will soon be history. Parent Citigroup combined Salomon Smith Barney's operations with Citibank's corporate bank and renamed the group Citigroup Corporate and Investment Bank. In a company-wide e-mail in May 2001, Chairman Weill told employees that Citigroup wished to exploit the strength of its Citi brand name, as well as strengthen the "common culture we are developing as Citigroup." (The name change was supposed to take place in the first quarter of 2002, but has been postponed.) Additionally, in a return to making money the old fashioned way, Salomon Smith Barney will use the name "Smith Barney" as the brand name for its private client business.

GETTING HIRED

Thin velvet rope

Although Salomon Smith Barney generally limits its formal recruiting process to the top undergrad and MBA programs, the firm does look further than the first tier for new talent. According to one banker, SSB also targets "select second-tier schools that have proven successful over time." Another insider says the firm recruits from other than the top schools "during better economic times when there are more jobs to be filled." Explains one source, "The firm is selective, but does allow for individuals with unique backgrounds to take a shot at explaining why they can add value." Another says SSB "keeps a relatively open mind about a candidate's backgrounds. However, if you are not able to demonstrate an ability to be aggressive about selling yourself, it can be hard to get in."

Once in the door, all recruits typically go through three rounds of interviews. As one insider points out, "The recruiting process is quick and very organized. Unlike some of our competitors, we don't drag out the interview process for four unnecessary rounds." The first round usually occurs on a recruit's campus, the second off campus, and the third at SSB's offices. During the entire recruiting process, candidates will meet with between 10 to 15 bankers at the associate through managing director levels. According to one New York employee, "Questions are definitely behavioral-based, weighted on fit," rather than quantitative-based. Another source says that although interviewers will pose "a few light technical questions at some point," they won't throw out any "screwball questions about Rubik's cubes or physics."

Summer lovin'

Most employees agree that it's easier to land a full-time position at SSB having worked as a summer intern for the firm. Although difficult to land, SSB summer internships are "key to getting a full time job here," says one employee. One summer alumnus says, "Unlike other top firms, which hire about 80 [summer associates] per summer and hire half of them [for full-time positions], we only hire between 40 and 50, but at least 90 percent receive full-time offers."

OUR SURVEY SAYS

The competitive advantage

"If you can succeed at this firm, you can succeed anywhere," says one New York insider, sounding a little like Sinatra. SSB's extremely competitive, fast-paced culture is "designed to let those who perform flourish," says another. The internal competition among employees is team-oriented and collaborative, not ruthless. "You are constantly surrounded by extremely bright individuals, who push you to perform at your best," says one contact. When describing SSB's corporate climate, many insiders use the words "friendly," "entrepreneurial," "open-minded," and "meritocracy." At SSB, "people take their work seriously, but not themselves," says one contact. Speaking about who is most likely to succeed at SSB, one banker says, "Only the people who are the most determined, but who also seek a friendly environment, find themselves staying at the firm." Despite the passage of time, some feel the firm's merger history still haunts the culture. One insider in London admits that your standing with the firm is based somewhat on where you were before the mergers. "People are aware who the Salomon people are, who the Schroders people are," says that source, who concedes that the firm is developing a "unified" culture.

Clearly, SSB's well-known training program is one of the firm's strengths. Numerous firm contacts call SSB's program the "best on the Street." Despite receiving such high marks for its training year after year, SSB is unafraid to make changes to the comprehensive 10-week program. Reports one insider, SSB is "constantly tweaking the program, scrapping initiatives that don't work." As far as the specifics of the program, inside sources seem to have conflicting opinions. One source calls the accounting training "superb," but the finance training just "average." However, another says, "No other bank comes close in terms of teaching financial statement analysis."

You'll live at the office

SSB certainly hasn't been gaining ground on the top I-banks without its junior folks working long hours. Analysts and associates both log, on average, a minimum of 80 hours a week, which includes frequent weekend office visits. Of course, analysts work more, regularly putting in 100-hour weeks during busier times. While most sources report having to put in little to no "face time," some say they're still forced to spend a significant number of unnecessary hours at the office. One insider says, "25 to 35 percent of hours worked are needless, resulting from the inefficiency and abusiveness of senior bankers." Another agrees, saying, "Many hours spent in the office are due to senior manager's inability to focus, and to realize the amount of time and effort it takes junior people to complete something as requested." With or without the needless time spent at the office, SSB analysts and associates eat many a dinner in cubicle city (if working past 6 p.m., employees are given a $20 dinner allowance). Says an associate in New York, "Just because there's very little, if any, face time required, doesn't mean you'll be able to go home before midnight from Monday to Thursday very often."

How 'bout a little something, you know, for the effort?

Most insiders call SSB's pay package at best average, compared to its competitors. One source calls SSB's compensation "consistently lower than the industry average," but another says it's "adequate when compared to other banks." Even so, with SSB gaining ground in the league tables, some employees think they're being slighted. An insider says, "The firm's compensation is barely above average, which is pretty disappointing given the relative performance of the firm over the past two years." Another employee echoes that opinion. "Given the strength of the bank, we should pay higher than the Street. But this just isn't the case."

Showing some respect

With few exceptions, junior employees at SSB report receiving a great deal of respect from their superiors. One source says SSB senior managers are "very respectful of subordinates' skills and opinions," while another says senior bankers are "always professional and respectful." One insider offers, "If you are good, managers will respect your work, however, they never respect your time." While many contacts say senior managers lack arrogance, "there is some of the 'don't waste my time, you lowly analyst' attitude from the senior people," says one source. Another employee, speaking in a macro sense, disagrees. SSB's "culture doesn't reward people who treat subordinates poorly." The source goes on to say, "Expectations are high, but realistic. And VPs and MDs are reasonable."

The office atmosphere is pretty typical. SSB's offices seem utilitarian, if not overly aesthetic. "Cubicle city," says one contact. "Nothing fancy here at Salomon Smith Barney. The conference rooms are plain [and] even MDs offices are less than spectacular. At least analysts don't work in bullpens." The firm also provides a refuge from those late nights, both at the office and on the town. "The lounge on the 36th floor is a God-send for the overworked and the hungover," says one party animal. Salomon Smith Barney hasn't gone back to suits and ties and "currently, there is no talk of going back to business attire."

For detailed 40- to 50-page insider reports on top finance employers like Goldman, Morgan Stanley, Merrill, Salomon Smith Barney, Lehman Brothers and more, get Vault Employer Profiles. Go to http://finance.vault.com.

"If you can succeed at this firm, you can succeed anywhere."

— Salomon Smith Barney insider

Merrill Lynch

4 World Financial Center
250 Vesey Street
New York, NY 10080
Phone: (212) 449-1000
www.ml.com

DEPARTMENTS

Corporate and Institutional Client
Group • Investment Management •
Private Client Group

THE STATS

Chairman and CEO:
David H. Komansky
**President and Chief Operating
Officer:** E. Stanley O'Neal
Employer Type: Public Company
Ticker Symbol: MER (NYSE)
2001 Revenue: $38.8 billion
2001 Net Income: $573 million
No. of Employees: 57,400
No. of Offices: 900

KEY COMPETITORS

Credit Suisse First Boston
Goldman Sachs
Morgan Stanley
Salomon Smith Barney

UPPERS

- Good relations with superiors
- Name recognition
- Outstanding perks and benefits

DOWNERS

- Research facing legal troubles
- Lagging in pay
- Unpredictable schedules

EMPLOYMENT CONTACT

Investment Banking
Carrie Higginbotham
Assistant Vice President,
Undergraduate Recruiting

Denise Patton
Vice President, MBA Recruiting

Sales and Trading
Claudine Rippa
Vice President

Merrill Lynch
4 World Financial Center
250 Vesey Street, 2nd Floor
New York, NY 10281-1302
Fax: (212) 449-3130
www.ml.com/careers

THE BUZZ
WHAT EMPLOYEES AT OTHER FIRMS ARE SAYING

- "Strong showing lately"
- "Stick with retail business"
- "Nearly as good as Goldman and
  Morgan Stanley"
- "Falling with all the layoffs"

THE SCOOP

Bulge bracket behemoth

Merrill Lynch is among the biggest of the big; with approximately 57,000 employees (as of December 2001), it's second only to Morgan Stanley, and has one of the largest sales forces (over 20,000 financial consultants). The firm is in the middle of a cost-cutting initiative headed by Chief Operating Officer and Chief Executive Officer-in-waiting E. Stanley O'Neal. O'Neal's goal is to streamline Merrill Lynch and return it to elite status, a job made somewhat more difficult by the fallout from the terrorist attacks on the World Trade Center. Three Merrill Lynch employees died in the attacks and 9,000 employees in the complex were temporarily relocated.

From humble beginnings to Wall Street player

Charles Merrill formed an eponymous underwriting firm in 1914; a year later, Merrill took on Edmund Lynch as his partner, and the firm was renamed Merrill, Lynch & Co. Following the market crash of 1929, Merrill decided to focus on investment banking and sold off its retail operations to E.A. Pierce, a brokerage firm. A decade later, Merrill recaptured the retail business when Merrill, Lynch & Co. merged with E.A. Pierce.

Charles Merrill (who ran Merrill Lynch until his death in 1956) was a true renaissance man. In addition to his activities in the financial world, he founded *Family Circle* magazine (you've likely seen it at the grocery store checkout line) and even played semi-pro baseball as a young man. He quickly decided his fortune lay not in the hit-and-run, but in sales and trading. In 1971 Merrill Lynch became the second Big Board member to have its shares listed on the New York Stock Exchange (the first was Donaldson, Lufkin & Jenrette, now a part of Credit Suisse First Boston). Later that year, the company unleashed its "Merrill Lynch is bullish on America" ad campaign. For better or worse, the firm has been linked to its bull mascot since then.

Bitter times for the bull

Merrill Lynch is the nation's largest securities firm and a global powerhouse. But 2001 proved a difficult year for the bullish brokerage firm. The firm cut approximately 15,000 jobs in 2001, including 9,000 in the fourth quarter alone. The layoffs, along with other one-time expenses, led to a loss of $1.26 billion for the fourth quarter, the firm's first quarterly loss since 1998. But Merrill says the workforce cutbacks are part of a plan to slash costs by $1.4 billion a year and increase profitability.

Heir to the throne

E. Stanley O'Neal, the firm's chief operating officer, is heading the cost-cutting plan. O'Neal was named the successor to CEO David Komansky in August 2001 after a lengthy wait. Komansky indicated in late 1999 that he would name a successor ahead of his retirement in 2004, and O'Neal seemed a shoe-in for the job in February 2000 when he was named head of the company's brokerage division. But Komansky stalled on making a formal announcement, and told CNBC that he was considering "at least three" people to take his place. After 15 months of debate, Komansky and the board chose O'Neal.

O'Neal faced significant challenges soon after his designation as Komansky's successor. The firm evacuated its headquarters in the World Financial Center after the terrorist attacks of September 11, 2001. Three Merrill employees died in the attacks and 9,000 workers were evacuated. (Most were able to return to the World Financial Center, which sustained only minor damage, within a few weeks.) Some observers were surprised that O'Neal was the one who took command on September 11. According to *The Wall Street Journal*, O'Neal made key decisions such as splitting up the firm's senior management immediately after the attack (reducing the possibility that the company would be incapacitated by a sudden loss of its leadership). O'Neal also restructured the management team shortly after the attacks, naming executives to positions such as chief legal counsel and head of institutional securities — despite the fact that, according to an interview with the *Journal*, Komansky felt the firm needed a measure of stability after the trauma of the attack.

Rumor mill

The events of late 2001 brought the rumormongers out of the woodwork. After watching O'Neal take charge on September 11, some thought Komansky would retire much sooner than 2004. The rumor picked up some steam in February 2002, when the *Journal* reported that Merrill had formed an executive committee to discuss strategic and operational issues at the firm — and that Komansky wasn't on the committee. Instead, the nine-member team was headed by O'Neal and included division heads, the CFO, general counsel and vice chairman.

Though Komansky denied the rumors, it turns out they were right on target. In July 2002, Merrill's board named O'Neal CEO effective December 2002. Komansky will stay on as chairman until April 2003, when O'Neal will assume that role as well. O'Neal will be the first African American to head a major Wall Street firm.

Looking to sell?

In November 2001, the *Journal* speculated that Merrill Lynch, after years of being linked to various suitors, would finally agree to a merger upon O'Neal's ascension to leadership. In fact, the *Journal* reported that Komansky talked to Goldman Sachs, Deutsche Bank and Bank of America in the summer of 2001 before naming O'Neal COO. Industry insiders believe that while O'Neal might eventually be open to a sale or merger, he'll probably want the chance to run the firm for a while. "Could Stan be the one to sell this thing at some point? Absolutely," Richard Strauss, an analyst at Goldman Sachs, told the *Journal*. "But he ain't going to do it until he drives this Ferrari for the next five years."

End of an error

In what some saw as the final nail in the coffin of the New Economy, Merrill Lynch's famed Internet analyst Henry Blodget announced his resignation in November 2001, accepting a lucrative buyout the firm offered its employees in late 2001 (Blodget reportedly pulled in $12 million for the year). Blodget rose to fame in November 1998 while at CIBC Oppenheimer, predicting that Amazon.com's share price would reach $400. The online retailer was then selling for $240 per share, but soon met Blodget's ambitious target. Blodget, along with his counterpart at Morgan Stanley, Mary Meeker, became stars of the New Economy. Conversely, their reputations suffered when Internet stocks began plummeting in value in 2000 and 2001. Blodget told *The New York Times* that he would write a book about the Internet bubble and then seek work at a money management or hedge fund firm.

Not so fast, Hank

In April 2002, not long after Henry Blodget left Merrill, news surfaced that the former star analyst had been the focus of an investigation into Merrill's research practices. The investigation, led by New York State Attorney General Eliot Spitzer, centered around phone calls and e-mails made by the firm's Internet research group, which Blodget oversaw. Spitzer discovered that Merrill analysts had publicly hyped stocks, while privately referring to the same stocks as "junk" and "crap." Merrill said the e-mails were taken out of context.

After tech stocks tanked, regulators began scrutinizing possible conflicts of interest between a firm's investment bankers and analysts, whose negative research can hurt bankers' chances of obtaining advisory work. Spitzer's office obtained a court order forcing Merrill's research department to make several changes, including disclosing to investors whether it has or intends to have an investment-banking relationship with a corporate client, and adding in its reports how many buy and sell recommendations it has in a particular sector.

These changes, however, didn't end Spitzer's spat with Merrill. When Spitzer later announced that he might bring criminal charges against Merrill, the firm retained former New York Mayor Rudy Giuliani to help negotiate a settlement with the state attorney general. Soon after Rudy became a Merrill consultant, the firm's CEO, David Komansky, publicly apologized for the firm's malpractices. During Merrill's annual shareholder meeting in April 2002, Komansky called the internal e-mails that went public "very distressing and disappointing," and said they fell "far short" of the firm's standards in research. Komansky also voiced plans to take "meaningful and significant actions to restore investor confidence." However, the firm continued to deny that it had broken any rules, saying the e-mails were taken out of context. Still, Merrill began negotiating a settlement with Spitzer.

A deal was reached in May 2002. Merrill agreed to pay $100 million, remove any consideration of investment-banking fees when analyzing research analysts' compensation, disclose relevant investment-banking relationships in research reports and appoint a compliance monitor to oversee the research department. Spitzer, along with the Securities and Exchange Commission and other state attorneys general, are probing research practices at other firms, and the Merrill settlement is being considered a framework for any future deals.

Financial finesse

Despite the firm's fourth-quarter setbacks, Merrill was the leading underwriter of stocks and securities related to stocks and the second-ranked adviser on mergers and acquisitions in 2001. Merrill lead managed 14 IPOs in 2001. Among some of the firm's biggest offerings: Petco Animal Supplies' $287.5 million common stock offering, CNOOC Limited's $1.3 billion stock deal, and Alliance Data Systems' $156 million IPO. Merrill was the lead acquirer adviser on 11 of the top 35 M&A deals in 2001, including General Electric's purchase of Security Capital Group for $4.7 billion in December, AT&T Wireless's acquisition of TeleCorp Wireless for $4.3 billion in October and Alltel's purchase of Century Tel for $9.2 billion in August.

GETTING HIRED

Tough sell

Like all bulge-bracket firms, positions at Merrill are hard to come by. "The overall markets dictate whether it is extremely difficult or nearly impossible to get into Merrill Lynch," reports one associate. "The work is difficult, the hours are long and the lifestyle is tough — but many, many people want to work for Merrill Lynch and competition is tough and only gets tougher to move up within the firm." Another contact echoes that assessment, noting that the recent slump has made landing a job at Merrill even more difficult. "Merrill Lynch has become extremely selective in this market downturn," says that source.

Who do you know?

Resumes submitted to Merrill through college career centers and direct mail are sorted by Merrill's recruiting personnel; all qualified applicants are invited for interviews. The first round of interviews is held on the applicant's campus, and those candidates who make the cut are invited to further rounds at the New York office. Make sure you're at your most charming at cocktail parties, lunches and other informal Merrill gatherings. "Each social outing prior to interviews is very important in determining who makes the closed list," reports one insider. Who you know is important, say others. "Merrill Lynch Investment Banking has a target roster of schools numbering in the dozens," reports one insider. "If you're not from one of these schools, and don't happen to know a bigwig, getting attention from recruiting is tough."

But bigwigs aren't the only ones with influence, continues that contact. "Resume books with hundreds of resumes — Penn has over 400 — are handed out to analysts to comb through. Our selections, mostly people we know, with a few others we're in some other way impressed by, are then given first-round interviews. From there, it's all about who you meet and how you do."

Meet the bankers

Insiders report that Merrill's interviews (even the initial on-campus screening interviews) "can last a lot longer than the typical half-hour interviews that other firms conduct." The firm doesn't shy away from technical questions. "I went through the typical full-time hiring process at business school," reports one associate. "With an investment-banking internship under my belt, I did the standard on-campus interview, followed by a group-specific interview [with] five people, followed by an office-specific interview [with] another 5 people. The questions were based primarily on my summer experience — I was asked to describe the deals I worked on, the strategic rationale and the valuation methodologies used." Those looking at smaller offices outside of New York might meet most or almost all of the relevant employees at the office, say sources.

OUR SURVEY SAYS

Proud to be a Merrill-ite

One insider says that employees are "proud to be part of Merrill Lynch, but not heady about it." The people there are "hard working, driven and extremely bright but down to earth with a relatively good sense of reality," continues that banker. Merrill has a reputation for a gentler culture than its competitors. "Historically, you must remember, Merrill was a 'huge lumbering elephant' because that was the culture in the dominant retail side of business," says one source. "However, things are changing as Merrill becomes one of the top three investment banks, and we're becoming more like Goldman or Morgan Stanley day by day." One contact adds, "We're different from other places. The people are nicer than at other banks." That doesn't mean things don't get dicey. "While the overall culture at Merrill Lynch is much more collegial than at most Wall Street firms, investment banking, and M&A in particular, suffers from the same sharp elbows that afflict all of the Street," says one banker.

Naturally, though, Merrill's size fosters many subcultures, and insiders say that Merrill's culture varies "from department to department." "I found the culture to be very fragmented, though I doubt it is more so than other bulge bracket firms," continues another banker. "For example, M&A has a very different culture than many of the industry groups in investment banking. M&A bankers consider themselves to be the 'Marines' of investment banking and will go to extraordinary lengths to serve their clients. Many of the industry groups still have an 'old-school' entitlement culture where the attitude is that their clients are lucky to have their attention. As you can imagine, this results in a very different work-life balance between the two types of groups."

The firm's junior bankers report a fair amount of respect from their more senior colleagues. "Directors and vice presidents work associates hard, but managing directors ensure proper care and feeding of the associates," says one contact. Another says his bosses treat him as well as any associate in investment banking — which, admittedly, isn't always a love-fest. "While investment banking is billed as a meritocracy, one's title and tenure is still extremely important in terms of getting respect from senior bankers — there is a bias that junior bankers don't have much to add to a discussion that is valuable," gripes that insider. "Generally, I found senior bankers to be disinterested at best and condescending and verbally abusive at worst to associates. Investment banking is simply not a culture where anyone says, 'Please,' 'Thank you' or 'Good work.'" On the other hand, the firm's training can be helpful. "Both formal and informal training is great," enthuses one associate. "Most associates are MBAs and only need a little specific training — the real training starts when you get to work on live transactions, interact with clients and have real money on the table."

Do you read Kafka?

The major drawback of working for Merrill, most agree, is the "horrendous" bureaucracy, which "can sometimes combine with office politics to make life miserable and incomprehensible." An insider repines, "Sometimes, for no apparent reason, you get blamed for things you didn't do and get assignments you're not supposed to have, and there's no one to complain to — life becomes like a page from a Kafka novel." Another source agrees, "While I'm in the world outside, I'm proud to be working for Merrill. But on the inside, I know that bureaucracy and politics can make life pretty miserable." source finds that the bureaucracy can be circumvented. "Merrill Lynch runs relatively flat in terms of day-to-day decision-making, but tends to get bogged down in large-scale company-wide initiatives," says that banker. "In other words, if a decision needs to be made quickly to take on a new client or hire a high-profile banker, senior bankers have a lot of latitude to do so." That associate finds that with a major change, like a change in benefits or compensation, "it can take months, if not years, to work its way through the system. The general rule is: if you can keep your request out of HR, you can [shave] light-years [off] the decision-making process."

Merrill offices: Be impressed

Merrill Lynch's offices are "impressive and large." While "they're not furnished in a particularly lavish fashion, they're always tastefully decorated." The digs are "very comfortable and functional — Merrill doesn't tend to go for as much marble and oil paintings as some of its competitors," critiques one source. Insiders say the firm spends most of its decorating cash on impressing clients. One insider notes, "The conference rooms and other areas visited by clients are very nice, but some of the analyst bullpens are kind of dumpy." Another banker concurs, saying that when clients visit they "are hosted in very nice conference rooms and dining rooms — that is what really matters."

How low can they go?

One area where Merrill lags is pay. While the firm is around the industry average, insiders complain Merrill is slow to match competitors' increases. Gripes one banker, "[The firm] doesn't ask, 'How much do we have to pay to get people to stay?' but, 'How little do we have to pay people to get them to stay?' They look at Morgan Stanley and Goldman Sachs and then price at the lowest." In general, though, "the firm works hard to be fair and is successful," concedes one associate. Private Client Services employees are more pleased. One employee in that department notes that his base salary is more than 10 percent higher than offers he received from several competitors. The firm's 401(k) is standard, while employees rave about the health insurance, "one of the best plans in corporate America."

Perks at Merrill, according to employees, are "the same as those you get at other banks. If you stay past a certain hour, you get dinner and transportation home." Officially, you have to stay past 8 p.m. to get a car, and past 7 p.m. to get dinner. The firm's dinner plan utilizes restaurants with which Merrill has negotiated discounts. Some insiders say they get sick of the food, "but a lot of the associates love it." Those who work on Saturday or Sundays get three meals covered.

Other perks include "free travel and accommodations when you travel with clients." "When you travel," one analyst notes, "you have it pretty good because you use airlines and hotels that must be up to the standard of your clients." The firm still has casual dress, except for client contact, and officially has no plans to change. However, the industry seems to be in disarray on this subject — one banker laments that "the Street doesn't know what it wants to do regarding formal attire" — so a change is not out of the question.

Write your schedule in pencil

Merrill employees have the typical investment bankers' gripes about their hours. "It is not purely the hours that are difficult, it is the unpredictable nature of when a project may become hot and consume every moment of your time and every ounce of energy for days on end," complains one insider. Another source has a theory for the unpredictable schedule. "[The hours] are driven primarily by inefficiencies in information flow," he says. "The majority of time, the hours beyond 50-60 per week are the result of poor communication by senior bankers — either because they: a) neglected to tell junior bankers about the depth of an assignment until shortly before its due date, b) did not clarify with the client the level of detailed work required for a given assignment or c) created an unnecessary and unreasonable expectation with the client about the timing of the delivery of the work."

Living large

The lifestyle at Merrill certainly doesn't help employees stay in shape. One New York analyst complains: "I worked so many hours at the office that I gained a substantial amount of weight. I got fat, to avoid euphemisms. The problem is, you spend so much time sitting at your desk, with no time to exercise, and you're always eating a lot at meetings at night or ordering food from different restaurants. There's no company gym for easy, during-the-day access to weights or jogging." There is an "executive gym" in the building for those high up on the ladder; as for the hard working junior employees, "some associates go to the nearby Marriott, some go to another club."

Credit Suisse First Boston

11 Madison Avenue
New York, NY 10010
Phone: (212) 325-2000
www.csfb.com

DEPARTMENTS

Financial Services • Investment
Banking • Securities

THE STATS

Chairman: Stephen R. Volk
CEO: John Mack
Employer Type: Subsidiary of Credit
Suisse Group
No. of Employees: 25,150
No. of Offices: 46

KEY COMPETITORS

Goldman Sachs
Merrill Lynch
Morgan Stanley

UPPERS

- International reach
- Top-notch perks

DOWNERS

- A lot of bureaucracy
- Organization in disarray after
  merger, layoffs, restructuring

EMPLOYMENT CONTACT

US
Investment Banking
Rachel Graves, MBA Recruiting
Pauline Ma, Undergraduate Recruiting

Fixed Income
Cynthia Marrone, MBA Recruiting
Lindsay Hobbs, Undergraduate
Recruiting
Hallie Silver, MBA and Undergraduate
Dedicated Programs

Equity
Courtney Kirkland, MBA Sales and
Trading Recruiting
Jennifer Murphy, Undergraduate
Sales and Trading Recruiting
Beth Kramer, Research

Private Client Services
Eileen Duff
Recruiting Manager

For international contacts and mailing
addresses, go to
careeropportunities.csfb.com

THE BUZZ
WHAT EMPLOYEES AT OTHER FIRMS ARE SAYING

- "Overtaking Morgan"
- "In disarray due to merger"
- "Smart folks, tough times"
- "Cutting edge, cutthroat"

THE SCOOP

A bulging bracket

Credit Suisse First Boston (CSFB) is a firm in transition. The investment bank is a wholly owned subsidiary of Credit Suisse Group, the Zurich, Switzerland-based financial services firm. CSFB has broken into the bulge bracket of investment banking since the 1988 purchase of CSFB's predecessor, First Boston, by Credit Suisse Group. This process seemed to be complete in 2000 with the purchase of Donaldson, Lufkin & Jenrette (DLJ), an investment banking competitor and an established player in the American securities markets. However, CSFB's establishment in the top echelon has stalled. A Securities and Exchange Commission investigation and changes at the top have left CSFB very much in disarray.

From New York to Zurich

The mega-bank has a history that spans nearly 70 years. First Boston began as the investment-banking arm of First National Bank of Boston. When the Glass-Steagall Act and other legal reforms imposed barriers among commercial banks, investment banks and insurance companies, the investment-banking arm became the independent First Boston. In 1988 Credit Suisse, the Zurich-based bank, renamed itself CS Holdings and became a parent company/shareholder of a newly renamed CS First Boston. The alliance became more formalized in 1997, when CS Holdings swallowed the whole investment banking unit and both parent and child emerged with new names: Credit Suisse Group (a global bank headquartered in Zurich) and investment-banking arm Credit Suisse First Boston (headquartered in New York).

CSFB slowly shed its reputation as a second-rate player throughout the late 1990s. The firm saw a chance to become an unquestioned leader in the industry through acquisition and did exactly that, announcing the purchase of DLJ in August 2000 for approximately $11.5 billion. The deal was not universally loved — some analysts predicted culture clashes, and the union resulted in the elimination of 2,500 jobs. Some senior managers abandoned the new firm shortly after the merger. Ken Moelis, who had served as DLJ's head of corporate finance and was named co-head of investment banking at the new firm, left CSFB for competitor UBS Warburg in November 2000. Also irksome was a September 2000 report in *The Wall Street Journal* stating that Joe Roby, DLJ's president and CEO, received a six-year contract worth over $82 million to act as chairman of the combined firm.

Despite these setbacks, the new CSFB was a reasonably successful firm, staying near the top of the league tables in 2001. Profits were down somewhat, but the firm's performance was on par with the rest of the industry. However, there was trouble looming.

Welcome Mack

In early 2001, the National Association of Securities Dealers announced a probe into the IPO practices at major Wall Street firms. It quickly became clear that CSFB was a focus of the probe. The NASD was investigating allegations that brokers coerced clients to pay higher commissions and buy aftermarket shares in exchange for larger allocations of future IPOs. In May 2001, the NASD charged six CSFB employees with violating NASD rules; the firm later concluded in an internal investigation that three brokers had violated firm policy and dismissed those brokers.

Embarrassed by the investigation and hoping to stave off a possible criminal indictment, Credit Suisse management decided to make a change. In what *BusinessWeek* called a "ruthless corporate ambush," Allen Wheat, CSFB's CEO since 1997, was summoned to London in July 2001 by Credit Suisse Group Chairman and CEO Lukas Mühlemann, who promptly dismissed Wheat. Mühlemann immediately hired John Mack, a Wall Street veteran with a reputation as a cost-cutter. Mack had resigned from Morgan Stanley in January 2001; he reportedly lost a power struggle for control of that firm to executives from the old Dean Witter, which merged with Morgan Stanley in 1997.

Though CSFB initially denied that the IPO probe was a factor in Wheat's dismissal, among Mack's first moves was the hiring of legal experts Stephen Volk and Gary Lynch as vice chairman and global general counsel, respectively. Both were veterans of prestigious law firms. Volk was a partner at Shearman & Sterling while Lynch, the former head of the SEC's enforcement division, was a partner at Davis Polk & Wardwell. (Volk was elevated to chairman in January 2002, a month after Roby was named chairman emeritus and senior advisor.)

So we meet again

Besides dealing with the IPO probe, Mack's initial goals included cost-cutting and establishing a single culture across the firm. One example was Mack's relationship with superstar banker Frank Quattrone. Quattrone had worked for Mack at Morgan Stanley but left for Deutsche Bank in 1996, seeking more autonomy. Unsatisfied with his role at Deutsche, Quattrone came to CSFB in 1998, where he excelled.

Quattrone was allowed to run CSFB's technology banking practice as a virtual fiefdom, controlling most aspects of life in the tech group and making it a firm-within-a-firm. The model was successful and CSFB became a leader in tech M&A and underwriting during the Internet boom.

When Internet and tech deals dried up in late 2000, Quattrone's influence waned. Additionally, though Quattrone wasn't named in the IPO probe, some members of his group were. This led to speculation that Quattrone would leave CSFB, though Mack was quick to make him feel wanted, calling him a "first-class banker" and a "rainmaker."

Despite Mack's effusive praise, Quattrone and other senior bankers who negotiated guaranteed compensation at the height of the tech boom were asked to renegotiate their deals. According to *The Wall Street Journal*, approximately 350 bankers and traders agreed to changes in their deals, saving the firm a whopping $400 million over three years. Quattrone, who may have pulled in as much as $100 million during the good times, reportedly agreed to drop a clause that gave his tech team a cut of the group's annual profits.

The pay reductions weren't the only cuts ordered by Mack. In October 2001, he announced a plan to cut $1 billion in costs by the end of 2002. The cuts included finalizing the integration of DLJ, as well as approximately 2,000 layoffs. In March 2002, new investment banking-chief Adebayo Ogunlesi stood before an auditorium full of CSFB bankers and announced that the pink slip recipients would most likely be senior executives. According to *The New York Times*, Ogunlesi told employees CSFB had 25 percent to 50 percent more senior managers than comparable Wall Street firms, and that cuts would be necessary and made swiftly. Less than one month later, CSFB cut 300 investment-banking jobs, which, according to an internal memo, "covered all levels of professional staff, every product and industry group."

Making the SEC go away

In January 2002, CSFB finally settled the troublesome IPO investigation. The firm agreed to a hefty $100 million settlement. The firm will pay $30 million in fines and surrender $70 million in profits it made from managing IPO stocks during the tech surge of the late 1990s and early 2000. The payment is the fifth-largest fine sanctioned against a brokerage firm, and will be divvied up by the SEC and the NASD. As part of the settlement, CSFB neither admitted to nor denied the allegations.

The year 2002 began with a bang for CSFB. The investment bank announced it was acquiring the assets of HOLT Value Associates, chief provider of independent research and valuation services to asset managers. Based in Chicago, HOLT offers a valuation platform and database covering 18,000 companies in 28 countries. The firm has more than 350 institutional clients, and some of the world's foremost asset managers, who double as core clients of CSFB.

M&As and accolades

Despite the internal and external turmoil, CSFB has remained a top investment bank. The firm was the fifth top merger adviser in 2001, sporting a total deal value of $47.7 billion. Among some of the star deals: Comcast Corp.'s purchase of AT&T Broadband for $71 billion in July 2001 (named a "Breakthrough Deal" by *Investment Dealers' Digest*); EchoStar Communications' buyout of Hughes Electronics for $29 billion in August 2001; Phillips Petroleum's takeover of Conoco Inc. for $23 billion in November; and Washington Mutual's procurement of Dime Bancorp for $4.9 billion in June 2001. *The Banker* named CSFB the "M&A House of the Year" for 2001.

CSFB's achievement in the underwriter arena is none too shabby, either. The firm raked in 21 IPOs in 2001. Notable offerings include Kraft Foods' $8.7 billion IPO in June 2001 (a deal CSFB co-led) a hefty $418 million IPO for Weight Watchers International in November 2001 (also co-led by CSFB) and VCA Antech's $140 million offering in November 2001 (CSFB led this one by itself).

But CSFB scored the most points in secondary market offerings. The firm completed 71 deals in the secondary market in 2001, according to Thomson Financial Securities Data. CSFB managed Raytheon's October 2001 offering of $9.6 billion and had a hand in Earthlink's $200 million August 2001 offering and Duane Reade's offering of $241 million in June 2001.

CSFB's research staff is also a source of pride. The firm moved from No. 4 to No. 2 in the 2001 *Institutional Investor* "All-America Research Team" rankings for U.S. equity research, placing 52 analysts on *II*'s coveted list. CSFB was third in the fixed-income rankings with 32 analysts, up from 10 analysts the previous year.

The firm was one of several investment banks to adopt new research practices in 2002. CSFB will begin rating all stocks on a three-tier system in September 2002. The companies will be designated outperform, neutral or underperform. Previously, CSFB's research had rated firms strong buy, buy, hold or sell. The new system will conform to a simplified industry standard enacted in response to complaints about research analyst independence.

GETTING HIRED

This is how they do it

The firm's on-campus recruiting program is managed on a firm-wide basis and organized by each of the bank's target schools. Each school is assigned an "ambassador" (a member of the firm's operating committee), a "team captain" (a director or managing director) and a "team leader." In addition to the standard I-bank campus presentation — which provides an overview of the firm, a Q&A session and, in some cases, dinner — CSFB also participates in other get-to-know-recruit events such as golf tournaments and various student-organized functions. Candidates can expect to go through three rounds of interviews. The first round is usually held on-campus, with the second and third rounds at CSFB offices. One insider says the interviews "pay attention to the technical side," but admits that the first and second round interviews are "fit-oriented," while the final round contains "more technical questions."

CSFB hires summer associates for its investment banking, fixed income and equity divisions. The firm has a flexible sales and trading summer associate program, which allows summer associates to focus on fixed income or equity, or pursue a rotational program that offers exposure to both. CSFB also has an equity research summer program, in which hires are assigned to work with a research analyst for the summer. According to the firm, all summer associates are assigned mentors and reviewed periodically.

OUR SURVEY SAYS

Bigger, not better

Big mergers, big layoffs and big market declines certainly hasn't boosted morale at CSFB. Not long ago, sources called the work environment at CSFB "well balanced," "collegial" and "entrepreneurial." But now, insiders say, it's become "very political," "terrible" and, even "the worst." Asked about the firm's culture, one recently laid-off employee says, "People are demoralized, and ex-DLJ employees feel incredibly marginalized." The source goes on to say that former DLJ employees have a "secret code: Whenever they find out that they're speaking with another ex-DLJ employee, they make a comment such as 'What a pit this place has turned into.'" The source does admit that "a good portion of the bad morale can be attributed to a merger that just didn't go well," but says, "new management is also to blame." Another disgruntled contact says, "I was disgusted by CSFB's treatment of employees during their mass layoffs. An entire trading desk found out they were laid off by e-mail. And some MDs let people go over the phone — talk about spineless." The contact adds that, overall, management at CSFB is "poor," and the firm "lacks a sense of team."

CSFB, not unlike several big I-banks, expects its employees to "grunt hard and work." However, unlike some finance behemoths, CSFB also "knows how to let them relax when appropriate." And employees do enjoy a large degree of "interaction with senior management." One former associate reports: "We would go out at least once a week. Anytime there was someone new in our group visiting from one of the other CSFB offices, it was basically their duty to take you to a bar." A former analyst notes that the best aspect of working for the firm was "definitely the people. I've made some great friends at the firm, both in my analyst class and in my group. I still keep in touch with many of them — I was also struck by how genuinely nice people were compared with what I had expected when I went into investment banking." Another former employee also praises the people. "Some of the people from DLJ were incredibly bright. You can learn a lot from them."

Some contacts say the firm could be a little nicer when it comes to diversity. An associate in one of the international offices, for example, says he considers the number of women there to be below the industry average. A former female employee of the firm's LA office admits that CSFB "pays attention to diversity," but, like most firms, "There are very few women at the senior levels." The source adds that CSFB "has a mentoring program, but it doesn't work well."

How 'bout a little help?

Support services, such as word processing and graphic design, receive low marks from firm contacts, and are described by one insider as "one of the weakest points" at CSFB. Administrative assistants are rated in similarly poor fashion. Says one contact, "Secretaries are terrible." The grumbler goes on to complain, "My phone never got answered — [my secretary] was technically supposed to be able to do word processing as well, but I wouldn't for a second trust him to do any of it."

Sources also give CSFB's formal training low grades. Describing the firm's one-month program in New York, one contact says, "It's nice for the social aspect because it gives you a chance to know your peers, but there's very little technical training." The source underscores this, saying that CSFB "is not a very strong bank for

© 2002 Vault Inc.

technical knowledge. There's not enough time spent on the technical side." A CSFB trader says, "No real help or training was provided. The other associate in my group felt threatened by my presence, so she never helped me. Although the traders did offer to help, I never had any formal training."

Pretty perky

Insiders say the firm has made lifestyle improvements to retain talent. To help with the long hours, CSFB has improved the meal policy. "We used to have one of the stingiest meal allowances on the Street," reports one insider, "and they have relaxed that considerably." Despite having to work in a cubicle, one associate in London considers the company's accommodations rather swanky because they have "the largest corporate gym in Europe and a fantastic cafeteria." For those looking to re-energize in New York, the firm also has a health club in its Manhattan offices.

Working at CSFB offers other, more basic benefits. "[The firm offers] lots of health care options, including one in which you can save money for health care expenses tax-free," says one insider. "So, say you know that later in the year you'll have $2,000 in medical expenses that won't be covered by insurance. You can save for that in a pre-tax account. If you didn't have that account, you might have to earn $2,800 to pay for the $2,000 in expenses."

Those who believe casual attire at the office should be a necessary perk beware: One CSFB employee predicts the firm is "going back to formal [attire] in the near future."

Burning out, not fading away

Like most employees on Wall Street, CSFB's workforce contends with "long," "intense" workdays and "excruciatingly tight deadlines." According to one analyst, "The hours vary. I pulled almost no all-nighters, but I worked a lot of days until four or five in the morning." Another source says, "You burn out by the time you're 30. Most people only last until they're about 35, then go off and do something else." Many employees comment that their jobs "require a high level of energy and dedication." Simply put, "the hours are not good," says a former employee, who frequently clocked in 80 to 100 hour workweeks. As far as face time is concerned, one trader says, "You don't leave until the MD is gone, and he would often stay later, because he didn't want to go home to his family. So sometimes we were all stuck there twiddling our thumbs."

Fidelity Investments

82 Devonshire Street
Boston, MA 02109-3614
Phone: (800) 544-6666
www.fidelity.com

DEPARTMENTS

Brokerage • Corporate Systems and Processing • Employer Services • Financial Intermediary Services • Management and Research • Strategic Investments

THE STATS

Chairman and CEO: Edward C. "Ned" Johnson III
Employer Type: Private Company
No. of Employees: 33,200

KEY COMPETITORS

Charles Schwab
T. Rowe Price
Vanguard Group

UPPERS

• Great benefits, especially for women
• Top-notch name brand

DOWNERS

• Lack of teamwork on equity side
• Lots of company politics

EMPLOYMENT CONTACT

Fidelity Investments — Resume Central
82 Devonshire Street, Z 2 F2
Boston, MA 02109
Fax: (617) 476-6150
resumes@fidelity.com
jobs.fidelity.com

THE BUZZ
WHAT EMPLOYEES AT OTHER FIRMS ARE SAYING

• "Gold standard buy-side"
• "Massive bureaucracy"
• "Top of the line"
• "Losing its shine"

THE SCOOP

From one fund to many

Edward Crosby Johnson II founded Fidelity Management and Research (FMR Corp.) in 1946 to act as investment advisor to the Fidelity Fund, which was started in 1930. During the 1970s, Fidelity began to make funds directly accessible to individual investors and set an industry standard by eliminating mutual fund sales charges. An early leader in discount brokerage, Fidelity was the first to see that the future of financial services depended on empowering individual investors to take advantage of investment opportunities. Fidelity also provides insurance both through its own life insurance unit and through affiliations with insurance.com and John Hancock Financial Services.

Fidelity Investments is the housemark for FMR Corp., the holding company through which CEO Edward "Ned" Johnson III controls the empire of financial institutions that his father established. The Johnson family (including Abigail Johnson, who was named president of FMR Corp. in May 2001) controls 49 percent of the company; the remaining 51 percent is owned by Fidelity senior managers. Ned has received some kudos: He was No. 2 on *SmartMoney*'s list of the 30 most influential people in the world of investing, behind only Federal Reserve Chairman Alan Greenspan. The company itself has won a number of awards: Research firm J.D. Power and Associates ranked Fidelity No. 1 in customer satisfaction and the firm's online trading division has been similarly honored by Gomez.com, *Forbes* and *Money* magazine.

Mutual fund behemoth

This financial services conglomerate offers mutual funds, life insurance, discount brokerage and retirement services. It's the world's largest mutual fund firm, managing more than 300 funds for approximately 17 million investors. Fidelity also has large holdings in telecommunications, real estate and transportation. Additionally, more than 80 corporations with a total of 1.6 million employees use Fidelity for human resources outsourcing, including payroll, health care, stock options and pension management.

With $873 billion in assets, Fidelity earned $77 billion in new money in 2001; more than $36 billion poured into the approximately 4,600 mutual funds managed by other firms but sold by Fidelity through its FundsNetwork program.

WTC aftermath

The mutual fund industry wasn't immune to the fallout from the September 11 terrorist attacks on the World Trade Center in New York and the Pentagon in Washington, D.C. The resulting economic decline (which built on a recession that had been festering for most of the year) caused Fidelity and many of its competitors, including Charles Schwab and Merrill Lynch, to trim headcount. After cutting approximately 230 employees through July 2001, Fidelity made an additional 94 cuts in November 2001. None of the cuts, however, were at the manager, analyst or trader levels.

Serving the rich

In response to the ongoing economic slump, Fidelity has begun to push its way into the high-end market, targeting individuals with at least $1 million to invest. The idea is hardly original — Charles Schwab acquired U.S. Trust, a well-known asset manager to the wealthy, in 2000. And rivals such as Putnam Investments and Merrill Lynch announced similar initiatives in mid-2001. Specifically, Fidelity announced it would be offering tax-friendly accounts to clients with $1 million or more and opening nine new offices for individual clients.

GETTING HIRED

Having the love will get you in Fidelity

While Fidelity doesn't specify educational requirements, the firm does look for entrepreneurial candidates who can succeed in a fast-paced environment. Most new hires have some financial or business background, but there are also opportunities for those with technology and computer expertise. Fidelity's employment web page, jobs.fidelity.com, discusses the different departments within the firm and the skills that they require. The web page also allows applicants to search a job database, build their resumes online and submit resumes via e-mail.

Fidelity prefers MBAs for positions such as quantitative equity analysts, regional service representatives, product/service consultants, investment managers, quantitative analysts and performance analysts. For MBAs applying for analyst positions, having a love for the stock market seems to be the most important qualification. For those sending in a resume, insiders recommend attaching a stock report. "They love that," says one insider. "It will definitely increase your chances of getting an interview." After landing an interview, recruits can expect to meet "with everyone, on multiple occasions. You're put through the ringer," says an asset manager who interviewed with 10 people before getting the job. He adds, "The firm seems very selective, and it takes months to get through the process."

OUR SURVEY SAYS

Understanding of the underlings

Fidelity's corporate culture wins high marks from employees for being "enlightened" because of its "high degree of tolerance in dealing with its people." According to one recent summer associate, "Fidelity understands that workers can't always be perfect. They don't have a problem with people being grouchy." Unlike many companies in the industry, Fidelity "assigns a great deal of autonomy, both personally and professionally" to its employees. However, one insider says the mutual fund monster has its share of bureaucracy. "Culture really depends on which part of the company you work in, but overall, it's political," he says, adding that at Fidelity "it isn't what you know, it's who you know." Another source says that the firm appears to be a place where the highly educated receive preferential treatment. "They really cater to people with advanced degrees. It appears to be a place where if you leave, go and get an MBA, and then return, you'll be very successful."

It's lonely at the stocks

Recent hires say that one of the "striking" characteristics of working for Fidelity is that its "workplace has a major dichotomy between the fixed income and equity divisions." The culture in fixed income is "completely different" from the culture in the equity division. Employees in the fixed income division praise their "team-oriented work place" and feel that "the best part of working for this company is your coworkers — the best in the game." However, an associate in the equity division laments his department's "individualistic, even 'dog-eat-dog' environment." "Equity," he notes, "is not very social at all." He adds, "It's not for someone who really likes a team effort environment. Not that it's not friendly, but although you interact with other people, you work a lot on your own. It's also stressful, so if you can't handle up and down stressful times, you should look elsewhere."

Another equity employee says that Fidelity "and its culture are more solitary than at other companies. In general, your job's going to be solitary if you work in the buy-side mutual environment." But, the employee adds, Fidelity "is even more solitary than usual — absolutely no after-work social life. It's stressful during the day, but then people go their separate ways after work. It's not a place for someone who wants work to be the center of their lives." And maybe that's why "the hours are not bad," says one employee. Another contact agrees, but he says the "hours depend on where in the company you work." The contact goes on to say that although Fidelity "has a reputation for overworking their people, I generally found this not be the case."

King Ned

It's "impossible to talk of Fidelity without mentioning Ned Johnson somewhere," insiders assert. "Ultimately, this place is an autocracy, and one man is ruler — Ned Johnson," one longtime employee comments, adding ruefully, "Ned Johnson has the power to make decisions with no checks on that power. He's a smart guy, but occasionally he makes a very non-optimal decision. And we have to bear the consequences of his occasional wackiness." Another agrees. "This is Ned's candy store. He was given this firm by his father. He'll come up with the quirkiest, strangest idea in the middle of the night, and everyone has to deal with it. It's very frustrating."

Great for women, good for all

A woman who recently interned in the fixed-income division states that Fidelity "is very anxious for women to work for it. My immediate superior was a woman and was very candid with me when soliciting my assistance in identifying good female candidates." One contact notes, "One of the most powerful people around the company is a woman — Abigail Johnson." Another, when asked about the effect of Abigail Johnson on the workplace, replies, "I don't think it matters. There were a few other women where I worked. I felt like we were treated fine. They don't treat women any different, there are just fewer of them. In a lot of ways that can be an advantage — there are more opportunities." Another contact agrees that there's "no bias," though this is not exactly an advantage. The contact says, "Women seem to be treated equally as poorly as the men."

Employees are particularly appreciative of Fidelity's many family-friendly programs, which, according to one female employee, ensure that Fidelity is a "good place for working women and families." Another contact agrees, noting, "there are a ton of people here on maternity leave." Fidelity's family programs include adoption assistance, childcare assistance, vacation programs for school-age children, college planning and scholarship information, elder care resource and referral, an employee assistance program and mortgage assistance. Other perks that draw praise include Fidelity's comprehensive training opportunities and an "excellent" retirement benefits plan consisting of a 401(k) package with a matching contribution.

In addition to the "great benefits," including an "on-site gym at many locations," one insider says Fidelity gives "good compensation." However, the contact adds that the offices themselves are "nothing special but not bad," and because the firm "has so much market space in Boston, they can, to a degree, control your income." Another employee praises compensation. Fidelity "pays very well, with bonuses almost as an expectation rather than a possibility." And the contact agrees that Fidelity's offices are nothing extraordinary, calling them "very run-of-the-mill."

Lazard

30 Rockefeller Plaza
New York, NY 10020
Phone: (212) 632-2000
www.lazard.com

DEPARTMENTS

Asset Management • Capital
Markets • Investment Banking •
Principal Investing

THE STATS

Chairman: Michel David-Weill
Head: Bruce Wasserstein
Employer Type: Private Company
No. of Offices: 25

KEY COMPETITORS

Allen & Company
Dresdner Kleinwort Wasserstein
Goldman Sachs
Morgan Stanley

THE BUZZ
WHAT EMPLOYEES AT OTHER FIRMS ARE SAYING

- "Great M&A shop"
- "Workaholics"
- "The glory days are gone, but
  with Bruce at the helm it's
  bound to come back"
- "Stuck up"

UPPERS

- Excellent pay
- International prestige

DOWNERS

- Killer hours
- Management struggles may lead to
  more changes

EMPLOYMENT CONTACT

Investment Banking
Suzanne Zywicki
Lazard
30 Rockefeller Plaza
New York, NY 10020-6300

Capital Markets
L. Gregory Rice
Managing Director — Equities
F. Harlan Batrus
Managing Director — Bonds
John Rohs
Managing Director — Research

Lazard
30 Rockefeller Plaza
New York, NY 10020-6300

Asset Management
Amy DeAngelo
Lazard Asset Management
30 Rockefeller Plaza
New York, NY 10020-6300

THE SCOOP

A classic

Lazard might be called the classic advisory boutique, specializing primarily in providing mergers and acquisitions advice. The firm also has a small underwriting and trading practice and a respectable asset management arm with approximately $70 billion in assets under management. Despite the firm's specialization, Lazard's profits and influence are hardly limited. Quite the opposite, in fact: Lazard is known for a superstar culture. Its elite, well-connected bankers are known as the trusted advisers to the princes of business. The firm touts itself as "the only private partnership in global investment banking."

French bred

The Lazard family's U.S. business ventures can be traced back to 1848, when the clan immigrated to the United States from France and opened a dry goods enterprise in New Orleans. In 1849 the family moved to San Francisco after a fire destroyed the New Orleans operation. The Lazards arrived just in time for the gold rush and the resulting economic boom caused by arriving prospectors. The company began banking operations in Paris in 1852, adding offices in London in 1877 and New York in 1880.

Much of the firm's growth is attributed to Alexandre Weill, a cousin of the Lazards who opened the New York office. The company has remained in the hands of the Weill family for more than 120 years. Michel David-Weill (the family hyphenated its name to David-Weill in the 1920s to add aristocratic luster) took the helm in 1977.

Internal conflict

David-Weill's leadership of the firm came under fire in the late 1990s, forcing him to change the structure of the firm to placate investors and partners. Several high-profile partners (including Edouard Stern, David-Weill's son-in-law) left the firm, reportedly amid complaints about David-Weill's leadership style and the firm's direction. Lazard Frères (as it was then known) underwent a sudden reorganization. The firm's three main offices (in New York, London and Paris) were consolidated and managed by a seven-member executive committee headed by David-Weill. Additionally, the firm dropped the Frères from its name, becoming known internationally as Lazard. Finally, David-Weill agreed to appoint a CEO who would manage some of the firm's day-to-day operations. After a short search, David-Weill settled on Lazard veteran William Loomis, the first American to be named CEO.

The new structure didn't make the complaints about David-Weill's management style disappear. Demands from Lazard partners and outside shareholders continued, with some requesting a public offering or additional changes to the firm's ownership structure. Also at issue was the compensation structure. Some were upset at David-Weill's take (it was reported that he was paid approximately $100 million) and the overall firm compensation formula, which heavily rewarded offices that did well. (Since the New York office was generally the most successful, this formula had the effect of disproportionately rewarding New York and U.S. partners.) The opposition was headed by Vincent Bollore, a French industrialist who quietly amassed a large ownership stake in Rue Imperiale de Lyon, which controlled 17 percent of Lazard's shares, and by London-based UBS Warburg. Though David-Weill won the standoff (Bollore sold his interest in Rue Imperiale to French bank Credit Agricole, another Lazard shareholder, in early 2001), he made more concessions to his critics. Lazard's outside ownership structure was simplified (several companies had held significant stakes in Lazard) and Loomis was named CEO in late 2000.

Lazard's strife resurfaced in late 2001 after Loomis resigned suddenly in October. The firm said Loomis wanted more contact with clients and time to pursue personal interests, but observers saw him as another casualty in the Lazard power struggle. According to *The Wall Street Journal*, Loomis never enjoyed widespread support and was caught in a struggle between David-Weill and London and Paris partners. The renewed bickering gave David-Weill's old nemeses, Bollore and UBS Warburg, the chance to make another play for the firm. Bollore began buying up shares in Eurazeo while UBS was upping its interest in Immobilie're Marseillaise. (Both companies are part of the intricate web of Lazard owners.) David-Weill's immediate response to the new coup attempt was to placate the cost-cutters at the firm. Lazard cut 25 percent of its U.S. investment-banking staff in late 2001. The firm had cut 50 back-office personnel earlier in the year.

Wasserstein the warrior

Facing dissension, David-Weill again hoped to square things by naming a new head. This time, he went for a rainmaker. The firm named Bruce Wasserstein, the superstar banker who founded M&A powerhouse Wasserstein Perella, head of Lazard in January 2002. Wasserstein sold Wasserstein Perella to Dresdner Bank in January 2001. He resigned from the company in November 2001 after a disagreement with

Dresdner's management. David-Weill is clearly betting on Wasserstein's M&A prowess to restore some of Lazard's lost luster.

Another fly in the ointment

The firm's enemies list keeps on growing. In January 2002, it was revealed that Jon Wood, head of UBS Warburg's proprietary trading unit, was launching a campaign to change Lazard's management structure. According to *The Wall Street Journal*, the Bahamas-based trader has spent years purchasing shares in companies that make up the dizzying web of Lazard owners. Wood hopes to force more consolidation that would end David-Weill's near monopoly on power. Wood's actions are somewhat aggressive, as UBS Warburg has tried to avoid stepping on toes throughout the power struggles of the past few years. However, observers feel the increased pressure may force still more concessions from the top of Lazard's management pyramid.

GETTING HIRED

The model employee

Lazard's investment-banking division recruits at undergraduate colleges and business schools, but other departments such as asset management fill their open slots primarily through word of mouth, sources say. A recruiting schedule for investment banking and contact information for other departments are available on the firm's web site, www.lazard.com. Insiders advise showing up for your interview at the firm with a "nice expensive suit." "The people they hire — there's no way to say this, really — but they tend to be attractive people," says one Lazard employee. "They're not looking for the nerdy number-cruncher that you get at some of the banks like Goldman. They want it so that when there's a meeting, you can tell Lazard walked in the door."

B-school insiders report mostly enduring two-on-two interviews. The firm recruits at most of the top-tier MBA schools including Columbia, Wharton, Harvard and the University of Chicago. At some schools, after the initial screening round, "they call you later on that night and have you come back and do some more interviews, and they will give you the offer then." Asked where the firm fishes for undergrads, one employee says simply, "the Ivies." The contact adds, "Almost everyone here knew someone who worked here before they got hired," which is somewhat of an exaggeration, as the firm does extensive on-campus recruiting.

A source says his interviewer asked "questions on experience and quantitative skills." Reports one associate, "One question they like to ask is, 'What was the hardest thing you did — what was the most complicated deal?' If you brought up an M&A deal, from talking to you about it, they can tell where you are." The contact adds, "I strongly stress to anyone who wants to work there as an associate that you've got to be a banker. They expect you to walk in the first day and be ready. My first day, my phone rang, and they said, 'You're late.' I said, 'I'm late? I just walked in the door.' It was a secretary of one of the senior people, and she tells me, 'There's a meeting up on 62 and you've got to get up there.' I get up there and there's the CEO and he's talking about what type of company he wants to acquire. I start taking notes. That evening and the rest of the night I cranked out merger models."

Born to bank

Like other Wall Street firms, Lazard aims to hire full-time associates through its summer associate program and through on-campus recruiting efforts. Lazard also maintains a summer analyst program for college juniors, but it's not exactly open to just anyone. "Not all, but many internships are reserved for clients' kids or friends of the firm," reports one insider. The firm contests that statement, saying that summer hires are culled from on-campus recruiting. No matter how you get in, you'll still have to prove yourself. "Those [internships] that lead to hires are more, but not always, meritocratic." That contact advises candidates to consider divisions other than M&A to start. "Getting hired in a less attractive division can lead to promotions or transfers to better areas."

OUR SURVEY SAYS

Work hard, play hardly

To say Lazard "demands total commitment" is an understatement. "Working hours are just crazy," says one insider, who sometimes wishes for "more time for family, friends and non-professional areas of interest." Says another: "You will definitely work over 100 hours during an average workweek." Another insider puts the figure at "110 to 130" hours weekly. One employee criticizes the "superhuman expectations" at the firm. "You can't work any harder than they work," a former Lazard banker attests. "There were people carried out by ambulance — they had collapsed from exhaustion," that banker continues, rehashing a well-worn anecdote about life at Lazard.

How bad it is for Lazard bankers depends almost entirely on where one is on the totem pole, according to sources. Contacts concur that "analysts have no life." Explains one insider, "The attitude is that the analysts are not bankers. It's 'I want to work you for two years and then spit you out, and you're lucky to be here.'" That source continues: "The analysts do not exercise, they do not leave, they are there all the time." "The analysts for the most part are extremely bitter," says one associate. "I think they're going to do better in the future, because they're starting to realize that it's not good," says that contact. Despite Lazard's hard-work reputation, the firm reported that in 2000, 10 out of 24 second- and third-year analysts stayed on at the firm after the completion of the analyst program.

Associates don't have it much better, insiders say, but "they know what they're getting into" and morale is pretty high. "The first three years as an associate — you're throwing those years away," says one banker. "You're just trying to survive." Why do associates put up with the intense work? For the promotion to VP that happens in three or four years. "If you can survive the four years, you're looking at a pretty good lifestyle," explains one insider. "A VP at Lazard is very different from a VP at other places. At other places, the VP gets dragged down to do associate work and still gets dragged into the office on weekends. A VP at Lazard — they really know their shit, and if they want to, which pretty much everyone wants to, they refuse to do associate-level work. They want to be working on getting clients and things like that." During the week, insiders report, VPs are there "until nine, and even MDs put in long hours." On the weekends, "they'll be at the Hamptons with a fax machine."

On the plus side, some insiders report doing meaningful work at least some of the time. "I get to do interesting things which Lazard is comfortable doing, but there tends to be resistance to new ideas," says one source. "I also do more mundane work, being low enough on the totem pole." That source continues, "I personally have gotten a lot of respect and recognition for my intelligence in conversation and to some extent responsibility." The firm was one of the last to go business casual, but some worry that privilege might be pulled. "Now that the dot-coms have crashed and burned we don't expect [business casual] to last, but it's been nice," says one source, who adds, "we're waiting for the memo to go back to suits and ties."

Paying for your time

The amazing luxury that the Lazard lifestyle affords is a top reason the firm's bankers endure the almost unconscionable hours. "Bankers at Lazard are usually paid 25 to 50 percent more than the market salary [for] comparable positions at other banks," says an analyst. "They basically tell you that their goal is to be the highest-paying firm, and they're looking to start up private equity stuff in order to expand what they can do as far as compensation," reports another banker.

Insiders also agree that Lazard is at the top of the list when it comes to prestige. "It's an amazing place," says one source. "They really do have great relationships with the CEOs of major companies." Says another, "We're the cutting edge of management and finance theory. The culture is very focused on production, merit and profits." A former banker says, "They're not spinning their wheels, working their hours. They really put some time and thought into the work they're doing." However, one source calls Lazard "very political" and says, "communication between New York and the foreign offices is poor."

Good ole boys and girls

One employee maintains that the firm is "relatively progressive, with active recruitment of women and minorities," but notes that "there are very few women investment bankers at Lazard, not because we don't hire them, but because many of them leave due to the inhumane working environment." One insider calls recruiting for women in the marketing and accounting divisions "great." But, he says, "Otherwise, it could use some improvement."

"We're the cutting edge of management and finance theory. The culture is very focused on production, merit and profits."

— *Lazard insider*

Lehman Brothers

745 Seventh Avenue
New York, NY 10019-6801
Phone: (212) 526-7000
www.lehman.com

DEPARTMENTS

Corporate Advisory • Equities •
Fixed Income • Investment Banking •
Operations and Corporate Services •
Private Client Services • Private
Equity • Risk Management

THE STATS

Chairman and CEO:
Richard S. Fuld, Jr.
Employer Type: Public Company
Stock Symbol: LEH (NYSE)
2001 Revenue: $22.39 billion
2001 Net Income: $1.3 billion
No. of Employees: 13,100
No. of Offices: 66

KEY COMPETITORS

Credit Suisse First Boston
Goldman Sachs
Merrill Lynch
Morgan Stanley

THE BUZZ
WHAT EMPLOYEES AT OTHER FIRMS ARE SAYING

- "Unsinkable"
- "Living in the past"
- "Deserves more recognition"
- "Consolidation target"

UPPERS

- Collegial culture
- State-of-the-art offices in New York

DOWNERS

- One of the first banks to go back to suits and ties
- Skimps on bonuses

EMPLOYMENT CONTACT

Investment Banking
Analyst Recruiting
Candace Darling
Associate Recruiting
Bess Frank

Sales, Trading and Research
Analyst Recruiting
Kathleen Frisina
Associate Recruiting
Stephanie Amanatides

745 Seventh Avenue
28th Floor
New York, NY 10019

Private Client Services
Associate Recruiting
Valerie DeMartino
399 Park Avenue
5th Floor
New York, NY 10022
For additional contacts, see
www.lehman.com/career

THE SCOOP

Southern roots

Lehman Brothers was founded in 1850 in Montgomery, Ala., by brothers Henry, Emmanuel and Mayer Lehman. The enterprise began as a commodities brokerage and trading firm and opened a New York office in 1858. In 1887 Lehman acquired a seat on the New York Stock Exchange and underwrote its first stock offering two years later. Continuously expanding over the last 152 years, the company is currently a full-service global investment bank providing a wide range of financial services, including fixed-income and equities underwriting, sales, trading and research, M&A advisory, public finance and government advisory, private equity and private client services. Lehman's investment-banking group serves 10 industry segments: communications/media, consumer/retailing, financial institutions, financial sponsors, health care, industrial, natural resources, power, real estate and technology.

American Express acquired Lehman in 1984 as part of Amex's strategy to become a full-service institution covering all consumer and business financial needs. But Amex changed its tune 10 years later, deciding to refocus on its core businesses. Amex spun off Lehman Brothers into an independent company, and the new firm stumbled out of the starting gate, implementing significant cost-cutting measures to stay afloat. The new structure worked wonders. Lehman Brothers became one of the most profitable Wall Street firms and has avoided layoffs even in the leanest of times. When many competitors were eliminating staff in 2001, Lehman increased headcount 15.5 percent, even though revenues and net income fell 13 percent and 29 percent, respectively.

WTC woes

Of course, Lehman Brothers has an excuse for its weakened financial performance. The firm was hit hard by the September 11th terrorist attack on the World Trade Center in New York. One Lehman Brothers employee died in the attack, and the firm was forced to evacuate its offices in the nearby World Financial Center. Lehman temporarily housed much of its operations in a back-up facility in Jersey City, N.J., and had its investment banking, equity research and private equity temporarily working out of a Manhattan hotel. Though the firm initially wanted to return to the World Financial Center, Lehman eventually opted to relocate. In October 2001, Lehman purchased a 32-story building in midtown Manhattan from Morgan Stanley. Though the price of the deal wasn't disclosed, *The Wall Street Journal* reported that

Lehman paid approximately $650 million for one million square feet of space that became the firm's new global headquarters.

Despite the setbacks caused by the terrorist attacks, Lehman Brothers still had a successful year by all standards. The firm's results were the second-best in its history, an accomplishment that didn't escape industry observers. *Investment Dealers' Digest* honored Lehman Brothers as "Bank of the Year." The trade magazine specifically cited the firm's quick recovery from the terrorist attacks, its gains in debt and equity underwriting and its ability to avoid layoffs. For example, Lehman Brothers lead managed the first post-September 11 IPO (Given Imaging, a $60 million deal) and the first major post-attack bond offering (Generel Electric Capital, a $2 billion global debt offering).

Dealmaker

Lehman's deal-making ability was not diminished in 2001. The firm lead managed 67 equity deals worth approximately $18 billion. Among the firm's top engagements was a $2.2 billion offering for Tyco International, a $1.4 billion convertible and common stock offering for Cendant Corp. and a $1.4 billion convertible stock deal for France Telecom. Lehman had a healthy year in M&A advisory as well, completing 156 deals worldwide worth $172 billion. The firm advised Chevron on its $43.3 billion purchase of Texaco and Bank of Tokyo-Mitsubishi on its $10.7 billion merger with Mitsubishi Trust & Banking and Nippon Bank. Finally, Lehman's fixed-income team underwrote more than 1,000 transactions in 2001 worth approximately $238 billion. Big debt deals included a $6 billion offering for GMAC, a $4 billion deal for Kraft Foods and a $3.8 billion debt offering for Qwest Capital Funding.

Deals for a dealmaker

Even with Lehman's relatively strong 2001 performance, the firm was reportedly seeking more bang for its buck. According to *The Wall Street Journal*, Lehman Brothers held preliminary merger talks with international banking boutique Lazard in the summer of 2001. The talks were very general, and were abandoned completely after the September 11th terrorist attacks changed the industry landscape.

Lehman did manage to add Cohane Rafferty Securities to its family in early 2002. The firm purchased Cohane Rafferty, a White Plains, N.Y.-based investment bank that caters to financial institutions, for an undisclosed sum in January 2002. Cohane Rafferty will keep its name and its headquarters and remain an autonomous unit of Lehman Brothers.

Broker misbehavior

Lehman's public image took a hit in January 2002 when a former broker and branch manager admitted he had falsified client account statements in order to collect higher fees. Frank Gruttadauria, who ran Lehman's Cleveland branch office, joined the firm in October 2000 when it purchased the brokerage business of SG Cowen. In a letter to the Federal Bureau of Investigation, Gruttadauria admitted to padding client account statements in order to collect higher fees and commissions. Gruttadauria then went on the lam, only to turn himself in February 2002. He was charged with fraud for perpetrating the scheme since 1987, when he worked for Hambrecht & Quist. Authorities believe Gruttadauria stole as much as $125 million. Some have questioned why Lehman wasn't more aware of the rogue broker's activities. Lehman faces several lawsuits in connection with the case. In a delicious twist, one lawsuit was filed by the co-founder of Mr. Coffee, Samuel Glazer. He is seeking full restitution for his losses and $500 million in punitive damages against Lehman Brothers and SG Cowen.

Dressing up

Lehman sprung a surprise on its bankers in March 2002 when it announced a return to formal business dress for its employees. The firm had followed other Wall Street firms in allowing business casual dress in 1999. However, Lehman management demanded a return to suits, ties and stockings, saying the wardrobe change was necessitated by increased client contact. The firm will allow business casual attire on a limited basis in the summer months.

GETTING HIRED

No cakewalk

Naturally, as the economy slumped it got tougher to land a spot at Lehman Brothers. "The necessary credentials for getting hired these days are very high," warns one source. "This has escalated significantly over the past couple years." Being a summer analyst or associate helps — "almost all full-time hires come from the summer program," observes one banker. Attending one of the firm's target schools also helps. "If you are trying to get a job after graduating from a school other than those where we recruit, it is pretty difficult unless you know somebody who can pass along your resume," remarks one insider. The schools are fairly typical of the bulge-bracket set; Ivy League and top-20 schools dominate, though the firm does recruit from other institutions. Nerds won't get a free pass. "[Lehman is] highly selective but ends up taking the "right" people, not always the person with the highest grades," says one banker. "It's important to fit the corporate culture above all other things. [You] must be a team player."

Expect "[two to] three rounds of interviews," says one source. "The first round with an associate. Second round is with a vice president or above. Final rounds in New York with four separate interviewers ranging from associate to an SVP." The final round interviews can last approximately 30 minutes each, say interview veterans. "Most questions were personality-related, with a few basic market questions," remembers one employee, who adds that questions change depending on major. "If you majored in finance, you should expect to be asked related questions, such as firm valuation." The firm notes that the interview process can vary across different regions and departments.

Overall, though, most Lehmanites agree Lehman Brothers uses the interview to get to know potential co-workers. "Lehman focused a lot more on trying to suss out my character and personality rather than testing me on finance questions," recalls one London banker. "They were more interested in my intelligence than whether I knew a formula." Lehman is famous for its on-campus "Trading Game" in which the firm simulates trading pits from the Chicago Futures Exchange. Firm representatives observe the game to gauge the skills of potential traders. "It's a way of gaining visibility on campuses more than anything," says one insider.

OUR SURVEY SAYS

The "one team" firm

Lehman Brothers' employees say the firm is a good place to work, though it is fraught with the usual pitfalls of the aggressive, competitive field that is investment banking. The firm has "a 'one team' atmosphere in which your co-workers help each other out and work toward a common goal," remarks one insider. Since the firm boasts a "fairly lean structure," you "won't have to worry about bureaucracy as much as you might at another firm."

As another plus, Lehman insiders say the firm lacks the infighting among departments that plagues some other firms. The firm focuses on "maximizing the profit for the firm as opposed to the division," says one source. Of course, there are some drawbacks. "Everything is politics," complains one contact. "Remember, this is an investment bank," one insider cautions, "and, like anywhere else, there is a healthy amount of BS necessary to move up through the ranks of the firm."

The return of the suit

The firm shocked the khaki-clad banking world in March 2002 when it announced it was going back to full-time formal dress, with casual Fridays in the summers. Lehman employee reactions range from peeved to apathetic. "It is terrible," rants one sharp dressed young banker. "It was very expensive for analysts, who rarely meet with clients, and it is extremely uncomfortable to wear suits when working till 4 a.m." Still, don't expect a revolution by the tie-wearing masses. "I didn't hear much of a reaction. Some people said, 'Too bad, [casual dress] is good for morale and it doesn't cost the firm anything,'" according to one source, who speculates that "[CEO] Dick Fuld said, 'I've never liked this and people aren't going to quit because of it, so let's take it away.'"

Decent bosses

Junior-level employees are generally satisfied with their bosses. "If you do quality work and show you are a hard worker, you will gain respect from others around you," observes one banker. "Senior bankers always encourage you to talk, to bring ideas to the table," says one contact. Of course, your experience might be different. "I have worked with several senior bankers who do have a total lack of consideration for your time," contends one source. "I have worked with a few individuals for whom this is not accurate. This really varies on an individual basis."

Pinching pennies

Though Lehman is described as a firm where pay is "competitive with the Street" and insiders say, "compensation never ends up at either extreme," Lehman bankers are feeling the effect of cut corners. Lehman is "generous when times are good and tight when times are bad," says one contact. "Last June, our bonuses were less than the average on the street," fumes one analyst. "Our high was Merrill's low. It is frustrating to analysts." The firm provides a 401(k) plan "but only matched up to $1,000, compared to matching of one to one from other competitors," says one contact. Employees are also eligible to buy Lehman Brothers stock at a 15 percent discount five times a year.

Perks are standard. "The company provides meal allowances of $20 for dinner on weekdays and lunch and dinner on weekends," says one banker. "Car service is provided after 9:00 p.m. on weekdays and on weekends. Discounted gym memberships are available to clubs around the area, but there is no gym facility in the building unless you are a managing director."

The Lehman clock

Work schedules are "brutal" at Lehman, albeit no more brutal than most investment -banking firms. Some departments complain of face time requirements (though such requirements are officially discouraged) and unpredictable schedules. "As an analyst, I work whenever I am told to work. I have very little control over my hours. It is very frustrating to try and make plans, which often get cancelled," fumes one young banker. There's "lots of face time even though they allegedly don't believe in face time," remarks one employee from the investment management unit. In sales, "face-time hours are fortunately kept minimal, but I still packed six hours of work into a 12 hour day," jokes one source. "It is less the duration and more the uncertainty and unpredictability of hours that is hard to tolerate," summarizes one banker.

Everything you always wanted to know about banking

Lehman Brothers takes the time to get their employees up to speed. "The training program was thorough and excellent," raves one contact, calling it "extensive, broad-based, and in-depth." "I spent three months in a classroom learning about the various businesses of an investment bank, and continue to learn on the job," says one trader. The training consisted of "lectures in the morning," says one banker. "In the afternoon, they'd bring in someone from a different department to talk about what they do within the firm."

You'll get training for professional certification, including the Series 7 exam, and time to study for it. "The training was very well-planned and had good content, although much of it was already learned in college," says one brainiac, who found the informal training more effective. "While the training program was very comprehensive, all of the real learning I have done has been on my desk." Still, some feel they're out of the loop and would benefit from more classroom time. "Ongoing training on a monthly or bi-montly basis would be beneficial to the progression of analysts, as some analysts do not get the deal exposure that they desire," remarks one source.

New digs, great chairs

"We just moved into new space after the events of September 11," reports one source, referring to the purchase of a building built for Morgan Stanley. "Our new building and trading floor is technologically advanced, as well as very comfortable." But expect little personal space. "The new space is very nice, just not much of it," complains one insider. Most people, though, are happy with the space and location, including one banker who raves about "the greatest chairs ever."

J.P. Morgan Chase

270 Park Avenue
New York, NY 10017
Phone: (212) 270-6000
www.jpmorganchase.com

DEPARTMENTS

Asset Management • Commercial
Banking • Consumer Banking •
Credit Cards • Diversified Consumer
Lending • Global Markets •
Investment Banking • Private
Banking • Private Equity • Treasury
and Securities Services

THE STATS

President and CEO: William Harrison
Employer Type: Public Company
Stock Symbol: JPM (NYSE)
2001 Revenues: $50.4 billion
2001 Net Income: $1.7 billion
No. of Employees: 95,800
No. of Offices: 66

KEY COMPETITORS

Bank of America
Citigroup
Merrill Lynch
Morgan Stanley

THE BUZZ
WHAT EMPLOYEES AT OTHER FIRMS ARE SAYING

• "One of the more aggressive and
  opportunistic banks in the world"
• "Bad marriage"
• "Handling the merger pretty well"
• "A mess"

UPPERS

• Diverse workforce
• Global reach due to merger

DOWNERS

• Lacks definite culture and character
  due to merger
• Not at the top of the league tables

EMPLOYMENT CONTACT

Human Resources
J.P. Morgan Chase & Co.
270 Park Avenue
New York, NY 10017

THE SCOOP

Coming together

J.P. Morgan Chase & Co. (known informally as Morgan Chase) is the product of a merger between two diversified financial institutions, J.P. Morgan and Chase Manhattan. Morgan Chase provides the full slate of investment-banking services, as well as commercial-banking services such as accepting deposits and issuing loans to consumers and businesses.

The merger, which was announced in September 2000 and completed on the first day of 2001, was valued at approximately $38.6 billion. The combined firm instantly became the third-largest financial institution (in terms of assets) in the U.S. (behind Citigroup and Bank of America). The combination resulted in approximately 5,000 layoffs. William Harrison, formerly chairman at Chase Manhattan, was named Morgan Chase's president and CEO; J.P. Morgan's CEO Douglas Warner was appointed chairman.

Pistols at dawn

Chase Manhattan's history can be traced back to 1799, when The Manhattan Company was chartered to supply water to New York City. Included in the company charter was a provision that capital not needed for the water-supply business could be diverted toward the founding of a bank. Thus, The Bank of The Manhattan Company was formed. Historians are unclear whether Aaron Burr, one of the backers of The Manhattan Company's water business, intentionally inserted the clause so a bank rivaling Alexander Hamilton's could be formed. The two Founding Fathers had a long-running dispute, which came to an abrupt end in 1804 when Burr killed Hamilton in a duel. (The pistols have been preserved as part of Chase's historical collection.)

The bank continued to grow, surviving the Great Depression (with a little assistance from the Rockefeller family) and two World Wars. In 1955 The Bank of The Manhattan Company merged with Chase National, a bank founded in 1877 by currency expert John Thompson and named after former Secretary of the Treasury Salmon Chase. The Chase Manhattan Bank, as it became known, went seeking another commercial merger partner in the mid-1990s, settling on Chemical Bank, then the third-largest bank in the U.S. following its 1992 merger with Manufacturers Hanover. The 1996 coupling made Chase Manhattan one of the largest banks in the United States.

Chase continued its acquisition strategy in late 1999 and early 2000, starting with its purchase of Hambrecht & Quist, a San Francisco-based boutique specializing in the tech sector. The December 1999 purchase cost Chase $1.35 billion. The bank's next target was Robert Flemings Holdings, a London-based bank that Chase purchased in April 2000 for $7.9 billion. The purchase added some needed underwriting muscle, especially in Asia. In August 2000, the firm finalized its purchase of The Beacon Group, a New York boutique founded by former Goldman Sachs partner Geoffrey Boisi, who joined Chase as its lead investment banker. (Boisi left the firm May 2002, reportedly because of clashes with CEO Harrison.) In December 2001, Brown and Company, the online brokerage unit of J.P. Morgan Chase & Co., signed an agreement to purchase Dreyfus Brokerage Services, Inc., the online trading unit of Mellon Financial Corp. The takeover included approximately $6 billion in assets and 75,000 accounts.

The venerable house of Morgan

J.P. Morgan's roots go back to 1838, when American George Peabody opened a London merchant bank. Junius S. Morgan became Peabody's partner in 1854, and eventually the firm became known as J.S. Morgan & Company. Seven years later, Junius' son, J. Pierpont, established J.P. Morgan & Company, a New York sales office for securities underwritten by his father. Working on both sides of the Atlantic, the Morgans brought capital from Europe that was crucial to U.S. growth. In 1895, five years after Junius' death, J. Pierpont consolidated the family businesses under the J.P. Morgan name.

The firm's growth continued unimpeded until the enactment of the Glass-Steagall Act in 1933. Because of the newly formed barriers between commercial and investment banking, the firm experienced many changes. Several partners, including Harry Morgan, the grandson of J. Pierpont, left the firm to form the investment-banking firm Morgan Stanley. Following a merger with Guaranty Trust Company, J.P. Morgan moved into the commercial and personal loan business.

In the 1960s, J.P. Morgan began underwriting securities in Europe, where there were fewer banking regulations. The company craved such business in the United States, especially once corporations began looking to bonds as a cheaper alternative to bank loans. In 1989 J.P. Morgan received permission from the Federal Reserve to enter debt underwriting; one year later, the door to equity underwriting was opened.

The honeymoon's over

Hopes for the J.P. Morgan/Chase Manhattan union were high, with analysts using Citigroup as the model of a multi-purpose financial services behemoth. But the new company's first year was a rough one. J.P. Morgan Chase had to weather a recession, an economic collapse in Argentina, the bankruptcy of a major client and the effects of the terrorist attacks on the World Trade Center in New York. "One year after the J.P. Morgan/Chase merger, the jury is still out," Mike Mayo, a banking analyst at Prudential Securities, told Reuters in January 2002. He cited concerns that the firm may have laid off too many workers in critical areas (Morgan Chase will cut approximately 8,000 jobs as a result of the merger) and potential inefficiencies in areas like risk management that may have led to large financial losses. For example, Morgan Chase was a major lender to Enron, the Houston, Texas-based energy giant that declared bankruptcy in December 2001. Analysts estimate that J.P. Morgan Chase might have lost $800 million in bad loans to Enron in the fourth quarter of 2001 alone. Additionally, the firm was an adviser on Enron's proposed merger with Dynegy. That engagement fell through after Enron's financial woes became apparent, causing J.P. Morgan Chase to lose millions of dollars in fees.

More troubles surfaced in July 2002. *The Wall Street Journal* reported that congressional investigators were examing deals set up by J.P. Morgan Chase and Citigroup that helped Enron and other energy companies structure transactions that would not appear on the firms' balance sheets — deals like those that eventually brought Enron down. The *Journal* cited presentations to potential J.P. Morgan clients going to back to 1998 in which the firm bragged that the complex transactions would be "balance sheet 'friendly'" — evidence, critics say, that proves that the banks knew about the questionable nature of the deals but promoted them anyway. Both J.P. Morgan and Citigroup denied the accusations, which experts warned could lead to legal liabilities.

The firm had less trouble, relatively speaking, in Argentina; that country's economy virtually collapsed in late 2001, causing it to default on its debt. Morgan Chase was believed to have less exposure in that country than its rivals, especially in the consumer debt area.

Like most Wall Street firms, J.P. Morgan Chase was affected by the terrorist attacks of September 11. The firm had a major branch in the mall underneath the World Trade Center complex. All the employees from that location made it out of the building safely, but two Morgan Chase employees who had a meeting elsewhere in the World Trade Center were killed in the attacks. Additionally, the firm may be on the hook for some property stored in its vault at the WTC branch. Morgan Chase initially had said that everything stored in the vault was irretrievable, but some materials were recovered in December 2001. Some customers, claiming the firm was negligent in not building sturdier boxes in the vault, filed a class-action suit. The suit is still pending.

Shortly after the terrorist attacks, the firm announced that Chairman Sandy Warner would retire at the end of 2001. CEO William Harrison assumed his duties. Warner and Harrison stressed that the decision was mutual, but some were skeptical, believing that Warner was the victim of a cost-cutting initiative. "It sends a signal that the bank is being aggressive about cost cutting, and that extends to the highest levels," Reilly Tierney, an analyst at Fox-Pitt Kelton, told *Investment News*. Still, there's optimism the firm can turn things around. "Once the economy recovers, things won't look so dire," Steven Wharton, an analyst at Loomis, Sayles & Co., told *The New York Times* in February 2002. "The question is whether J.P. Morgan can weather the near term, because obviously that will be difficult."

M&A, IPO report card

J.P. Morgan, which attempted to bolster its stocks business, ranked number nine among competitors in its share of global equity and equity-related underwriting in 2001 and 2000. The firm fell from No. 5 in 2000 to No. 6 in 2001 in worldwide M&A advisory, though it did manage to have a hand in 14 out of the 35 top U.S. M&A deals of 2001. The firm was the lead acquirer adviser in Comcast's $72 billion buyout of AT&T Broadband (announced in December 2001); Phillips Petroleum's purchase of Conoco for $23.6 billion in November 2001; and Procter & Gamble's acquisition of Connectiv, for $5 billion in May 2001.

J.P. Morgan was the lead manager of eight IPOs in 2001. Among the largest deals was The Princeton Review's $59.4 million offering in June 2001. The firm also lead managed Wright Medical Group's July 2001 IPO worth $93.8 million and co-led Aramark Worldwide's $690 million offering in December 2001. J.P. Morgan was also busy in the secondary market. The biggest deals to note: Sprint PCS's $1.7 billion offering in August 2001; Northrop Grumman's $708 million offering in November 2001; and a $779 million deal for King Pharmaceuticals, also in November 2001.

IPO no no

In April 2002, the National Association of Securities Dealers (NASD) notified J.P. Morgan that the firm could face civil charges for commissions violations made during the tech boom of 1999 and 2000. The charges were a part of a two-year NASD investigation of several Wall Street firms that supposedly gave investors big blocks of coveted IPO stocks in return for investors' profits from the offerings. Investor kickbacks to banks were allegedly disguised as commissions. Before implicating J.P. Morgan, the NASD hit CSFB, the leading tech stock underwriter during 1999 and 2000, with a hefty fine for commissions violations.

GETTING HIRED

Separate but equal

Morgan and Chase separately hire new associates and analysts in much the same way they did before the merger. Each entity recruits at a number of the top-tier schools, but candidates from other schools are also considered. For both Morgan and Chase, at least two rounds of interviews are required. The final round is typically conducted in a Super Saturday format, with candidates spending the day at the firm and interviewing with a number of managers — at least four to six people. While some interviewers will ask complex questions intended to measure an individual's quantitative skills, others may simply engage in a few minutes of small talk to gauge how well an individual will fit into the organization. After offers are extended, candidates are often invited to a sell day, during which they meet more managers and learn more about the firm before deciding whether or not to accept the offer.

Joining J.P.

The Morgan side of the J.P Morgan Chase empire recruits at about 50 undergraduate and business schools for positions in global markets, investment banking, asset management services and consulting. Typically, Morgan makes on-campus presentations, giving a company-wide overview of its business, and later makes division-specific presentations in association with school clubs. Some of these are social events such as cocktail parties or lunches, and lucky schools such as UCLA get "beer blasts." Morgan also hosts "get to know you" dinners at the major business schools. "The people at the early events keep track of who they met," says one insider. "And if they have something to say about you, it's funneled to the decision makers at the firm."

First interviews tend to be lengthy and require contact with various levels of employees, including associates, VPs and MDs. Often, candidates go through two first round interviews, which are generally conducted on campus, unless the candidate applied online and doesn't attend one of the schools where Morgan recruits. In such cases, the candidate is interviewed by phone. Second-round interviews often follow the familiar Super Saturday format, in which a candidate will interview with anywhere from five to eight people in total. Depending on the position, offers are normally extended from a few days up to a month following second round interviews. For one investment management associate, though, "It was a relatively quick interview process. The second round was held the day after my two on-campus interviews. And I literally walked in the door after the second round and the phone was ringing."

According to another associate, candidates can expect questions such as "What do you think of the market?" and "What do you like to do?" The contact adds, "I was never asked to lever and unlever a beta, and there were no math questions. The interviews were more or less to see if you can interact without being a total goof." Another source says, "Personal fit is first priority. They want to know your background and thought process." He admits there were "some technical questions, which mostly came during the second round interviews with two MDs, who played a blatant good cop, bad cop routine."

A research analyst, who did not attend one of the firm's target schools, says he interviewed with managers from three different industry groups. This source says the questions he was asked ranged from the standard accounting and finance questions to other common questions such as "Why J.P. Morgan?" and "Why research?"

Chat with Chase

Undergrads applying to Chase need at least a 3.0 cumulative GPA and "strong quantitative, analytical, and computer skills and excellent oral and written communication skills," according to the firm. The same basic requirements go for MBAs, although there's no minimum GPA requirement. The first step is an on-campus interview, and then it's on to a Super Saturday. Usually, on the Friday night before the Super Saturday, undergrads have a dinner with Chase analysts. On Saturday, candidates typically interview with four bankers. The MBA process is pretty much the same, excluding the dinner. For MBAs, "Final rounds are five two-on-one interviews, and all interviewers must agree [in order] to hire a particular candidate," reports one source.

In general, Chase bankers note that interviewers are trying to "get a feel for who you are." Says one source, "It is really about your personality and vision, which should be clear." Typically, offers are extended the Monday or Tuesday following Super Saturday.

OUR SURVEY SAYS

Mix is a match

Blending the cultures of Chase Manhattan and J.P. Morgan has proven to be a considerable challenge. While the popular public image of Morgan was that of a starched-shirt, mahogany-paneled firm cloistered in 19th-century beliefs and manners, the company was known on Wall Street as being rather progressive. Chase, on the other hand, was in a state of flux even before the Morgan merger. Although the commercial bank had a reputation among its customers as being focused on customer service, it had been in search of a corporate identity as it sought to combine previous acquisitions into a cohesive unit. Following the merger, rumors flourished that loyalists from both firms were eyeing each other with suspicion. And many expressed little confidence in the marriage prospering. But, according to many insiders, especially those among the lower ranks, the combination was agreeable.

"From day one of the announcement, it was business as usual," says a J.P. Morgan associate, formerly with Chase Manhattan's investment-banking unit. "I was staffed on deals right away." He adds, "Nobody cares whether you've been in this organization or that one. There's no bullshit about whether you're from Chase or J.P. Morgan. It was a very easy transition." The contact goes on to say that "overall, the merger was good. If anybody has anything negative to say, I believe it's more a result of the bad market." A sales associate agrees. "The merger hasn't gone incredibly smoothly, but it's more a function of the market than the merger itself. Any difficulties we experienced more or less happened at any other firm." Although this contact admits, "There is a little of that looking down at Chase people," he says, "everyone's on equal footing." He adds that the huge firm-wide layoffs, a result of the merger and the poor economy, "should be over."

Another insider predicts that other I-banks might soon be going through mergers not unlike the Morgan/Chase marriage. "Eventually, all those old security firms such as

Goldman and Merrill will need a big balance sheet to get things done. It's moving towards the Citibank/Solomon way of doing things. So you can come here and work at a place that's already gone through their merger. Or you can go somewhere else, and go through their merger. We're done with the hard part."

A (mostly) happy step-family

Most insiders have only good things to say about their experiences working at Morgan Chase. "They're serious about business, but it's a pretty human and laid back place," says one banker. "It's an organized, well-managed place, where it's important to have a personality. People talk to each other about their holidays and interests, sports and the news." Another associate agrees, calling the firm "relaxed, not too uptight, but professional." An analyst says, "I would say that the job isn't perfect, but management is committed to making the analyst experience worthwhile. People are always willing to help their coworkers, the lifestyle is great and the pay is quite good." A co-worker agrees that "working here is fulfilling," and even though dealing with "the bureaucracy isn't, things are improving." Furthermore, little time is "spent on internal or dead-end projects," freeing analysts and associates up to learn more about developing deals. One analyst says he's lucky to work with someone who "has delegated responsibility downward, so I can get my hands on as much as I feel comfortable with — and sometimes more." Others caution that not all the bosses at Morgan Chase will hand over the reins of responsibility so freely. One insider moans, "Analysts are first and foremost data retrievers." However, this contact deems it a necessary function because "it forces the analyst to understand the business."

As for interaction with senior bankers, associates and analysts say they feel respected by managers and receive good feedback from them. According to one contact, "Senior bankers typically show concern for the development of junior resources." Another says he enjoys working at Morgan Chase because "analysts are praised for doing good work." Proclaims one confident insider: "I take my job seriously, and as a result, the senior guys pay attention — and don't give me trouble when I argue with them." One sales associate says he enjoys the firm's "hands-off" attitude. He explains, "Managers let you run your own business. If you're hitting numbers, no one cares what you do or how you do it." An experienced commercial banker has a similar, but slightly different spin. She says, "Most managers are reactive but like their subordinates to be proactive."

According to one investment banker, "Relationships with one another outside of work are encouraged — group heads encourage MDs to interact with analysts and associates. And different groups work really well together. It's very normal to mix all together. In our group, people go out for monthly drinks."

Looking for ladies

Employees, for the most part, give the firm high marks for diversity, especially regarding women. A New York source says the firm actually "seeks out women and minorities." Another agrees, saying the firm "goes out of its way" in this area. Reports one source, "There are quite a few women, including senior MDs." And an insider in consumer banking says there's "lots of female AVPs and VPs," but admits, "you don't really see too many senior VPs." One contact thinks the firm "could use more women," and says, "we're trying to hire more." He adds, "At a certain level, I think managers' compensation is linked to hitting diversity targets, so some MDs actually fight over qualified women."

A London insider says, with respect to the firm's hiring practices in Europe, "We have every nationality, especially in our core markets — French, German and Italian. I also work with Russians, Hungarians and Lebanese. Actually, Brits and Americans are minorities." However, he adds, "I don't think Europe is as far along as the U.S. in hiring people of African descent."

Even prior to the merger, the parent companies had records of being diversity-friendly. Before combining, each firm made several appearances on the "50 Best Companies in America for Minorities" list, as compiled by *Fortune*. J.P. Morgan had also instituted a Diversity Steering Committee (DSC), composed of managing directors from each business group to oversee the issues affecting the firm on a global basis. Additionally, J.P. Morgan was the first firm on Wall Street to grant benefits for partners in same-sex relationships.

Dressed for success?

Both firms have casual dress codes. Unfortunately, say some employees, the firm is becoming a little too casual for their tastes. While officially, "no jeans, exposed toes, navels or tattoos" are allowed in the office, some report that it's "slipped to the point where some people are coming in wearing jeans." One insider finds the attire violations disturbing. "I think it hasn't improved the overall attitude. Wearing a tie on the trading floor didn't slow me down before." One bemused analyst describes his co-workers' style of dress as "J. Crew and Banana Republic at war." Some, however, report that insiders welcome the dressed-down look. An investment-banking associate, with a bit more exotic taste than the mass market, says, "I usually wear a Hawaiian shirt every Friday. If I don't have it on, secretaries scold me. Even the MDs like it. Basically, if it's not interrupting work, people appreciate that kind of stuff."

"Nobody cares whether you've been in this organization or that one. There's no bullshit about whether you're from Chase or J.P. Morgan."

— *J.P. Morgan Chase insider*

Janus Capital

100 Filmore Street #300
Denver, CO 80206
Phone: (303) 333-3863
www.janus.com

DEPARTMENTS

Asset Management • Marketing •
Research • Sales

THE STATS

Chairman: Thomas H. Bailey
Employer Type: Subsidiary of
Stilwell Financial
No. of Employees: 1,475
No. of Offices: 6

KEY COMPETITORS

Fidelity Investments
Franklin Resources
Putnam Investments

UPPERS

• Comfortable offices
• Relaxed culture

DOWNERS

• Hit hard by layoffs

EMPLOYMENT CONTACT

Human Resources
100 Filmore Street #300
Denver, CO 80206
Fax: (303) 321-2125

THE BUZZ
WHAT EMPLOYEES AT OTHER FIRMS ARE SAYING

• "Top in its industry"
• "Not as smart as everyone
  thought during tech boom"
• "Very respected"
• "May be past its prime"

THE SCOOP

New beginnings

Janus Capital was founded by Tom Bailey in the summer of 1969 in Denver, Colo. Bailey named his firm after Janus, the two-faced Roman god of new beginnings. Since its inception, the company has grown into one of the largest mutual funds in the world, with 1,475 people and approximately $170 million (as of June 2002) in assets under management. With an entire family of retail mutual funds and a burgeoning business in separate accounts and sub-advisory relationships, Janus is one of the fastest-growing mutual fund companies in the U.S., and an increasingly important player overseas. Janus is a unit of Stilwell Financial, a Kansas City, Mo.-based holding company that controls several money managers.

Despite its quick ascent, Janus has had some growing pains, falling on tough times riddled with scandal before recovering. In November 1976, the Securities and Exchange Commission claimed Janus' partners were getting favorable prices on trades both for their personal accounts and for the firm, then giving false statements to the SEC on the matter. And in the early 1980s, soaring returns made the Janus Fund a popular spot for investors. Too popular, as it turned out — the fund was briefly oversubscribed, with more orders than legally authorized shares. The firm was forced to give refunds to thousands of investors. By 1984 Janus sold 80 percent of the company for $18 million to Kansas City Southern Industries (KCSI), a railroad company that had some financial services holdings. Bailey retained approximately 17 percent of the company.

After the boom

The firm's funds boomed in 1998 and 1999 as the company aggressively snatched up technology stocks. When those stocks flopped in 2000, the company's funds slumped as well, and investors fled the firm. In January 2001, Jim Craig, who had been elevated to chief investment officer, left Janus. A year later, the firm named Helen Young Hayes to replace Craig. Hayes became one of the few women at the top of a large investment management firm, and there was speculation that she might succeed Bailey when he retires.

Bailey bails

In June 2002, founder Thomas Bailey finally announced when he would be stepping down as the firm's president and CEO. Bailey, who spent 33 years as the head of the firm, said he would officially hand over daily operating duties to Janus's management committee effective July 1, 2002. The management committee, along with parent Stilwell, will search for Bailey's replacement. "This is a bittersweet moment for me because Janus has been — and continues to be — an important part of my life," Bailey said in a written statement. "I've spent half my life — and nearly all my professional years — at Janus. But it's time to shift my focus to my responsibilities as a trustee and away from my day-to-day operational role as CEO." Bailey remains as Janus' chairman of the board and continues to work with Janus trustees, focusing on monitoring fund performance.

Cutting back

Like most of its competitors, the firm cut payroll costs in the economic downturn of 2001. Janus cut 468 workers in February 2001, then added 45 more layoffs in April 2001. The cuts, approximately 16 percent of the company's workforce, were mainly in the operations division. The job cuts continued into 2002. In February 2002, Janus announced 222 more job cuts. The layoffs affected customer service reps and those who set up accounts and processed transactions. The cutbacks echoed diminished demand in the direct sales unit of the fund industry. Almost half of Janus' retail stock funds were closed to new investors and customers frequently use the company web site and automated phone systems.

GETTING HIRED

Janus maintains an employment page on its web site (www.janus.com) where potential employees can search for positions and apply online. The firm "only recruits from the top schools," according to one insider. Expect "four interviews," including a meeting with human resources and "managers and supervisors" from your prospective department.

OUR SURVEY SAYS

Insiders at Janus describe a "casual" culture where they "do not feel intimidated talking to the heads of the company." The surroundings are comfortable, as the firm provides "nothing but the best for office location and equipment." Despite the luxury, insiders say turnover is high. "But they do attempt to maintain the best talent," reports one source.

UBS Warburg

1/2 Finsbury Avenue
London EC2M 2PP
United Kingdom
Phone: (44-20) 7567-8000
www.ubswarburg.com

299 Park Avenue
New York, NY 10171
Phone: (212) 821-3000

DEPARTMENTS

Equities • Financial Control • Fixed
Income • Information Technology •
Interest Rate Products and FX •
Investment Banking • Operations

THE STATS

Chairman and CEO: John Costas
Employer Type:
Subsidiary of UBS AG
No. of Employees: 17,000
No. of Offices: 65

KEY COMPETITORS

Credit Suisse First Boston
Lehman Brothers
Merrill Lynch
Salomon Smith Barney

UPPERS

- A firm on the rise
- Relaxed culture

DOWNERS

- Most sales staff based in
  Stamford, Conn.
- Second-tier image in U.S.

EMPLOYMENT CONTACT

Human Resources
UBS Warburg Center
677 Washington Boulevard
Stamford, CT 06901
Phone: (203) 719-3000

THE BUZZ
WHAT EMPLOYEES AT OTHER FIRMS ARE SAYING

- "Gaining ground"
- "Second-tier U.S. player"
- "Rising stars"
- "Overly aggressive"

THE SCOOP

Neutral parent

UBS Warburg represents the investment-banking operations of UBS, the Swiss-based financial services behemoth with more than 70,000 employees worldwide. Besides investment banking, UBS offers private and corporate banking services through UBS Wealth Management and Business Banking and asset management and mutual funds through UBS Global Asset Management. After a tumultuous history of mergers and acquisitions, the firm hopes to become a major player in the U.S. market. In May 2000, the firm listed its shares on the New York Stock Exchange and made it clear that UBS Warburg had expansion and acquisitions on its agenda. The firm didn't disappoint: UBS Warburg later acquired PaineWebber for $11.8 billion.

Multi-merger history

The company's story begins in 1872 with the founding of the Swiss Bank Corporation (SBC). SBC grew internationally (the London office, the bank's first outside Switzerland, opened in 1898) and, by the 1990s, had established alliances or subsidiaries in the world's financial centers. In the mid-1990s, the firm became a major player in the investment-banking world by purchasing the securities business of S.G. Warburg Group, a firm started in London in the 1930s by Siegmund Warburg, a German who fled Nazi persecution. The investment-banking division of the new firm was dubbed SBC Warburg, which expanded into the U.S. with its September 1997 acquisition of Dillon, Read & Co., a New York I-bank founded in 1832. The investment-banking division was then named SBC Warburg Dillon Read. In June 1998, SBC merged with UBS (Union Bank of Switzerland), taking the name UBS AG. UBS had been formed in 1912 by the merger of two regional Swiss banks, the Bank of Winterthur and Toggenbirger Bank.

Early analysis of the UBS/SBC/Warburg combination wasn't favorable, and much of the criticism was directed at the integration of SBC Warburg into UBS. Profits for 1999 were lacking and critics were vocal, most notably *The Economist*, which called UBS "a directionless and unhappy institution." Things picked up in 2000 when UBS reported profits of $4.8 billion, an increase of $600 million over the previous year.

New millennium, new order

In February 2000, UBS restructured into its current format, and it was then that the bank renamed its investment-banking operations UBS Warburg. In May 2000, UBS began trading on the New York Stock Exchange (the first financial services firm based outside the United States to trade on the Big Board). UBS CEO Marcel Ospel told CNBC that the NYSE listing would enable the company to "act in the United States on the acquisition front." Additionally, Ospel emphatically denied the possibility of the firm retreating from the investment-banking business. "These rumors have absolutely no substance; to the contrary, investment banking is very important for our group, we are determined to grow it with a focus to here — North America."

Thank you, PaineWebber

The initial focus of UBS Warburg's expansion plans turned out to be PaineWebber, the 121-year-old investment bank. In July 2000, UBS announced it was acquiring PaineWebber for $10.8 billion in cash and stock. The purchase connected PaineWebber's considerable U.S. retail presence (the firm was the nation's fourth-largest broker at the time of the deal) with UBS Warburg's growing banking practice. PaineWebber was initially absorbed in the UBS Warburg family as UBS Painewbber. Acquiring PaineWebber added more than 8,000 brokers and 2.7 million clients to the UBS portfolio. "The combination of UBS' international reach and product range, with PaineWebber's leading position in the U.S. market for affluent and high net worth individuals, will create a premier global investment services firm," Ospel said in the release announcing the coupling.

Initial reaction to the deal was mostly positive, though there was some concern that despite adding millions of retail clients the firm hadn't done much to improve its position in investment banking. (UBS reportedly had designs on a deal that was more investment-banking focused; according to Bloomberg, the firm held merger talks with Lehman Brothers in early 2000.) Optimists said the larger retail base would naturally lead to more investment-banking business.

PaineWebber payoff

That optimism was well founded. In 2001 the firm became Europe's top investment bank, based on revenues generated from investment-banking activities. According to *The Wall Street Journal*, the firm reported a 7.5 percent European market share in investment-banking revenues 2001, up from 4.5 percent in 2000 (when it held sixth position). And in the U.S. the firm broke into the top 10 in overall I-banking revenues. UBS Warburg nearly doubled its U.S. market share in 2001 to 3.2 percent, good enough for ninth place in total I-banking revenues. UBS Warburg also broke into the U.S. top 10 list of equity underwriters. The firm reports that U.S. investment -banking operations now represent about 40 percent of total revenues, compared with less than 15 percent previously.

At the beginning of 2001 UBS announced that it would turn PaineWebber's private client business into an independent unit. (PaineWebber's institutional clients remained with UBS Warburg.) The move, which restores some independence to the house of Paine, reflects UBS's desire to increase its foray into the growing wealth management industry. UBS said it had planned for some time to separate the private client operations. "What we thought was that we have some pretty fantastic people running our wealth management in the U.S. and it would make sense to link that with our private client business in Europe," UBS Warburg CEO John Costas told *The Wall Street Journal*. He also said the separation would not impact any of the benefits already produced by the combination of UBS Warburg and UBS PaineWebber.

M&A muscle

UBS Warburg's strength lies in its M&A advisory practice. According to Thomson Financial Securities Data, the firm ranked first in global M&A deals announced and not withdrawn in 2001, advising on 239 deals worth $228 billion. In 2000 the firm ranked seventh in announced M&A deals, advising on 291 deals worth $317 billion. The firm also picked up the coveted "Privatization Advisory Team of the Year" from *Privatization International* in 2001.

Picking up a piece

In February 2002, UBS Warburg acquired the North American energy-trading operations and systems of Enron, the Houston-based energy giant that collapsed in 2001. Included in the deal was Enron's online trading platform, which accounted for more than $1 trillion of business since it debuted in November 1999. UBS Warburg edged Citigroup in the bidding and renamed the operation UBS Warburg Energy. The unit provides real-time bid and offer prices for North American natural gas and power products via its web site, UBSWenergy.com. For what used to be the source of most of Enron's income (90 percent of Enron's $100 billion in 2001 revenues), UBS Warburg paid no cash up front, but agreed to give Enron at least 33 percent of the new organization's profits for up to 10 years. The Enron deal will serve as UBS Warburg's entry into energy trading, further expanding its worldwide trading operations.

GETTING HIRED

The few, the proud

Landing a position at UBS Warburg isn't as easy as it used to be. "Hiring standards have become much more rigorous over the last few years," says one firm insider. "Now the firm is purging the weaker links, and it has become very difficult to get hired into a smaller number of available slots," offers a source. One New York banker says, "The bar has been raised substantially as a result of increased management expectations and the drop off in the market." Putting it bluntly, one contact says, "It's tough. Only a select few can make it."

UBS Warburg targets its recruiting efforts on the top-10 MBA programs and selected top 20 undergrad institutions. But, as one insider points out, the firm "also looks at people from 15 or so others institutions that are non-target schools — and a lot of those recruits get hired." In addition to targeting the typical top schools, the firm recruits from "Howard, Morehouse and Spelman for diversity initiatives," according to another source.

Insiders note that UBS Warburg's interview process is pretty typical of the industry. Potential employees go through two to three interview rounds, the last of which is usually a "Super Saturday" format in which a recruit meets with several senior employees during the course of an entire day. Throughout all rounds, interviewees can expect both technical- and character-based questions, although one associate admits, "There's no firm-wide set questions. It's up to each interviewer." According to one contact, questions can run the gamut from "the stock market," "the industry," "accounting" and "valuation," to "personal background" and "team-player mentality." Another source says interview questions are "standard, relating to past experience, applicable computer skills and general knowledge of the industry."

OUR SURVEY SAYS

Definitely relaxed, but no kicking back

According to insiders, UBS Warburg lacks the cutthroat atmosphere typically associated with investment banking. In fact, most say the firm is "relaxed" in many ways. The culture is "relaxed and focused on quality of life," says one source. "In general, people here are a little more relaxed and friendly than at other firms," says another. Yet another contact calls the firm "down to earth and relaxed." A laid back environment, however, doesn't necessarily equal a slow pace. It's "relaxed but diligent" says one trader. A banker offers, "We have a fast-paced and aggressive, but collegial culture." Many insiders agree that UBS Warburg is "team-oriented," "fast-paced," "vibrant" and "challenging," as one contact says.

Next to "relaxed," insiders are partial to the word "open," which many use in describing the interaction between senior and junior employees. One contact says senior managers are "easy going and have an open door policy. If you have a problem and you say something, it's respected, and will be attempted to be worked out." Another insider says relationships are "very good" and calls managers "open and honest." Yet another says, "For the most part, senior management and junior management interact openly." However, at least a few sources admit encountering some less-than-approachable higher-ups. An associate says, "A couple of groups have managers who are terrible to junior staff, while others have great managers who treat junior staff with dignity." Another source echoes the opinion. "It's a mixed bag. Some managers are thoughtful and respectful, and others are ogres." The non-ogres, however, seem to have a profound effect on their subordinates. An insider says, "I have a great manager who has provided me with a lot of feedback on how to excel in my job." Another contact says, "One of the best aspects of the firm are the relationships built with senior managers."

Middle of the street

UBS Warburg's pay and work hours are right in line with the industry average, say insiders. The firm "pays what the Street is paying," says one banker. "Generally, we find out about [our] bonuses after other firms announce theirs." Another source concurs, saying UBS Warburg "pays based on a survey of and interviews with other firms. Compensation is well in line with peers, if not slightly above." At least one employee says it wasn't always this way. UBS Warburg "historically paid somewhat under-market, which led to a stream of people leaving for greener pastures. However, in the last two years, my compensation has been very competitive with the best bids I've seen elsewhere." Insiders report some fine perks as well. One salesman says, "I use the car service to and from work every day — who wants to ride the subway if you don't have to? — and we get meals delivered from all of Mario Batali's restaurants. I never pay for my own lunch." Other sources also say that lunch is often, if not always, provided. Some employees, however, don't have it as good. Even so, they seem quite satisfied with the $30 dinner stipends offered by the firm for those that work late.

As far as hours go, one I-banking associate admits, "They suck, but they're no worse than any other bank." Typically, the firm's investment-banking analysts work about 70 to 80 hours week, with 100-hour weeks not uncommon. I-banking associates work about 10 hours less, and traders, as is customary, work even fewer hours. Face-time is nearly non-existent. One source says, "If there's a lot going on, we're there a lot. But if there's down time, we're not in the office just to be there."

(You can get some) satisfaction

Overall, employees don't have many gripes about working at UBS Warburg. Most are pleased with their situations, though, of course, things could always be better. Says one employee, "It's a solid firm that gives you a good opportunity to learn and grow. Politics exist, as with any firm, but are not overbearing. However, there is room for improvement — from a compensation and training standpoint for junior bankers." Another insider says, "I wish we were having a better year, I had more people working for me, and I was being developed more as a manager. But, I enjoy my work, and it keeps me challenged." Location is another common, minor gripe. The firm's American sales and trading headquarters is located in Stamford, Conn., a New York suburb in wealthy Fairfield County. The Stamford office itself receives high marks. The trading floor was recently redone and can now fit up to 1,400 traders (up from 800) and is as big as two football fields, according to the firm. Says one trader, "I don't know any other firm that has more space on the trading floor than we do. If you're a quarterback and would like to practice your throw, this is the place to be." However, pigskin haters, culture-seekers, and late night French martini drinkers probably won't find that the salacious digs outweigh the bore of the 'burbs. "The office is awesome," says another trader. "It's only the location I mind." The firm counters that most of the sales staff in Stamford lives in the area, making for an easy commute.

"Some managers are thoughtful and respectful, and others are ogres."

— *UBS Warburg insider*

Citigroup

399 Park Avenue
New York, NY 10043
Phone: (800) 285-3000
www.citigroup.com

DEPARTMENTS

Citigroup International • Consumer
Group • Corporate and Investment
Bank • Global Investment
Management and Private Banking
Group

THE STATS

Chairman and CEO: Sanford I. Weill
Employer Type: Public Company
Ticker Symbol: C (NYSE)
2001 Revenues: $83.6 billion
2001 Net Income: $14.1 billion
No. of Employees: 268,000

KEY COMPETITORS

Bank of America
Bank of New York
Deutsche Bank
J.P. Morgan Chase

UPPERS

• Major global brand name
• Worldwide reach

DOWNERS

• Big bank bureaucracy
• Undefined culture due to merger

EMPLOYMENT CONTACT

Debbie Bertan
Citigroup
One Court Square
14th Floor/Zone 1
Long Island City, NY 11120

THE BUZZ
WHAT EMPLOYEES AT OTHER FIRMS ARE SAYING

• "The model to beat"
• "Stodgy commercial bank"
• "Banking powerhouse No. 1"
• "Clueless"

THE SCOOP

The making of a giant

Today's Citigroup can trace its roots back to 1812, but the foundation for the financial services behemoth's present form was set in 1986, when Sanford (Sandy) Weill became chairman of Commercial Credit, a Baltimore, Md.-based loan company. Two years later, Commercial Credit purchased Primerica; the new firm adopted the Primerica name. In 1993 Primerica acquired The Travelers Corp. and adopted that name. The new firm purchased Salomon Brothers, the respected investment bank, in 1997 and combined it with Smith Barney to form Salomon Smith Barney.

In April 1998, Weill's Travelers merged with Citicorp to create Citigroup. The two companies were betting hard that Depression-era rules that regulated the financial services industry would be modified. In fact, rather than bet, the companies lobbied to make it so, pushing for the Financial Services Modernization Act of 1999, which made the arrangement legal. (*Crain's New York Business* claims Citigroup CEO Sanford Weill has the pen used by former President Bill Clinton to sign the act into law on display in his office.)

Citigroup's oldest ancestor is Citibank, the commercial bank founded in 1812 by Samuel Osgood, the first commissioner of the U.S. Treasury. The City Bank of New York (as it was then known) began by serving cotton, sugar, metal and coal merchants and became a pioneer in overseas expansion during the early 20th century. Since then Citibank has gone on to become the first commercial bank to make personal loans, the first to provide high-interest specified-term CDs and the first to introduce ATMs on a large scale. Today, Osgood's creation offers one-stop shopping to its customers, whether they be homeowners looking for a mortgage or institutional investors in need of derivatives to hedge bets on the market.

Branding strategy

Overall, the bank is making good progress toward the mission first articulated by former Citigroup co-CEO John Reed: to transform the Citigroup name into an internationally recognized and trusted brand name on par with the likes of Coca-Cola or Xerox. Industry observers predicted that if the Citicorp/Travelers combination proved successful, it would likely spur similar mergers in the future.

Lonely at the top

Wall Street dealmaker Weill snagged former Treasury Secretary Robert E. Rubin in 1999, making him director and chair of the Executive Committee. (It was rumored that Rubin was a CEO-in-waiting, a rumor he and the firm have consistently denied.) In February 2000, turmoil hit the chairman's office. Co-chairman and CEO John Reed announced his retirement, effective April 2000. While observers said that Reed and his co-chairman and CEO, Sanford Weill, had personality and style clashes, Reed said he merely sought the peace and quiet of retirement. According to published reports, Citigroup executives had complained that the presence of two CEOs was disruptive to Citigroup senior management. The issue finally came to a head in late February 2000, when the board of directors debated for several hours the fate of the company's two CEOs. Reed resigned, and Weill remained head of the bank. (To acclaim, as it turns out: *Chief Executive* magazine named Weill "CEO of the Year" for 2002.)

Citigroup's post-Weill succession plans remained unclear through mid-2002, especially after a reshuffling of the company's top management. The January 2002 announcement that Robert Willumstad was named president led many to speculate he was being groomed to replace Weill. But in June, Deryck Maughan, head of Citigroup's Internet business, was placed in charge of the company's international business. The promotion threw Sir Deryck (an Englishman who was knighted in January 2002) into the competition. Willumstad, along with Michael Carpenter, head of corporate and investment banking, and Thomas Jones, head of asset management, were also given greater responsibilities in the June 2002 restructuring. While Willumstad and Sir Deryck are considered front runners for Weill's throne, analysts say any of the men (Carpenter and Jones included) could be selected.

The rich get richer

Due in large part to some monumental acquisitions, Citigroup climbed over Deutsche Bank in 2001 to become the largest financial services company in the world, measured by assets. In July 2001, Citigroup acquired European American Bank (EAB) from ABN AMRO Bank N.V. for $1.6 billion plus the assumption of $350 million in preferred stock. The acquisition of EAB — one of Long Island's largest banks with $11.5 billion in deposits, $15.4 billion in assets, and 97 branches — increased Citi's branch network and strengthened its role as a middle-market business lender. Following the merger, EAB locations were converted to Citibank financial centers with the Citibank brand name.

The bank bought Mexico City-based Grupo Financiero Banamex Accival and its holdings, including Banamax USA Bancorp and California Commerce Bank, in August 2001 for $12.5 billion. The new entity became the largest banking group in Mexico. After integrating the Mexican bank's operations, Citigroup cut 2,700 jobs, which was nearly 1,000 jobs less than analysts expected. In January 2002, Citigroup paid $1.24 billion for Dutch insurer Aegon's stakes in two Banamex insurance partnerships and a fund management endeavor. With respect to foreign acquisitions, Citi has no plans to sleep: the bank is keeping an eye out for acquisitions in other emerging markets and is currently negotiating a deal in China.

Closer to home, Citigroup increased its presence on the West Coast by purchasing Golden State Bancorp for $5.8 billion. The May 2002 deal adds 300 branches to the company's fledgling California operations; the company already operated 80 Citibank branches there.

The bigger they are, the harder they fall?

Citigroup's 190 million corporate and consumer accounts in over 100 countries can be a double-edged sword: Its global presence ensures it will get hurt in almost every financial calamity in any sector worldwide.

For example, Citigroup was one of the largest lenders to North American energy giant Enron, which became the largest bankruptcy in U.S. history in 2001. As one of Enron's creditors, Citi had a lot to lose — over $1 billion — in the company's dissolution. Thankfully, Citigroup's losses amounted to much less than the whole billion, as a large portion of the loans were backed by assets or hedged with credit derivatives. For the fourth quarter of 2001, Citigroup only reported a $228 million pre-tax loss due to its dealings with Enron. Citigroup officials told *The Wall Street Journal* that, as of January 2002, the bank still had approximately $230 million outstanding in unsecured Enron exposure, and $650 million in secured loans.

But Citigroup's liabilities from Enron extend beyond bad loans. Investigators began looking into whether Citigroup and J.P. Morgan Chase, Enron's other big lender, knew about the illegal transactions that brought Enron down. Specifically, congressional investigators charged the firms with promoting complex deals with offshore partnerships that would enable energy firms (*The Wall Street Journal* reported that the deals were offered to companies besides Enron) to conceal their debt load from investors. The firms denied the charges, saying that they fulfilled their legal obligations in their dealings with Enron, but e-mail messages leaked during the investigation suggest that, at the very least, Citigroup and J.P. Morgan bankers understood the need to structure transactions in such a way to keep them off client balance sheets. The *Journal* quoted a Citigroup client presentation from 2001 bragging about how the bank could structure a deal that "eliminates the need for Capital Markets disclosure, keeping structure mechanics private." Additional information was disclosed about Citigroup's relationship with Enron. Investigators discovered internal documents deals where Citigroup bankers expressed doubts about the accounting procedures in one Enron deal. According to the *New York Times*, Citigroup told Enron management about concerns regarding the accounting methods used in a deal with Enron's Roosevelt partnership. Initially, the *Times* reported that an oral agreement was reached to use Citigrop's accounting methods, but the decision was soon reversed. In internal communications, Citigroup bankers stressed not including the discussions and oral agreement about the accounting procedures. "The paperwork can not reflect their agreement, as it would unfavorably alter the accounting," read one e-mail. Citigroup denied the existence of an oral agreement and said the e-mails represented preliminary, informal discussions about the deal in question.

Don't cry for Citi

Citigroup also incurred losses in 2001 in Argentina, where the bank has been a major player since 1918 and has over $8 billion in assets. After Argentina's four-year recession turned into a full-on financial crisis, the country began to freeze assets at most of the top banks in order to prevent a run on deposits. Citigroup announced that during the fourth quarter 2001 it took a pre-tax hit of $470 million due to Argentinean turmoil. According to *The Wall Street Journal*, the loss included $235 million in foreign exchange valuations and $235 million in credit losses, investment security write-downs and charges related to the exchange of Argentine debt securities for loans. In January 2002, Citigroup became the first foreign bank to divest some of its Argentinean holdings. Citigroup's Banamex sold its majority stake in ailing Banco Bansud to Banco Macro for $65 million, and paid Macro $150 million more to assume Bansud's loans.

Ironically, trouble in Argentina could ultimately prove to actually increase Citigroup's reach. FleetBoston, the largest bank in Argentina and a major Citigroup rival in the Northeast U.S., was hit hard by the Latin American country's troubles. According to *New York Newsday*, "[Fleet's] mounting troubles have created a buzz in the banking industry and among analysts that it is vulnerable to takeover." The *Newsday* piece added that many experts say a transaction between FleetBoston and Citigroup makes a whole lot of sense. Gerard Cassidy, analyst at RBC Capital

Markets in Portland, Maine, told *Newsday*, "The question is not if the company will be acquired, the question is when." Cassidy said a deal between Citi and Fleet would probably be worth more than $50 billion — placing it among the top 10 largest bank deals — and could provide cost savings of 20 percent as Citigroup cut overlapping operations in consumer banking, capital markets, corporate lending international and staff functions.

Good fortune

Citigroup made its first appearance in 2002 on *Fortune* magazine's annual list of "America's Most Admired Companies," coming in eighth. The publication cited Citigroup's delivery of more than $14 billion in profits for the year, "despite a recession, September 11 fallout, and exposure to Enron and Argentina." Citi also garnered the top spot in its industry (Banks: Commercial and Savings).

Giving props to the public

Citigroup made headlines in December 2001 when it announced it planned to spin off subsidiary Travelers Property Casualty, by selling 20 percent in an IPO and offering the rest of the company to Citigroup shareholders. The $3.7 billion IPO, completed in March 2002, was the largest insurance IPO ever, and the fourth-largest initial offering in U.S. history. Citigroup also sold $850 million in convertible notes along with the public shares.

Citi dumped

Berkshire Hathaway, the investment company of billionaire investor Warren Buffett, sold all of its shares in Citigroup in 2001, ending an investment of almost 15 years in the bank and its predecessors. According to Bloomberg News, Berkshire's 2.7 million shares were valued at more than $128 million if sold at Citigroup's average price in the fourth quarter. What exactly does the relatively small stock sale mean? Bloomberg said investors saw Buffett's ownership of Citigroup as a vote of confidence in chairman Sanford Weill. In the simplest of terms, as Michael Stead, chief investment officer of the $700 million SIFE Trust Fund, which owns 400,000 Citigroup shares, told Bloomberg, "It means Mr. Buffett thinks he has a better place to put his money."

GETTING HIRED

The program

Each year, Citigroup hires about 150 into its Management Associate (MA) program for the consumer group, Citigroup International, the global investment management and private banking group, human resources and financial management. (Note that the Corporate and Investment Bank, also known as Salomon Smith Barney, recruits separately.) The process begins on campus and is followed by a Super Saturday-style affair, where candidates are shuffled from one office to another for (usually) five 30-minute interviews with associates and VPs. One contact characterized her interview as "pleasant" and "not very stressful," but don't expect a chat over coffee — Citigroup interviewers will give out brainteasers, which in the words of one contact "sound like they probably got them out of a book."

Outside of the MA program, such as branch management or personal banking, the job-seeking process is less formal — one of our contacts, for example, reports obtaining an interview simply "by picking up the telephone book and calling someone at Citibank." One employee hired into Citigroup's asset management group says her interviews were "much more of a discussion as opposed to an interview."

Summers in the Citi

Citigroup offers summer associate programs in the consumer group, Citigroup International, human resources and financial management. Associates are assigned to a group to work on specific projects, rather than a rotational system. Check out Citigroup's web site, www.citigroup.com, for job listings, including a search agent that notifies you when jobs meeting your specifications pop up.

OUR SURVEY SAYS

Citi, and suburban, livin'

An accurate picture of Citigroup's culture is difficult to nail down, considering its gargantuan size. "Your perspective on the firm's culture will depend on which part of the bank you're in," says one contact, who adds the atmosphere at Citigroup is still "in flux" due to the merger and subsequent acquisitions. One employee says the firm's culture "is "professional, but it's now slightly distorted," because of the "massive diaspora in September." As a result of the September 11 terrorist attack on the World Trade Center, approximately 1,000 New York employees moved from their downtown Manhattan offices to a space in Stamford, Conn. "In Connecticut, there is an element of disconnect with the rest of the bank," remarks the source, who isn't happy about commuting to the suburbs or the manner in which the firm handled the whole situation. "Under the circumstances I feel as if we were deported. It's inhumane to make people commute that far after what they went through after September 11." The contact predicts that "as a result of the commute to Stamford, people are going to leave. They're not going to be able to take it. By December [2002] all the old people will have slowly disappeared." However, moving to the suburbs wasn't all bad. Some employees' hours have lessened because of the commute. "Sales associates used to work 8 to 6 or 8 to 7, but now most are 9 to 5," says an insider.

Despite the firm's growing pains and office space shifts, associates and analysts say the treatment they receive from senior managers is "very respectful." Whatever uncertainty there may be regarding the firm's culture, Citigroup employees generally give their company high marks in a number of areas, including work/life issues. In particular, sources say they're pleased that Citigroup initiated a company-wide business casual policy. One insider notes that "the farther away you are from client contact, the more casual you can be." A banker who describes the work environment as "very comfortable" says, "I don't think I could find a financial services company where I would have a better balance between my work and home lives." While one contact believes "[Citigroup] is one of the most diverse corporations in the financial industry sector," another says, "It's like everywhere else, probably right on par." One source says, "There are issues being addressed about gays."

Some employees warn that challenging work assignments can be hard to come by during the first couple of years at Citigroup. According to one source, "A number of people who entered the bank with me have left for this very reason." One insider says, "I'm not finding the work itself to be very challenging." A banker in the firm's Management Associate program disagrees. He praises the program for giving him "international exposure and a breadth of work experience." Insiders lay some of the blame on the bank's "lack of focus" and "bureaucracy." One contact explains another problem facing Citi employees. "Because of the bank's massive size, it becomes a morass when you're looking for something."

31 West 52nd Street
New York, NY 10019
Phone: (212) 469-8000
www.db.com

DEPARTMENTS

Asset Management • Corporate and Investment Banking (Global Markets, Global Equities, Global Credit Products and Global Corporate Finance) • Private Client

THE STATS

Chairman, Management Board and Head of Corporate and Investment Banking: Josef Ackermann
Employer Type: Public Company
Ticker Symbol: DB (NYSE)
2001 Revenue: $28.6 billion
2001 Net Income: $167 million
No. of Employees: 94,780
No. of Offices: 2,300

KEY COMPETITORS

Citigroup
Credit Suisse First Boston
J.P. Morgan Chase
UBS Warburg

THE BUZZ
WHAT EMPLOYEES AT OTHER FIRMS ARE SAYING

- "Pretty strong showing lately"
- "Second-tier bank trying to pretend that it's first tier"
- "Trying to fit into the U.S. — and so far so good"
- "Disorganized leadership"

UPPERS

- Major global presence
- Relaxed culture

DOWNERS

- Bureaucratic due to mergers
- Not a brand name in the U.S.

EMPLOYMENT CONTACT

Corporate Finance
Nebal Fahed
Cfcampus.teamus@db.com

Sales, Trading and Research
Caryn Blumenfeld
Stcampus.teamus@db.com

Global Technology and Operations
Jacqueline Murray
Gtopscampus.teamus@db.com

THE SCOOP

German giant

Deutsche Bank AG is the second largest financial institution in the world in terms of total assets, with approximately $900 billion in assets (as of January 2002). In early 2001, the company initiated a reorganization that established two distinct business groups: the Corporate and Investment Bank Group (CIB), which includes corporate finance, sales and trading, and transaction banking; and the Private Clients and Asset Management Group (PCAM), which contains the bank's personal banking, private banking and asset management operations.

Founded in Berlin in 1870, Deutsche Bank initially expanded throughout Germany and later throughout the rest of Europe. The company first made its mark in the U.S. in the 1880s when it helped finance the construction of the railroads that linked the East and West coasts. In the late 1800s, Deutsche Bank grew in large part due to several mergers with, and acquisitions of, European banking firms.

Like most German corporations, Deutsche Bank's actions during World War II are a sensitive subject. The company has admitted that it helped finance the construction of the Auschwitz concentration camp. To its credit, the bank participated in the $1.25 billion settlement fund offered by Swiss and German companies to Holocaust victims. And Deutsche Bank mentions unseemly events such as the 1933-1934 ouster of Jewish board members in the history section of its corporate web site.

Purchasing power

The company's growth continued after the war, but it wasn't until the late 1990s that the firm made the move that placed it among the major international players. In June 1999, Deutsche Bank acquired Bankers Trust (BT) for approximately $9 billion. BT had purchased Alex. Brown & Co., a U.S. investment bank with nearly 200 years of history, two years earlier, giving Deutsche Bank significant corporate lending and underwriting prowess. Although the combination initially faced skepticism, the doubting subsided after Deutsche Bank integrated BT.

In September 2001, Deutsche Bank announced an agreement to buy Zurich Scudder Investments from Zurich Financial Services in a deal valued at $2.5 billion. The announcement came after two disappointing years for Scudder, ending speculation that its Swiss parent company would put it on the chopping block. At the time of the deal, Zurich Scudder had $300 billion in assets, bolstering Deutsche's total assets under management to $900 billion.

Deutsche tried to become even more formidable in 2000. The firm announced plans to merge with German competitor Dresdner Bank AG in March. The deal fell apart one month later, reportedly over the fate of Dresdner's investment-banking unit, Dresdner Kleinwort Benson (now Dresdner Kleinwort Wasserstein). Deutsche bank wanted Dresdner Kleinwort Benson closed or sold; Dresdner's people resisted, and the dispute scuttled the deal. After the merger failed, Dresdner CEO Bernhard Walter resigned. Some thought Deutsche Chairman Rolf Breuer would also be forced out, but he stayed on until May 2002.

Year of the ax

The year 2001 will go down as one of the most brutal years for global German banks. Deutsche, like its fellow German über-banks, was forced to cut thousands of jobs. In all, Deutsche announced 9,200 layoffs as a result of the worldwide economic slowdown. Early in the year, the bank unveiled plans to cut 2,600 jobs as part of its company-wide restructuring. In November, the bank announced plans to slash 3,300 positions in its private client and asset management division, and another 1,200 in its technical support division. As the year came to a close, the bank's corporate and investment-banking division took the hit, as 2,100 more layoffs were announced in December. That same month, the bank revealed plans to sack 1,500 employees as a result of the integration with Zurich Scudder.

Bringing out the bankers

Deutsche made several moves in 2001 to solidify its presence in the U.S. The firm switched over to American accounting standards, and in October the bank listed its shares on the New York Stock Exchange. Deutsche also announced that it would be cutting the traditional German management board from eight members to four in order to simplify decision making at the highest level. The downsizing of the board — which *The Wall Street Journal* has called the "most exalted council in German finance" — signaled an important change from a consensus-driven German management style, where the board members take collective responsibility for decisions, to the more American management style of a strong chief executive. Newly appointed Chairman Josef Ackermann, who succeeded Rolf Breuer in May, will oversee the board and is expected to run the kingdom of Deutsche much like an American CEO (German law doesn't allow a corporation to have an actual CEO).

Ackermann's takeover of the board, and of the bank itself, also signals a monumental strategy shift for the world's second largest bank. Unlike his predecessor, Ackermann comes from an investment-banking background. Before his retirement, Breuer oversaw the Private Clients and Asset Management Group, while Ackermann ran the Corporate and Investment Bank Group. Observers feel that the firm appointed an I-banker in order to send the message that it intends to focus on strengthening its position in the lucrative global investment-banking market.

On its way to the bigs

Under Ackermann's leadership, Deutsche's Corporate and Investment Bank Group has gained ground on the big banks of the bulge bracket. In 2001 Deutsche Bank surpassed Goldman Sachs and Morgan Stanley in total investment-banking revenues. According to Thomson Financial Securities Data, in 2001 the bank ranked seventh in U.S. M&A and eighth in global M&A, a decent jump from its 12th place finish on the global list in 2000.

The Wall Streeet Journal reported that Deutsche's investment-banking unit "continued to score unexpected victories [in 2001], winning high profile advisory roles in competition with more-established firms." The *Journal* cited Deutsche's advisory role on EchoStar's $30 billion purchase of Hughes Electronics, the second largest deal in 2001. The *Journal* also mentioned the bank's coup in gaining an advisory role with Electricite de France (EDF) on its takeover of Montedison, despite Goldman Sach's relationship with EDF. Although Deutsche's M&A operations have been competing near the highest level, the company's equity underwriting practice has lately appeared amateurish by comparison. The bank did not participate in any IPOs in 2001.

GETTING HIRED

Pick your team

Both analysts and associates are recruited by, and hired directly into, specific departments. Different departments and different offices have different procedures. One Deutsche recruit had three rounds of interviews. The first round interview was an on-campus one-on-one in which recruits "tell the interviewer what group they want to join," says that insider. During the second round, held at the firm's offices, the source says, "You meet a few people from the groups you want to join." And during the third, a Super Saturday also held at the bank's offices, "You meet everyone from the specific group you want to join." During the entire interview process, recruits can expect to interview with a total of about 10 people, who, according to one source, ask both "hard and soft questions."

The firm says that it looks for candidates who demonstrate "initiative" and "excellence" and who will work well in a team environment. One financial analyst reports that the firm "looks for smart people and thinks that grades are very important in determining mental horsepower. Also, the company looks for a strong work ethic, and an outgoing and engaging personality, because you have to get along with clients when away from the office and with peers when working 100 hours a week."

In addition to the usual top undergrad and MBA programs, the bank "hires from other schools, but [those] candidates must be more proactive," according to one source. Another contact says getting hired is "becoming much more demanding than it was even one or two years ago. It's not only due to the downturn in the market, but also the result of a more focused and organized recruiting effort, resulting in tougher standards." Another source agrees: "One year ago it was tough. Now it's impossible."

The firm also offers summer analyst and associate positions. Summer positions for investment banking are available in New York, Europe, Singapore and Hong Kong, and last anywhere from six to 10 weeks between June and September. A European-based trader says acceptance for summer internships is based on two 30- to 45-minute "two-on-one" interviews.

Back to school

Those who join the firm as full-time investment-banking analysts participate in four to six weeks of training in New York. Those who sign on as investment-banking associates attend a four-week training program in New York. Analysts in sales, trading or research are in for eight to 12 weeks of training in London; associates can expect either six to eight weeks in New York or eight to 12 weeks in London, depending on the division. In addition to the formal training, the firm offers continuing education classes. Deutsche "is quite accommodating to employees who show a desire to attend one-, two- and even three-day training courses," says one employee.

OUR SURVEY SAYS

Good times, bad times

Insiders describe Deutsche Bank's culture as "easy-going" and "generally more relaxed than U.S. investment banks." One banker says it's "professional and efficient, yet has a sense of humor." One trader admits that the bank's culture "was formerly a hybrid of many other firms' cultures because of the way it built a presence in the investment-banking world." But now, he says, "It's coming into its own. The atmosphere is academic but very commercial. Innovation is formally rewarded. Client skills are especially well-regarded. And junior employees are given much more latitude to take initiative and grow." Recent layoffs have hurt morale, of course. "The culture's weird now," says one analyst who didn't survive the purge. He concedes that Deutsche is "better at firing people — in terms of how many — than other banks," but adds that the "people who are still there are happy to have a job."

Although given the opportunity to grow, junior employees aren't necessarily given an easy time. While some insiders describe the relationship with their superiors as "great" and "more relaxed and congenial than that at U.S. banks," other employees use less amiable words to explain their experiences with the higher-ups. One Baltimore-based banker says, "There are great bosses in this firm, but there are even more lousy ones. If you're lucky, you stick with the good ones. But sometimes, you get stuck with the lousy ones, who make life seem like an eternal punishment." Another banker says managers provide "no training, no guidance," and adds, "no one cares."

Come together

The 1999 merger of Deutsche and Bankers Trust (which owned Alex. Brown at the time) plays a significant role in explaining the firm's current work environment. A Deutsche insider and former employee of Alex. Brown speaks favorably of the merger. "Things have moved very smoothly. The merger wasn't 100 percent seamless, but it was a fluid transition." Another insider agrees, saying "the merger played out well." That source, however, also notes that the firm has become "more bureaucratic since the merger, which was expected, but not necessarily welcome." However, a former Deutsche insider and, prior to that, Bankers Trust employee, says the merger for Bankers Trust "wasn't smooth, because BT employees remained relatively independent" from Deutsche. He adds that Alex. Brown "merged more successfully because it was put in charge of the investment-banking operations" at Deutsche. The contact goes on to say, "Although they wanted to make it seem like a merger, it wasn't. It was an acquisition. They lost a lot of talent that they couldn't replace, and they're still reorganizing." Another source agrees that the BT/Alex. Brown coupling was — and still is, to some extent — an issue. "BT had more of a cowboy culture, while Alex. Brown was a white-shoe firm," reports that insider, who adds that the Deutsche acquisition of Alex. Brown was flawed in its own way. "Deutsche paid $2 billion for Alex., then killed its name. So [the deal] was worth zero in the end."

Standard practice

Insiders generally agree that Deutsche Bank "pays according to the industry's prevailing standards." According to one source, "High achievers are compensated far in excess of the average." Another contact admits that while the bank normally pays on par with the industry, for 2001 "bonuses are going to stink due to the economy." At least one employee says the firm "is still trying to find its way" with respect to compensation. He explains, "A big part of 2000 bonuses were paid out in options, which are now well underwater. As a result of their decline in value, the options were repriced this year for certain high-level executives." The contact adds that "in 2001 bonuses were focused more on cash, albeit at a level lower than 2000."

Deutsche bankers report working an average of 60 to 70 hours a week, with 100-hour workweeks possible, but not frequent, during peak periods. Some employees say they commonly make weekend office visits, while others say they rarely have to come in on a Saturday or Sunday. One investment-banking analyst in Baltimore who rarely works weekends says, "There's not much work to do, yet people still stick around the office, putting in face time." Another Baltimore banker remarks, "Hours in 2001 have been much lower than hours in 2000." If this trend continues, it should give the bank's Oriole fans a chance to catch more games at Camden Yards. Deutsche gives its employees "discounts to museums and ball games," says one Baltimore-based insider.

"High achievers are compensated far in excess of the average."

— *Deutsche Bank insider*

Putnam Investments

One Post Office Square
Boston, MA 02109
Phone: (617) 292-1000
www.putnaminvestments.com

DEPARTMENTS

Institutional Management •
International • Investor Services •
Putnam Retail Management

THE STATS

President and CEO:
Lawrence J. Lasser
Employer Type: Subsidiary of Marsh
& McLennan Companies
2001 Revenues: $2.6 billion
No. of Employees: 6,000
No. of Offices: 3

KEY COMPETITORS

Alliance Capital
Fidelity Investments
Franklin Resources

UPPERS

• Industry leader
• Team-oriented culture

DOWNERS

• Stuffy, political

EMPLOYMENT CONTACT

Putnam Investments
Resume Processing Center
7 Shattuck Road, (C-36-H)
Andover, MA 01810
Fax: (617) 348-8925
Recruiter1@putnaminv.com

THE BUZZ
WHAT EMPLOYEES AT OTHER FIRMS ARE SAYING

• "The go-to investors for any
transaction"
• "Stodgy, weak performance"
• "Top-tier investment firm"
• "Trouble"

THE SCOOP

We've got the money

Putnam Investments is a global asset management firm that specializes in mutual funds and retirement plans. The firm boasts more than 700 institutional clients, over 14 million shareholders and retirement plan participants and more than 100 mutual fund offerings. With $302 billion in assets under management (as of May 31, 2002), primarily in mutual funds, Boston-based Putnam is the fourth-largest mutual fund manager in the U.S. Putnam also has offices in London and Tokyo. The firm is a wholly owned subsidiary of professional services firm Marsh & McLennan, which acquired Putnam in 1970. In past years, Putnam has accounted for about half of Marsh & McLennan's profits.

Illustrious beginnings

Putnam began managing money in the 19th century when clipper ship captains hired trustees to handle their financial affairs while they were away at sea. One of those trustees, Justice Samuel Putnam, wrote the following credo for professional investment management: "Those with the responsibility to invest money for others should act with prudence, discretion, intelligence and regard for the safety of capital as well as for income." Known as the "prudent man rule," this ideology has since become the industry standard for responsible money management, giving Putnam Investments bragging rights for its creation. In 1937 Justice Putnam's great-great grandson founded Putnam with The George Putnam Fund of Boston. This balanced mutual fund, a flexible mix of stocks and bonds, marked the beginning of Putnam's strength in both of those key areas of the investment business.

Putnam's new portfolio

Putnam made several moves in 2001 to attract new business. The company teamed with private equity firm Thomas H. Lee Partners to offer a fund targeted to wealthy investors. TH Lee Putnam Ventures is a $1.1 billion venture capital fund affiliated with Putman and Thomas H. Lee Partners. Limited partners include Credit Suisse First Boston, Merrill Lynch, Goldman Sachs and AIG. The fund looks for mid- to late-stage companies in the technology sector, and generally invests between $10 million and $25 million. As of mid-2002 the fund had invested approximately $600 million in more than 35 companies.

The firm also teamed with its competitors to reach independent financial advisers, launching a web site with Fidelity Investments, Franklin Templeton and PFPC, Inc. The site, AdvisorCentral.com, allows financial planners to access market data and conduct transactions over the Internet. The site allows the planners to access all of the participants' services from one portal, rather than having to visit each company's site individually. The cost of the site was split equally among the four firms.

GETTING HIRED

Minimum qualifications

Putnam looks for people with strong academic backgrounds and utilizes a rigorous screening process. Industry experience in the form of prior jobs or internships is preferred. To find out about open positions, visit the firm's web site, www.putnaminvestments.com. Job seekers can search for positions by location (in Massachusetts) and function. Candidates can send resumes via fax, e-mail or regular mail to the firm. Putnam does not accept resumes e-mailed as attachments. (Text is fine.)

Don't expect to stroll into a job at Putnam. Says one insider, "It is very competitive, but if you make it through our screening process, it can be a very rewarding place to work." Applicants are gained "mainly through referrals within the company" but are also recruited from "six or seven carefully selected schools." "This doesn't mean that you can't get a job if you don't attend one of them, but it certainly becomes harder," explains one contact. An applicant can expect at least two interviews before being hired.

OUR SURVEY SAYS

Inside info

Putnam strives to provide employees with an autonomous, yet "team-based environment" in which to work. Contacts describe the approach as one that fosters collaboration, but affords analysts and managers the opportunity to make their own decisions. According to one investment analyst, "[Managers] let you do your job and they listen — if not agree" with your opinions.

Additionally, insiders say the firm's breadth of financial instruments gives investment managers a wide assortment of products through which they can hone their investment skills. As is the case on Wall Street, analysts can expect to work long hours — 12 hours a day is not unusual. Although the firm has been described as "a bit political" and "stuffy," as an investment management firm, Putnam lacks the frenetic pace of investment banking.

For detailed 40- to 50-page insider reports on top finance employers like Goldman, Morgan Stanley, Merrill, Salomon Smith Barney, Lehman Brothers and more, get Vault Employer Profiles. Go to http://finance.vault.com.

BlackRock

40 East 52nd Street
New York, NY 10022
Phone: (212) 754-5560
www.blackrock.com

DEPARTMENTS

Account Management • BlackRock
Solutions • Funds • Information
Technology • Portfolio
Adminsitration • Portfolio
Management • Real Estate
(Anthracite) • Strategy

THE STATS

Chairman and CEO: Laurence Fink
Employer Type: Public Company
Stock Symbol: BLK (NYSE)
2001 Revenue: $533.1 million
2001 Net Income: $107.4 million
No. of Employees: 800
No. of Offices: 7

KEY COMPETITORS

Alliance Capital Management
Goldman Sachs
PIMCO

UPPERS

• Easy schedules
• Relaxed culture

DOWNERS

• Occasional brushes with
management

EMPLOYMENT CONTACT

careers@blackrock.com

THE BUZZ
WHAT EMPLOYEES AT OTHER FIRMS ARE SAYING

• "Cutting edge"
• "Smart, but think they're smarter
than they really are"
• "Respectable, friendly people"
• "Bully"

THE SCOOP

You don't know them, but you should

For a firm that few people outside the financial industry have heard of, BlackRock has had a long and successful history. The company was created in 1988 as a unit of leveraged buyout firm Blackstone. Its bond savvy netted the company $239 billion in assets under management by 2002. The firm also offers equity (including mutual funds), liquidity, alternative investments, risk management and investor systems services to institutional and individual investors.

BlackRock has come a long way from its beginnings in 1988, when Chairman and CEO Larry Fink left his first finance gig at First Boston to join Blackstone. Fink, who holds bachelor's and master's degrees from UCLA, had gone to First Boston in 1976 and become a specialist in the then little-known area of mortgage-backed securities. By the early 1980s, Fink had parlayed the business from one of meager standing into a $100-million-a-year star in the First Boston lineup. The high-flying unit was hurt by interest rate declines in the second quarter of 1986 that hammered the mortgage-backed market. In March 1998, Fink and his team paired with a team from Lehman Brothers headed by Ralph Schlosstein to start an asset management unit at Blackstone (the new unit reportedly got 60 percent of the asset management group). By the end of 1991, the team had built up approximately $7 billion under management and a client list of heavy hitters (including Chrysler and GE). But Fink and Blackstone management disagreed over strategic planning issues; Fink wanted to add more partners, but Blackstone didn't want to dilute its equity.

Same game, new name

Again, Fink's team was on the move. PNC Financial Services purchased BlackRock (the team's name was changed in 1992) in 1995 for $240 million. By 1998 PNC had folded much of its asset management services under the BlackRock umbrella. In October 1999, BlackRock went public, selling a 14 percent stake for $126 million, the first time a bank had spun off an asset management unit as a public company. PNC kept a 70 percent stake in BlackRock, while BlackRock employees held the balance of the firm's stock, about 16 percent.

Although Fink and PNC CEO James Rohr both say that PNC gives BlackRock a wide swath to do its own thing, a March 2001 article in *Fortune* speculated that the independent-minded Fink may soon want to venture out on his own. However, having already demonstrated his prowess in the bond arena, Fink may be more interested in growing the equity management end of the business than engineering a break away from PNC. Referring to the firm's mutual fund business, Fink told *Best's Review* in July 2000, "People just don't know who we are." That, he said, "tells us we have a lot of opportunities" to make an impact in the marketplace. Fink and his group retain a 16 percent interest in the firm.

New business

In 2000 the firm began marketing BlackRock Solutions, its internal risk management system, and has attracted more than 20 clients. BlackRock Solutions advises clients looking to manage the risk exposure in their portfolios. The firm's other units have picked up as well; BlackRock raised $31 billion in new business in 2001. New clients include the New York State Teachers Retirement System, which hired BlackRock to manage a $100 million fund in January 2001, and office supply firm Boise Cascade, which picked the firm to manage a $320 million benefits plan in April 2001. Overall, BlackRock did marvelously well in 2001, thanks to its fixed-income holdings, which more than offset declines in the dismal equity market. Assets under management rose 17 percent to nearly $239 billion, and net income increased by 23 percent, to $107 million. At the beginning of 2002, BlackRock announced that it opened an office in Boston to house a seven-employee small- and mid- cap value equity team. The team, made up of ex-Boston Partners Asset Management employees, is expected to increase BlackRock's existing presence in the sector.

GETTING HIRED

BlackRock is a fairly selective firm, say insiders. The hiring process is typical, with several rounds of interviews over the course of a few days. "I had three full days worth of interviews," reports one contact. "I met with two-thirds of my group." That source reports that he was "asked analytical, technical, financial and just personality questions." Another BlackRock employee reports meeting with a total of six individuals during the recruiting process. Portfolio management hopefuls might be better off sending their resume to the risk analytics division. The firm reports that all portfolio managers need expertise in portfolio analytics and financial modeling, and approximately one-third of all BlackRock's portfolio management team got their feet wet in risk analytics.

The firm recruits at more than 20 universities, including Columbia, Cornell, Harvard, NYU, Princeton and the University of Virginia. In addition, the company attends several job fairs each year in several cities, including New York, Washington, D.C., and Chicago. Consult the firm's web site, www.blackrock.com, for further details and recruiting schedules.

OUR SURVEY SAYS

The culture at BlackRock is "very relaxed," according to one insider. There's "no micro-management. The focus is on getting stuff done." Another source agrees, saying that though the firm has grown, it has still retained its culture. "The firm has a small firm feel to it although it is no longer small," says that contact. "It is a meritocracy." In fact, some say the firm is still small enough to allow for significant contact with senior employees. "[BlackRock is] small enough for one to make an impact and know many people at the firm — even the highest ranked," gushes one employee.

Unlike other small firms, junior employees at BlackRock aren't shackled to a cubicle. On average, employees work 50 to 70 hours per week, with weekend time being a rare occurrence. Compensation is competitive with most investment banks and asset management firms, and the firm allows business casual dress.

VAULT
PRESTIGE
RANKING
16

Vanguard Group

100 Vanguard Boulevard
Malvern, PA 19355
Phone: (610) 648-6000
www.vanguard.com

DEPARTMENTS

Asset Management • Research •
Sales • Trading

THE STATS

Chairman and CEO: John J. Brennan
Employer Type: Private Company
No. of Employees: 10,300
No. of Offices: 7

KEY COMPETITORS

Charles Schwab
Fidelity Investments
Merrill Lynch

UPPERS

• Flexible hours
• Respectful managers

DOWNERS

• Work sometimes not challenging

EMPLOYMENT CONTACT

Kathleen C. Gubanich
Vanguard Group
100 Vanguard Boulevard
Malvern, PA 19355
Fax: (610) 669-6605

THE BUZZ
WHAT EMPLOYEES AT OTHER FIRMS ARE SAYING

• "Top in its industry"
• "Massive amounts of red tape
  and difficult to work with"
• "Smart money"

THE SCOOP

Not like the others

As the manager of the second-largest group of mutual funds in America, Vanguard Group sticks to a no-frills business model in which it spends virtually no money on marketing. Instead, the firm chooses to pass along savings to its investors. U.S. mutual funds spend on average 1.24 percent of their assets annually; Vanguard — which manages approximately $600 billion in mutual fund assets — spends 0.27 percent.

Vanguard's cost cutting can be attributed in part to a unique ownership structure. Unlike all other mutual fund companies, which — whether public or private — have shareholders who look to earn money that is not distributed to those invested in the funds, Vanguard is run like a mutual insurance company. Under this structure, the funds themselves (and their investors) own the parent company. The firm is the fastest-growing mutual fund company, and analysts predict it will soon surpass industry leader Fidelity Investments. Vanguard has been praised as a top place to work by *Fortune* (the company made its "Best Places to Work" list) and *Computerworld* (Vanguard was No. 6 on its 2001 list of 100 Best Places to Work in IT).

Vanguard was founded by John C. Bogle in 1974 after Bogle was fired as CEO of Wellington Management. Bogle had written a senior thesis at Princeton that described his theory that mutual funds should be run with low overhead and no sales commission. Basically, Bogle's thesis described Vanguard, or at least the fundamentals of the firm — an investor-owned family of funds with low expenses. Vanguard is the first (and still the only) investor-owned fund company.

The index funds

In 1976 Vanguard launched the first index fund open to individual investors, a fund designed to mimic the Standard & Poor's 500. The fund was originally known as the First Index Trust but is now known as the Vanguard 500 Index Fund. Unlike other funds that are based on idea- and research-heavy management, index funds require no stock-picking prowess from managers. The index funds did not immediately take off. Now, however, these funds are the keys to Vanguard's rapid growth. In 2000 the Vanguard 500 Index fund surpassed Fidelity's massive Magellan fund as the largest mutual fund.

New funds, new shares

In late 2000, Vanguard announced an initiative to reward long-time shareholders for their commitment to the firm. Investors meeting certain criteria such as account size and longetivity were given the option of switching to Admiral shares in certain mutual funds. The Admiral shares reduced fees for those shareholders by .03 percent to .08 percent, a windfall for mutual fund investors with big accounts at Vanguard. The new shares proved popular. By mid-2002 loyal Vanguard customers had invested $68 billion in Admiral shares. The downside was that investors who didn't qualify for the Admiral shares saw their expense ratios rise by a couple of hundreths of a percentage point.

In 2000 the firm looked to expand on its offerings by announcing the creation of VIPERs — Vanguard's brand name for its version of exchange-traded index funds (ETFs). Like index mutual funds, ETFs are based on an index, but trade on a stock exchange. Vanguard ran into a snag when it tried to introduce VIPERs. Standard & Poor's, which receives a license fee from Vanguard for the Vanguard 500 fund (since it is based on the S&P 500 Index), claimed that extending a license to Vanguard would infringe on other contracts. Vanguard replied that the VIPER is essentially the same product as the fund, just sold in a different way. S&P disagreed and filed a lawsuit. A November 2001 appeals court ruling upheld a lower court ruling siding with S&P. Rebuffed, Vanguard has developed other new products, including a VIPER based on the Wilshire 4500 Completion Index.

Vanguard further expanded its product base in late 2001. In September 2001, the firm began selling life insurance to its clients. In keeping with its low-fee policy, Vanguard is selling the insurance online, sans investment advisers. A month later, the firm began offering private equity investments to its wealthier clients through a partnership with Hamilton Lane Advisors.

GETTING HIRED

The basics

Vanguard lists job openings and recruiting schedules at www.vanguardcareers.com. The firm allows applicants to submit resumes online as well as by fax or regular mail. Insiders say the firm recruits from a variety of schools in the Northeast and South, "including Penn State, the University of Pennsylvania, Temple, UNC-Charlotte,

Duke, Georgia Tech, NC State, Vanderbilt and others." One source says, "We're growing at such an incredible pace, so there are always openings." A Vanguard employee reports going through "one phone interview and one on-site visit that consisted of three or four interviews." Others report interviewing with an HR representative, a department manager and a principal. No matter who does the interviewing, candidates can expect both "behavioral-based and technical" questions.

OUR SURVEY SAYS

Frugal, but respectful

Insiders say their superiors treat them well. "Upper-level management are always on a first-name basis with other crew members," one source offers. "Generally," says another contact, "superiors treat you with respect as long as you share your opinions and views." Aside from kind bosses, perks include on-site cafeterias, health clubs and stores with dry cleaning and other services. And the firm's "university" offers training in management and other areas, and all employees receive a minimum of one week of training per year. However, the dress code (the firm is business casual only on Friday) does promote a certain level of formality among employees. In keeping with its philosophy of providing low-cost investment vehicles, insiders say Vanguard's offices are no-frills. They are "comfortable, but not extravagant," according to one source.

Sources say that the company is flexible about work hours (normal office hours are 8:30 a.m. to 5:00 p.m.), enabling some employees to come to work earlier (and thereby leave earlier) or work longer hours and have a four-day workweek. But Vanguard employees don't necessarily have it easier than those at other investment firms. Says one Vanguard employee, "I am paid for a 37.5-hour week, but routinely work 45 to 50 hours and take work home." The benefits probably soften the blow. In addition to the on-site perks, the company offers a 401(k) plan with a 4 percent dollar-for-dollar match and a pension plan that can raise your retirement savings to 14 percent of your annual salary. Vanguard also offers a "Partnership Plan" that offers bonuses starting at over $1,500 payable in June and a second bonus program that gives as much as 10 percent to crew members in December. One downer: the work assignments can leave something to be desired. One source complains his job is "very easy" and "only occasionally [requires] deep thought." The firm counters that its retention rate is three times the industry average.

Pequot Capital Management

500 Nyala Farm Road
Westport, CT 06880
Phone: (203) 429-2200
www.pequotcap.com

DEPARTMENTS

Asset Management • Research •
Sales • Trading

THE STATS

Chairman and CEO: Arthur Samberg
Employer Type: Private Company
No. of Employees: 200
No. of Offices: 4

KEY COMPETITORS

Putnam Investments
T. Rowe Price
Vanguard Group

UPPERS

- Potential to shine
- Relaxed culture

DOWNERS

- Killer travel requirements
- Tough to break in as a junior employee

EMPLOYMENT CONTACT

Human Resources
500 Nyala Farm Road
Westport, CT 06880
HR@pequotcap.com

THE BUZZ
WHAT EMPLOYEES AT OTHER FIRMS ARE SAYING

- "The 800-pound gorilla of hedge funds"
- "Niche"

THE SCOOP

Hedging from the bottom up

Founded in 1986 as a unit of another asset management company, Pequot Capital Management has become one of the largest hedge funds in the world. Pequot (pronounced PEA-kwat) follows a rather unusual investment strategy. Most hedge funds — especially the largest — invest in a broad range of vehicles ranging from equities to currency and interest rate hedges. (Indeed, it is currency and interest rate investment that resulted in the downfall of many hedge funds in the late 1990s.) But Pequot sticks mainly to equity investments ranging from venture capital and private equity to positions in mid- to large-cap public companies. Pequot, based in Westport, Conn., manages approximately $10 billion in assets. The company has 20 funds and approximately 170 employees.

The original Pequot Fund was a unit of Dawson-Henry Capital Management, a money manager in Southport, Conn. Pequot was the brainchild of Arthur Samberg, a Columbia MBA and current chairman and CEO at Pequot. According to *The Wall Street Journal*, Pequot, which was started with $3.5 million, grew quickly and was renamed Dawson-Samberg Capital Management in 1989. The renamed firm made a killing in the tech boom of the late 1990s. Pequot funds were early investors in America Online in 1994 and secured a chunk of Yahoo! when the company went public in 1996.

Pequot schism

Samberg and Dawson went their separate ways in January 1999 when Pequot was spun off as a separate company with Samberg as the head. While the company claimed the split was amicable, some say a division over the risks Pequot was taking was a factor. *Alternative Investment News* claimed that Dawson felt the company's investments were spread too thin and that Pequot was too tech-heavy, while Samberg pushed for more risk-taking. Dawson soon split from Samberg altogether, leaving to run Dawson-Giammalva Capital Management.

Rumors of a similar divide within Pequot surfaced in early 2001. This time Samberg was afraid the company was too big while Daniel Benton, Pequot's president, pushed the firm to focus on technology companies both in the public and private marketplace. Despite the reported conflict in investment styles, Pequot continued to grow. The firm opened offices in London and Taiwan in March 2001. That same month it closed a $725 venture capital fund dedicated to expansion-stage companies.

Samberg seems to favor less risky markets in general. In a February 2002 interview with the *Journal*, Samberg expressed reservations about the growing number of hedge funds, saying that days of sky-high returns for hedge funds have passed. On the flip side, the *Journal* cited Samberg as a stock market booster immediately after the terrorist attacks of September 11, 2001. According to the *Journal*, Samberg and other influential investors discouraged their employees and associates from betting against the stock market, helping to prevent a collapse when the market reopened a week after the attacks.

GETTING HIRED

With only 200 employees, Pequot is a very selective employer. The firm does accept resumes at its Westport, Conn., headquarters and maintains an e-mail account for employment questions (HR@pequotcap.com). But you'd better be on top of your game if you want to get in. And fresh graduates are all but excluded from consideration. The firm "rarely takes candidates out of school," according to one source. Pequot "prefers to hire from the sell side (banking or research) with one to three years of experience." Recruits should have a good story ready when interviewing. "Candidates generally need to show some compelling case for why they are specifically interested in the buy side — too many are just looking for better pay and an escape from the crappy conditions of the sell side."

OUR SURVEY SAYS

Flat structure

Insiders say the culture at Pequot is "extremely informal. You can dress and act as you please, as long as you are productive." That source continues, "We live well and enjoy many diversions to help with the inevitable stressful days when the market moves against us." Additionally, the firm provides "great ability to make an impact, the ability to be paid for performance, intelligent and likeable colleagues, and very little annoying bureaucracy or hierarchy. I could not imagine a better work environment."

Insiders boast of the firm's ability to retain its employees. "Extremely competitive compensation means that people seldom leave voluntarily. However, there is somewhat of an up-or-out mentality. Employees either need to show they can scale to the next level or they risk being asked to leave."

Meet your mentor

One area where Pequot lags is training. "We're not really set up for formal training which is why we generally prefer not to hire straight out of school." However, they hardly throw new hires into the deep end. "We do set up junior employees with mentors who help them learn the process of modeling, talking to companies and doing basic research," says a source. The support staff, such as it is, is generally praised. "Secretaries are well paid and highly professional. We do not have elaborate support structures, however, because we don't tend to produce much in terms of written material."

Another potential Pequot drawback is the travel schedule. "I am on the road about a week a month," says one mid-level employee. "More junior employees travel about twice that much to visit companies in which we are potential investors." Finally, insiders say diversity is not an issue. "For a small firm, I think we have worked hard to create a welcoming environment. We do mandatory training for all employees on gender and racial bias issues."

Bear Stearns

383 Madison Avenue
New York, NY 10179
Phone: (212) 272-2000
www.bearstearns.com

DEPARTMENTS

Asset Management • Custodial
Trust • Derivatives • Equities •
Fixed Income • Global Clearing
Services • Investment Banking •
Merchant Banking • Private Client
Services

THE STATS

Chairman and CEO: James Cayne
Employer Type: Public Company
Ticker Symbol: BSC (NYSE)
2001 Revenue: $8.7 billion
2001 Net Income: $619 million
No. of Employees: 10,500
No. of Offices: 22

KEY COMPETITORS

Deutsche Bank
J.P. Morgan Chase
Lehman Brothers
Merrill Lynch

THE BUZZ
WHAT EMPLOYEES AT OTHER FIRMS ARE SAYING

- "Almost bulge bracket"
- "Takeover target"
- "Strong firm with basic industry
  focus"
- "Still macho"

UPPERS

- Responsibility for juniors
- Top of the pay scale

DOWNERS

- Company strives to cut corners
- Sink-or-swim culture not good for
  those who can't swim

EMPLOYMENT CONTACT

Resumes must be submitted online
at www.bearstearns.com.

THE SCOOP

All grown up

Bear Stearns & Co. is younger than many of its high-profile rivals, but the firm's reputation stands up to those of its competitors. Known as "Bear" to Wall Street players, the venerable institution is one of the nation's top investment banking, securities trading and brokerage firms.

With about half a million dollars in capital among the three of them, Joseph Bear, Robert Stearns and Harold Mayer started Bear Stearns in 1923. The firm initially operated with a small staff out of a single office at 100 Broadway. Founded as a partnership, Bear Stearns originally focused on brokerage. After a few years of profit hibernation during the early 1990s, Bear bounced back, rapidly outgrowing its office space. To accommodate the expansion, Bear built a new midtown Manhattan headquarters and moved into the building in April 2002. Today, with a gamut of financial services available, Bear Stearns serves as financial advisor to many of the nation's major corporations, and its clearing operations are a top choice of brokerage and other investment firms, including many of its rivals.

Close, but no Cuban

One of the few companies in America that can boast of 76 consecutive profitable years, Bear Stearns' striking success is attributed in part by its leaders and its commitment to a strategy of controlled growth with an eye toward long-term results. But despite consistent returns — the firm has topped 18 percent in return on equity (a common yardstick for a well-performing I-bank) for four straight years — Bear Stearns has not broken into Wall Street's upper I-banking echelon. Apart from businesses such as public finance (underwriting and issuing municipal bonds), in which the firm ranks in the middle of the top five consistently, and mortgage-backed securities, in which it consistently ranks in the top three, Bear Stearns usually hovers around the bottom of the top 10 in the league tables.

Big deals

Though not considered a part of the bulge bracket, Bear is still a major Wall Street player. In recent years, Bear has been tapped for some of the world's biggest deals, especially in M&A. The firm advised Starwood Lodging in its high-profile $13.7 billion acquisition of ITT (in 1997), Walt Disney in its $18.8 billion acquisition of

Capital Cities/ABC (in 1996), and NYNEX in its $52 billion "merger of equals" with Bell Atlantic (also in 1996). In 2001 Bear Stearns came in 10th in U.S. M&A advisory, working on 60 deals worth $75.3 billion. Bear advised Hughes Electronics on its $29.1 billion merger with EchoStar Communications, a deal announced in August 2001. The firm also advised Amgen on its $16.5 billion purchase of Immunex, announced in December 2001. And in a deal announced on the same day as the Amgen/Immunex merger, Bear represented USA Networks in the sale of its entertainment assets to Vivendi Universal for $11.3 billion.

The firm has had success in the fixed income markets as well. The firm lead managed the largest municipal bond issue ever — a $3.5 billion issue for the Long Island Power Authority. In the corporate bond world, Bear Stearns has proven a heavy hitter in recent quarters, taking the lead role in a $8.4 billion offering for Ford Motor Credit Company, and a $1.36 billion offering for Lucent Technologies.

Size matters

Given the firm's cost-conscious reputation, it's no surprise that Bear Stearns focuses on lean staffing. The firm has fewer total employees than Salomon Smith Barney, Morgan Stanley or Merrill Lynch have brokers. The firm does not like that bloated feeling — as one firm insider put it while much of the rest of Wall Street was cutting its staff in the fall of 1998: "I don't know if you've noticed, but we don't come out and announce huge layoffs. Merrill laid off 3,400. It's because we staff very leanly." Bear Stearns avoided large-scale layoffs again in 2001 when competitors were eliminating staff. However, in early 2001 the firm did cut approximately 800 people, mostly from the technology department.

Specialist purchase

Bear took a step toward growing its business in February 2001 when it announced plans to buy Wagner Stott Mercator, said to be the fifth-largest specialist firm on the Big Board. (Specialist firms manage trades of specific stocks, as well as the trades of certain firms.) The purchase is being made in partnership with Hunter Partners, the seventh-ranked specialist firm. Bear Stearns owns 49.8 percent of Wagner Stott; Hunter owns the remaining 50.2 percent. Taking less than half interest in the firm means Bear won't have to report Wagner liabilities on its balance sheet; Bear will have to report profit and losses on its income statement, though. Wagner Stott counts Citibank and Merrill Lynch as its major clients, putting Bear Stearns in the unusual position of being in charge of the orders of two competitors. The transaction closed in April 2001.

Clearing the way

One of Bear Stearns' most profitable divisions is its clearing business. Clearing firms process much of the paperwork that goes along with brokering. The company is hired to execute trades, maintain client records, send out trade confirmations and monthly statements and settle transactions. Close to 2,600 clients employ Bear for clearing, and even rival firms such as Lehman Brothers have employed the department's services. Smaller brokerages are the firm's main customers for this service; the appearance of Bear Stearns' name on paperwork sent to investors is often a selling point.

Alan Greenberg: an "Ace" in the hole

With the odd business guidelines handed down to Bear Stearns employees from the desk of former chairman Alan "Ace" Greenberg, people might think that the investment-banking powerhouse is scraping for pennies. Greenberg earned a reputation for his humorous (and sometimes biting) memos, which were collected into a book called *Memos From the Chairman*. Greenberg's memos espoused the benefits of reusing rubber bands (if they're broken, simply tie the loose ends) and conserving paperclips. Ace even encouraged employees to inform upon colleagues who might be breaking one of the chairman's rules (this included professionals at all levels).

In June 2001, Greenberg announced he was stepping aside as executive chairman and handing the reins over to CEO James Cayne. (Greenberg stayed on as chair of the executive committee, continuing a 52-year career with Bear Stearns.) Unlike many sudden high-level departures, Greenberg's seemed truly amicable. Greenberg and Cayne had worked together for over 30 years, making a power grab by the younger executive unlikely. "I haven't had a contentious moment with Alan in 32 years," Cayne told *BusinessWeek* in July 2001. More important, Cayne denied that Greenberg's departure was part of a restructuring designed to make Bear Stearns more attractive to potential buyers. "[A]m I sprucing us up, going to market with a little apple in our mouths? Nah," Cayne told *BusinessWeek*. "We don't have the right to say we're not for sale because that's absurd. But we feel there is a compelling reason for a firm that's independent like us to be in the marketplace and remain independent."

GETTING HIRED

For investment banking, the firm targets approximately 12 business schools. At these schools, either the co-head of investment banking or another high-ranking official makes a presentation. At about five other business schools, the firm interviews but does not give presentations. Don't worry if your school is not targeted. The firm conducts "in-house interviews for those who write in" from out-of-the-way schools. Another note: Bear doesn't want resumes clogging up their mail room and e-mail inboxes. A message on the firm's web site, www.bearstearns.com, instructs applicants to submit their resumes through Bear's online application process. At Bear's target schools, interested parties can arrange an interview through the career services office.

Bear Stearns draws many of its associates from its summer programs. The summer hiring process is condensed into a three-week period. The first round is usually an on-campus, two-on-one interview. While students at some schools will travel to Bear's New York headquarters for second rounds, many will simply interview again that evening on-campus. The final round in New York is described as "the typical super day format with analyst-level candidates meeting mostly with associate and VP-level bankers and associate candidates meeting mostly with VP and managing director/senior managing director-level people." That source also reports that "one of the two co-heads of investment banking generally interviews every associate candidate."

The firm also generally targets about 40 undergraduate schools each year. It hires approximately 100 analysts into I-banking worldwide, and about 75 of them work in New York. Although Bear accepts resumes from all undergraduate schools, for summer analyst positions Bear likes to have representation from its core schools — the firm only recruits on-campus for summer analysts at Wharton, Dartmouth, Michigan and the University of Virginia.

Insiders say not to look for technical questions. "There is a uniqueness to our culture and we look for people who can both enhance it and excel in it," says one source. "We stay away from the brain teaser questions." Another contact concurs, saying Bear asks "the typical banker questions. 'Why banking,' 'why you' and 'why you with Bear?' Some technical questions for undergrad students with a business degree and MBAs, but nothing out of the ordinary — [it] all depends on the interviewer."

The firm doesn't recruit undergrads for sales and trading, although undergrads who complete the firm's operations training program can go into sales and trading. For associates in sales, trading, research and public finance, the firm recruits on campus at 10 business schools — NYU, Columbia, Harvard, Wharton, Chicago, Kellogg, Stanford, UCLA, Fuqua and Darden. Says a recruiter, "We do very well with Columbia, NYU and Chicago; those are our three best." Associates are hired into one of four departments: fixed income, equity, research or public finance. Candidates in these areas can expect one-on-one interviews, with probably two rounds. "For a full-time hire, you have to have six interviews," according to one insider. Summer hires generally go through an on-campus round and then one callback.

About 50 to 75 percent of the sales trading, and public finance associate class is hired through the summer program. In these departments, the firm hires about 20 to 25 summer associates and about 20 full-time associates. All fixed-income hires complete 12 weeks of rotations, covering six different desks, and are placed after that; the equity division hires students for both specific slots and as generalists. All research positions are hired on an as-needed basis.

OUR SURVEY SAYS

Early responsibility, with all its drawbacks

Insiders at Bear Stearns praise the firm as being "entrepreneurial" and "aggressive," though they concede the culture has its less appealing aspects. Sources say the firm offers "so much responsibility that it automatically becomes a rewarding experience." "You're going to a firm that's large and has its fair share of marquee deals, but you're not going to a factory," reports another insider. One source called the firm "flat," which enables everyone "to make an impact on every level." That autonomy does have its price. "The every-man-for-himself culture and the lack of honesty and fair-mindedness I see in the management outweigh, for me, the early responsibility and challenging, interesting work I have received," rails one insider. "Little effort is made to cultivate junior pros or to instill loyalty in the right kind of people. In short, the culture is broken."

Because "there's very little structure, you have to find your own way" at Bear Stearns. Says one source: "Every place says they're entrepreneurial — this place is entrepreneurial." The firm also allows for "individual stars to shine." Because of Bear Stearns' "thorough commitment to recognizing individual merit, those who perform well can really hold their heads up high." One junior banker explains,

"There's an openness here to new ideas. If I do something unique, it's going to get noticed and appreciated."

Survival of the fittest

While insiders note the lack of hand-holding that might be present at some other firms, at least one Bear employee says everyone has "the chance to become a star player for the firm." Some employees say the firm has a "survival of the fittest" mentality that "extends into all ranks." Bear is "very much a cowboy culture," continues another source. "[There's] lots of whooping and hollering emanating from the trading floor. A colleague put it best: 'Every man is his own corporation, with his own bottom line.'"

Bear employees are quick to point out that the firm is not a completely sink-or-swim environment, saying that they are provided support from senior employees. "Bear people are, above all else, individuals, and the culture not only accepts but applauds this." Still, the firm makes an effort to encourage teamwork. I-banking associates are assigned a junior and a senior mentor (a VP as the junior mentor and an MD as the senior mentor). There are those who downplay the competitive culture. "The bottom line is to make money," says one associate. "If all that they say about back stabbing and sink-or-swim were true, how the hell would we make any money?" "From a junior banker's perspective, the culture encourages development and rewards those who excel," brags another insider. "It truly is a meritocracy."

Associates, stick to your mentor

Speaking of senior bankers, Bear insiders give their superiors mixed reviews. "Success at Bear Stearns depends partly on good results and partly on patronage," says one source. "There is no formal evaluation process and no institutional method to ensure objective feedback. It is thus crucial to find a good patron to help your career along." Once you find that patron, never let them go. "My senior bankers have taken a true interest in my development; I feel that I can sit down in any of their offices at any time and be welcomed. They personally push me to the limits of my ability and are genuinely thankful for the work that I do for them." You'll rarely get stuck doing menial work. "Once in a while you've got to suck it up and work on that random annoying pitchbook that you just don't want to do, but the vast majority of the time, work assignments are appropriately assigned to analysts based on their prior experiences and abilities."

Whatever you get from your seniors, don't expect a great deal of formal training. "Come to Bear Stearns already knowing the job you are to do," warns one insider. "Otherwise it will be very difficult. Training simply is not a priority at this firm." Those outside the firm's New York headquarters report that some formal instruction is "offered over video conference."

No paper clips for you

The Bear Stearns support staff has been described by employees as "the best available." Unlike at other Wall Street firms, there are plenty of secretaries to go around, though some offices may have a limited number depending upon their needs. Word processing and data entry services are also available and interns are plentiful and available for all research needs. However, several employees confirm that "the firm does emphasize thrift." One banker says of the dearth of supplies, "No joke, if I see a paper clip on the floor or a pen on somebody's desk — if somebody's stupid enough to leave a pen on their desk — I take it."

VAULT
19
PRESTIGE
RANKING

Dresdner Kleinwort Wasserstein

1301 Avenue of the Americas
New York, NY 10019
Phone: (212) 969-2700
www.drkw.com

75 Wall Street
New York, NY 10005
Phone: (212) 429-2000

DEPARTMENTS

Asset Finance • Bank Debt •
Dresdner Kleinwort Capital •
Equities • Investment Banking

THE STATS

CEO: Leonhard Fischer
Employer Type:
Division of Dresdner Bank AG
No. of Offices: 38

KEY COMPETITORS

Goldman Sachs
Lazard
Morgan Stanley

UPPERS

• Friendly colleagues
• High-quality deals

DOWNERS

• Long hours
• Slow workflow, lots of downtime

EMPLOYMENT CONTACT

M&A Recruiting
Frances A. Lyman
1301 Avenue of the Americas
New York, NY 10019
Fax: (212) 969-7977
Recruit-M&A@drkw.com

Capital Markets Recruiting
Jacquelyn Johnson
75 Wall Street
New York, NY 10005
Fax: (212) 429-2545
NYMBA@drkw.com

THE BUZZ
WHAT EMPLOYEES AT OTHER FIRMS ARE SAYING

• "Premier, selective, old school"
• "Post-Bruce, not the place to be"
• "Rising star"
• "Nothing left"

THE SCOOP

German mergin'

In January 2001, Germany's Dresdner Bank purchased investment-banking boutique Wasserstein Perella for $1.4 billion in stock, and combined it with its London- and Frankfurt-based investment-banking division, Dresdner Kleinwort Benson (DrKB). Bruce Wasserstein, founder and head of Wasserstein Perella, Dresdner CEO Bernd Fahrholz and DrKB CEO Leonhard Fischer were tapped as the executive management of the new entity, Dresdner Kleinwort Wasserstein (DrKW). As part of the deal, Dresdner set aside $190 million for retention payments maturing in 2002-2003. "We want to keep the [Wasserstein] people medium-term," a Dresdner spokesman told Reuters. Famous dealmaker "Bid 'em up" Bruce Wasserstein reportedly banked $600 million in stock as a result of the merger.

A few months later, another giant German deal was hatched. In July 2001, German insurer Allianz purchased Dresdner Bank for $22 billion, placing DrKW under a larger umbrella. DrKW chief executive Leonhard Fischer survived as CEO of the investment-banking unit and, along with Fahrholz, was appointed to the managing board of the new Allianz Group.

See ya

Upon announcing the Dresdner acquisition, Allianz unveiled plans to spin-off DrKW in an IPO. The plan pleased DrKW bankers, who were promised an ownership stake in the independent unit. But in July 2001, Allianz scrapped its plan to separate DrKW, to the chagrin of DrKW employees, especially Wasserstein, whose vision of an independent global investment-banking powerhouse all but died. Allianz instead said it would create a division combining Dresdner's corporate banking and investment-banking operations in a structure comparable to Deutsche Bank's. (Incidentally, a Deutsche-Dresdner merger in 2000 was called off in its early stages because of disagreement over what to do with Dresdner's investment-banking unit.) As part of the restructuring, Dresdner also announced that 1,500 DrKW jobs would be cut in order to save $439 million annually. To support its 180-degree turn, Allianz cited weak equity markets, especially for investment banks, and the difficulty of separating the investment bank from the corporate bank (DrKW's corporate advisory business was said to be the only easily detachable unit). Following the announcement, the London *Sunday Times* reported that bets were being taken at DrKW on how long it would take Wasserstein to jump ship.

It didn't take long. Unhappy with Dresdner Bank's plans to assimilate DrKW into the larger company, Wasserstein resigned from DrKW in November 2001 — but not without a plan. Wasserstein immediately signed on to head up Lazard, the international M&A specialist. Lazard's chief executive, William Loomis, Jr., resigned in October 2001. Once Wasserstein was securely on board at Lazard, he didn't wait long before raiding his former firm. In January 2002, Wasserstein convinced six former DrKW colleagues, including Wall Street star Jeffrey Rosen, to join him at Lazard. The firm managed to replace the departed bankers with senior hires of its own and has kept headcount at approximately 7,000.

Fewer deals, but big ones

DrKW doesn't transact the same number of deals as some of its bulge-bracket competitors, but it has advised on some major deals, most notably the $165 billion Time Warner/America Online merger. The firm also advised UBS on its $12 billion acquisition of PaineWebber, Ralston Purina on its $11.7 billion sale to Nestle, Ernst & Young Global Consulting on its $11 billion sale to Cap Gemini, and BASF AG on its $6.9 billion sale of its pharmaceuticals unit to Abbott Laboratories. In 2001 DrKW ranked seventh worldwide in completed M&A deal value with $343 billion in total transactions, according to Thomson Financial Securities Data. (Ranked by number of deals, however, the firm came in 22nd place worldwide, completing 96 deals.) More recent deals include representing Philip Morris in the $5.6 billion sale of its Miller Brewing unit to South African Breweries, announced in May 2002; DrKW also secured $2.0 billion in financing for the deal.

DrKW has been busy raising cash for clients on the capital markets side. The firm was the bookrunner on 251 debt deals in 2001, raising a total of $47.5 billion. Notable transactions include the €1.25 billion offering for Aventis, completed in April 2001. DrKW was global coordinator and/or bookrunner on 15 equity issues worth $9 billion in 2001. The firm co-led France Telecom/Orange's €6.4 billion IPO; DrKW followed up with a €3.1 exchangeable bond offering.

GETTING HIRED

Doors of admission

For analyst candidates, DrKW holds two interview rounds — the first on-campus, the second at its offices. The second (and final) round is a Super Saturday-like format, in which recruits go into four or five rooms, each usually consisting of a pair of bankers. Explains one employee, "In one room you're asked technical and finance questions, in one room accounting questions, in another 'why banking.' You'll have a get-to-know-you interview in another room. And in one room a senior banker just talks about their background and experiences." The employee, who went through the entire process, says he "wasn't intimidated," but he calls it "one of the more difficult interviews" he had. Prospective MBA hires get first- and second-round interviews on campus, with a final round in New York. DrKW concentrates its recruiting efforts on about 30 schools, "including all the Ivy League schools, Chicago, Northwestern, NYU and Stanford," according to one source.

OUR SURVEY SAYS

Bruce no longer the boss, but the firm plays on

Less than two years after the Wasserstein acquisition, DrKW's "U.S. presence is still very much Wasserstein Perella," explains one source. "Obviously, though, we're a lot more globally focused, because we're backed by a huge bank." And although many outsiders predicted (and still are predicting) less deal flow with ex-chairman Bruce Wasserstein out of the picture, an insider says, "business is the same. Bruce was more running the place than being a banker. His participation in getting deals wasn't what it used to be." The contact does admit that employees "were upset about the change."

Sources say DrKW, with or without Bruce, is a place, where "you know you're going to have to work a lot, but the senior bankers aren't tyrants." One source notes that the bank has a "mentoring program, in which everyone gets a Big Brother or Big Sister." The source says another benefit of working at a smaller bank such as DrKW is "you work closely with senior bankers. I have never had an associate working between a director and me on a deal. You just don't get that experience at most places."

On the nightshift

Sources say the workload is characterized by periods of intense work with some lulls. "Sometimes, you could be working until four or five in the morning fairly constantly," reports one source. "But other times, there may not be anything to do." Another contact says, "For all the long hours, much of the day is spent waiting for work to trickle down." That said, one first year analyst says the hours are "pretty bad," and adds, "A good week is 70 hours, a really bad week is 110 hours. It's a function of not having a lot of analysts." And those few analysts will put in some all-nighters. According to one employee, "They're definitely looking for people who can work the late hours, people who understand the differences between a small firm and a large firm. It's not a firm where you can sort of hide in the corner and do one small part of a deal."

The long hours, however, come with advantages, namely large paychecks. "In the past, compensation has been high compared to other banks," says one investment-banking analyst, who reports that "the base salary for first-year analysts is $55,000, which goes up by $10,000 each year — $65,000 for second-years and $75,000 for third-years." The contact adds that if DrKW were to go public, analysts "would participate."

Banker buddies

Insiders report that DrKW is a "friendly" place to work. "People will typically eat together or watch TV in a conference room," says one former analyst. "People dress down and go to the gym together. At night, it's a different firm. Everyone knows everyone. You're very close with your analyst class."

Analysts and associates also get to know each other pretty well — through the firm's six-week training program, in which associates and analysts train together. It's not all fun and games, though. At the end of the program, says one source, "Everyone breaks up into groups consisting of one associate and four analysts, and each group does a mock deal and a presentation."

"They're definitely looking
for people who can work
the late hours, people who
understand the differences
between a small firm and
a large firm."

— *Dresdner Kleinwort
Wasserstein insider*

Deloitte & Touche

1633 Broadway
New York, NY 10019
Phone: (212) 489-1600
www.deloitte.com

DEPARTMENTS

Accounting and Auditing •
Information Technology Consulting •
Management Consulting • Mergers
and Acquisitions Consulting • Tax
Advice and Planning

THE STATS

CEO: James E. Copeland, Jr.
Employer Type: Subsidiary of
Deloitte Touche Tohmatsu
No. of Employees: 29,000
No. of Offices: 97

KEY COMPETITORS

Ernst & Young
KPMG
PricewaterhouseCoopers

UPPERS

- Excellent benefits for working mothers
- One of the final four

DOWNERS

- Uncertainty surrounding split of accounting, consulting practices

EMPLOYMENT CONTACT

Deloitte & Touche
1633 Broadway
New York, NY 10019
careers.deloitte.com

THE BUZZ
WHAT EMPLOYEES AT OTHER FIRMS ARE SAYING

- "Energetic place to work"
- "Boring"
- "Well regarded in its industry"
- "Accounting is hurting"

THE SCOOP

Number two

Deloitte & Touche (D&T), one of the Big Five professional services firms, is the American branch of Deloitte Touche Tohmatsu, a global leader in professional services with 95,000 employees in 140 countries. D&T offers auditing, tax and consulting services, which, combined, made the firm the second largest of the Big Five in 2001 (pre-Enron, pre-Big Four era). However, D&T's accounting and audit practices were the smallest of the Big Five.

The firm traces its roots back to 1845 when William Welch Deloitte, the grandson of a French count who fled a likely date with the guillotine during the French Revolution, opened an office in London at the age of 25. He first opened for business in the U.S. in 1893. Deloitte's firm merged with Haskins & Sells, a New York-based firm that opened in March 1895. Founders Charles Waldo Haskins and Elijah Watt Sells had met two years earlier when they were tapped by a Congressional commission to investigate operating methods of the executive departments in Washington, D.C. George Touch, who later added the "e" to protect against mispronunciation of his Scottish name, set up shop in 1883. His firm first opened in the U.S. in 1900. Touche Ross (as it became known) merged with Deloitte, Haskins & Sells in December 1989, creating the Big Five behemoth of today.

The last to go

At the beginning of the new millennium, while other Big Five firms were looking to separate their audit and consulting units, D&T took a different tact. Ernst & Young, responding to regulatory concern regarding a potential conflict of interest, sold its consulting unit in 2000. KPMG spun-off its consulting operations in IPOs in February 2001. And PricewaterhouseCoopers, which announced in January 2002 the spin-off of its consulting services, planned a split as early as 2000 (a sale of its consulting unit to Hewlett-Packard fell through in November 2000). Although D&T was receiving several offers for its consulting unit, the firm bucked the trend. "We get calls almost every day," CEO Jim Copeland told the *Financial Times* in July 2001. Copeland rejected the idea that offering consulting and auditing services to the same companies risked a conflict of interest. "As an organization, we have not been distracted by selling out consultancies and dividing the imaginary profits," Copeland said. But come 2002, Copeland and D&T were forced to change their tunes.

In February 2002, while the U.S. Congress was grilling Arthur Andersen on its involvement in the Enron scandal, D&T's parent Deloitte Touche Tohmatsu reluctantly announced that it, too, would be separating its auditing and consulting units. "It's ironic and sad that we are forced by perception to separate our firm," Copeland said during a speech at the National Press Club a few days after the announcement. "This separation will accomplish nothing." Andersen's questionable dealings with Enron forced many to rethink the Big Five common practice of providing both auditing and consulting services to the same client. D&T also announced that it would no longer handle both internal and external auditing for new clients, a move the other Big Five firms had announced previously. Copeland told Reuters, "Now, because of Enron and other high-profile failures, we are forced to dismantle the very model that represents today the best practice in auditing."

All talk, no action

For a few days in March 2002, it looked as if Deloitte's parent, Deloitte Touche Tohmatsu, would inherit the messy operations of troubled Big Fiver Arthur Andersen. Merger negotiations began between the two at about the same time Andersen learned that it faced potential indictment on obstruction of justice in the Enron investigation. the *New York Times* claimed a deal was imminent on March 11. On the same day, however, *The Wall Street Journal* cautioned against the early call: "The sale or merger effort could come to nothing. It is complicated by the huge liability that Andersen potentially faces for its handling of the Enron audits and the destruction of Enron documents." With Deloitte the second largest of the Big Five, about half the size of big dog PricewaterhouseCoopers, many thought a Deloitte-Andersen marriage made sense, because the bonded couple could present a serious challenge to PricewaterhouseCoopers. But a few days later, when negotiations between Deloitte and Andersen slowed, reports began circulating that other Big Five firms had jumped into the bidding. Ultimately, Deloitte Touche Tohmatsu, which had been considered Andersen most likely suitor, withdrew. "We tried to step into this situation with Andersen and be helpful," CEO Copeland told the *New York Times*. "Unfortunately, we were unable to find our way through to a solution." In an attempt to further separate itself from its former parent, Deloitte Consulting announced a name change in July 2002. The consulting concern will be known as Braxton effective fall 2002.

A big five in a row

In 2002, for the fifth consecutive year, Deloitte & Touche was named to *Fortune* magazine's list of the "100 Best Companies to Work for in America." D&T is the only major professional services firm to make the list every year since its inception. In addition, for eight consecutive years D&T has made *Working Mother* magazine's list of the "100 Best Companies for Working Mothers," an award based on a company's child care services, leave for new parents, flexible work arrangements, work/life benefits and opportunities for women.

Girl power

Among the Big Five, Deloitte & Touche has the highest percentage of women partners, a distinction the firm has held since 1997. The firm counted 16 percent women partners in 2001, up from 10 percent in 1997. In the early 1990s, however, the firm's practice of promoting women was anything but praiseworthy. In 1992 only 5 percent of D&T's partners were women. The small number of women in Deloitte's power structure was a factor in a high turnover rate for female employees. In order to understand why women were not represented at the top, in 1993 D&T created the Initiative for the Retention and Advancement of Women, the first such formal program dedicated to retaining and advancing women instituted by a professional services firm. According to D&T, the initiative's task force addressed issues such as why the company had a higher turnover for women than for men and why fewer women were being admitted to the partnership. Since the program's inception, the firm has implemented strategies that address advancement, work/personal life issues, and cultural issues. To even further female advancement, in June 2001, D&T unveiled Vision 2005, a plan to double the promotion rate of women to partner and director positions. If Vision 2005 is successful, women partners and directors will make up 35 percent of the company's leadership.

GETTING HIRED

For the most part, "there are very few technical questions asked during the interview process. There isn't much emphasis on grilling recruits to determine their technical abilities because the recruits' academic records should speak for themselves." Applicants to the more technically oriented areas are warned to be ready for an occasional question testing their aptitude, though it will not necessarily be the determining factor in hiring decisions.

There may also be "a little written test — something quantitative that's quick and dirty." More commonly, though, "most of the questions asked are 'What would you like to do? Where do you see yourself down the road? What previous experience do you have?'" All things considered, most people who have been through the process describe it as "fairly long and stressful" but "not as rigorous as investment banking interviews." Deloitte "lets you know shortly [afterwards] by giving a phone call and sending a basket of goodies."

OUR SURVEY SAYS

D&T likes to emphasize that "experience teaches better than training." The lack of ego is also refreshing, say employees: "People don't go around bragging about where they went to school. The jerk is the exception." D&T, a "strong partnership," is known for "intensely demanding schedules," but it does try to reward employees for their effort. For example, D&T consultants, who often put in significant travel time, are assured they'll be on the road no more than three days a week — which is better than the industry average. Even so, one insider says, "We're relying more and more on hoteling and telecommuting."

"People don't go around bragging about where they went to school. The jerk is the exception."

— *Deloitte & Touche insider*

Ernst & Young

5 Times Square
New York, NY 10036
Phone: (212) 773-3000
www.ey.com

DEPARTMENTS

Assurance and Advisory Business
Services • Corporate Finance •
Law • Tax

THE STATS

Chairman: James S. Turley
CEO: Richard S. Bobrow
Employer Type: Private Company
2001 Revenues: $9.9 billion
No. of Employees: 84,000
No. of Offices: 670

KEY COMPETITORS

Deloitte & Touche
KPMG
PricewaterhouseCoopers

UPPERS

- Family-friendly leave and
  scheduling policies
- Tuition reimbursement

DOWNERS

- Cramped working quarters for
  junior employees
- Long workdays

EMPLOYMENT CONTACT

Ernst & Young
5 Times Square
New York, NY 10036

THE BUZZ
WHAT EMPLOYEES AT OTHER FIRMS ARE SAYING

- "A top accountant"
- "Dinosaur-like"
- "Solid firm"
- "Snobbish"

THE SCOOP

At heart, a nice Midwestern firm

In 1894 Scotsman Arthur Young set up an independent accounting firm in Chicago. A few years later, American brothers Alwin and Theodore Ernst launched a tiny accounting firm of their own in Cleveland. Both firms, Arthur Young & Company and Ernst & Ernst, received a big boost during the financial chaos of the 1930s, as the Great Depression spawned new financial reporting regulations that increased the need for accounting and auditing services. In 1957 Arthur Young & Co. made news by appointing the first female partner in what was then the Big Eight, and Ernst & Ernst merged with British firm Whinney, Murray & Co. to become Ernst & Whinney. In 1989 Arthur Young and Ernst & Whinney finally found each other and merged to become Ernst & Young, the Big Five accounting firm that it is today.

Ernst & Young International, Ltd. (EYI), the umbrella organization for all of Ernst & Young's businesses, has offices in 130 countries throughout Europe, the Americas, the Pacific region, the Middle East and Africa. The United States member firm of EYI is Ernst & Young LLP (E&Y), a major component of the Ernst & Young organization with approximately 30,000 employees in 85 cities. In April 2002, E&Y moved into its new 37-floor U.S. headquarters at 5 Times Square in New York. The firm is expecting to grow its Manhattan staff from the current 4,600 to approximately 6,000.

While not the largest of the Big Five, Ernst & Young has consistently posted double-digit growth and has lead its competitors in tax services and technology. Today, the firm audits 113 of the Fortune 500 companies. Since 1992, E&Y's computer consulting business has swelled from $300 million to $3.6 billion in revenues. The firm has also been an industry pioneer, developing extensive proprietary software and online consulting services. However, E&Y has experienced a few setbacks, most notably a failed merger with KPMG that revealed cracks in Ernst & Young's worldwide structure. The firm has also been the target of a spate of lawsuits and accusations of conflicts of interest as it struggles to reconcile concurrent auditing and consulting relationships with certain clients.

Consulting: We'll always have Paris

Ernst & Young currently ranks as the second-largest integrated professional services firm in the U.S. At one time, consulting was a major component of the Ernst & Young machine, with 20,000 employees (12,500 professionals). Late in 1999, rumors started swirling that French consulting giant Cap Gemini was in talks to acquire E&Y's consulting unit. In May 2000, the rumors rang true, and E&Y sold its consulting services to the Paris-based company for $11.2 billion. The deal nearly doubled Cap's revenue and increased its worldwide employment by almost 20,000. By selling its consulting unit, Ernst & Young hoped to avoid potential conflicts of interest between its businesses; industry watchdogs repeatedly argued that Big Five firms let accounting irregularities slide in order to maintain consulting contracts. E&Y was the first Big Five firm to separate its consulting and accounting units.

A stymied plan

Ernst & Young tried to fatten itself up in 1998 by merging with its competitor KPMG Peat Marwick (as it was then called), another Big Five firm. But the planned merger foundered on the shoals of European regulatory concerns. (It didn't help matters that the merger of competitors Price Waterhouse and Coopers & Lybrand was also pending at the time.)

In September 2000, E&Y combined its operations in more than 60 countries into ten geographic areas reporting directly to the firm's global CEO. The geographic areas are as follows: The Americas, Australia, The Far East, France, Germany, Italy, The Netherlands, Nordic, Switzerland and the U.K.

Auditor independence issues

Like all the big accounting firms, E&Y has had to defend itself against charges of questionable or biased audits. In one case, the firm was investigated by the Securities and Exchange Commission (SEC) for its audit of Cendant Corp. The SEC questioned E&Y's practice of giving Cendant price breaks on its audits in exchange for consulting business. Additionally, *The Wall Street Journal* reported that E&Y's audit materials for Computer Associates was subpoenaed. Most recently, the SEC charged E&Y with violating auditor independence rules by marketing and installing PeopleSoft products. The Pleasanton, Calif.-based software maker is an Ernst & Young client. E&Y denies that its sales relationship is improper. The SEC wants the firm to terminate the marketing agreement and return fees for auditing work done during the agreement.

Tip top taxmen

In July 2001, E&Y was named the best tax and financial planner in the U.S. by *Worth* magazine's Reader's Choice Survey for the second year in a row. The survey assesses the performance of products and services based on how well they have served the interests of the magazine's readers, whose median net worth is more than $1.25 million.

Ernst & Young supplies customized tax information to clients in 13 countries through its international Online Tax Advisor service. The service debuted in July 1999 with U.S.-only advice, and currently offers advice in 11 different countries.

Treating you well

For four consecutive years E&Y has been named to *Fortune*'s "100 Best Companies to Work For," a list of firms that best help employees balance their work and personal life. In the 2002 rankings, *Fortune* says one of the reasons a company makes the list is its "willingness, like Ernst & Young, to scramble-to come up with creative ways to keep employees satisfied, and to treat them with respect and dignity." For E&Y, "that meant redeploying people, lending staff to clients with temporary shortages, and offering voluntary leaves of absence at 25 percent of pay."

Ernst & Young also has been named to *Working Mother*'s "100 Best Companies for Working Mothers" list for four straight years. The firm landed on *Traning* magazine's 2002 "Training Top 100," snagging the No. 7 spot for its training and education programs. In 1999 E&Y won *Business & Health*'s first "Productivity Plus Award" in recognition of the company's employee retention efforts and flexible work schedules.

GETTING HIRED

Breaking in

Ernst & Young sets its hiring goals in the spring of each year, organizing its strategic planning and forming "school teams," which each have their own budgets. Each team has a "campus ambassador" and "campus captain."

The qualities that E&Y says it looks for in recruits include "intellectual competence, flexibility, communication skills, team skills, leadership skills, motivation, customer service focus, selling and influencing ability and technical skills." Each interviewer focuses on one or two of these factors. Among the questions interviewers ask to identify these skills: "Tell me about a situation where you used your [skills in one of these factors]. What was your role? What did you do? What happened? What did you learn from this experience?" One insider says he had "five interviews, each a half hour long." He adds, "There was nothing too difficult about the interview process — just questions about prior jobs and experiences."

Some offices have "sell days" for Masters of Accounting students, including the New York and Chicago offices. At these sell days, the firm "discusses the Accelerated Solutions Environment, our unique approach to decision-making." The attendees are taken through exercises in which they discuss the sort of workplace they want. At the end of the sell day, after a tour of E&Y, comes the "breakthrough decision," when candidates learn how to break a wooden board with their hand, "meant to mirror their breakthrough career decision — that they should work at Ernst & Young." About half of those who receive job offers accept the positions.

OUR SURVEY SAYS

Structure without supervision

Ernst & Young's size brings both advantages and disadvantages. One contact notes that "it's a large firm, and if you're ambitious, it can be tough sometimes." The same contact also says E&Y is "great if you want to settle down, but if you want to be making the most money of anyone your age, or if you want to do everything that interests you, you might get frustrated. It's more structured. You get assigned to something and that's your project — hopefully you'll like it, because that's what you'll be doing for a while." Structure, though, doesn't mean that management is always keeping a close watch over employees. One Los Angeles-based insider cites the "lack of management" as the best thing about working at E&Y. He adds, "I'm free to work on my own schedule, without someone looking over my shoulder, provided that the work quality is good." Note, however, that the rigid structure reported by some working in U.S. offices doesn't necessarily exist in other countries.

Going abroad?

E&Y insiders tend also to comment on the firm's increasing international outlook and encouraging attitudes towards going abroad. One contact notes that 30 to 40 percent of his officemates actively chose international assignments. "It's really encouraged," he says. "I guess because of globalization, and they know that a lot of these people would just leave if they couldn't go abroad. It's very easy to transfer between countries."

Paying fair

Pay doesn't seem to be one of E&Y's strong suits, though it is competitive with other Big Five firms. "As for compensation," one contact says, "the general pattern is that you make a fair salary, but nothing spectacular." The same individual notes, however, that the pay is "good lifestyle money," and that "you'll never have to beg on the floor of a car dealership for a loan." One employee says the incentive plan "is rare for this type of firm." He adds, "I think that the plan is fairly written and gives me good long-term upside potential."

T. Rowe Price

100 East Pratt Street
Baltimore, MD 21202
Phone: (410) 345-2000
www.troweprice.com

DEPARTMENTS

Brokerage • College Funding •
Mutual Funds • Private Account
Management • Retirement Plans

THE STATS

Chairman and President:
George A. Roche
Employer Type: Public Company
Ticker Symbol: TROW (Nasdaq)
2001 Revenue: $1.0 billion
2001 Net Income: $196 million
No. of Employees: 3,600
No. of Offices: 26

KEY COMPETITORS

Fidelity Investments
Janus Capital
Vanguard Group

EMPLOYMENT CONTACT

staffing@troweprice.com
www.trowepricecareers.com

THE BUZZ
WHAT EMPLOYEES AT OTHER FIRMS ARE SAYING

- "Good money management shop"
- "Stale environment"
- "Top in its industry"

THE SCOOP

Investing pioneer

Thomas Rowe Price, Jr., began his investment firm in 1937 after a dozen years at Mackubin Goodrich & Co., a Baltimore-based brokerage firm now known as Legg Mason. Price had a theory that companies with new products, services or technology could enjoy a sustained growth curve, and that investing in these companies during this growth stage would prove profitable. The goal was to buy stocks in such firms and hold them for the long term — an idea practically unheard of in post-Depression America. Through his company, Price promoted his philosophy by providing advice to investors on picking stocks. In 1950 he introduced his first mutual fund, the T. Rowe Price Growth Stock Fund.

Although Price's reputation as a stock-picker is impeccable, his reputation as a manager is less impressive. Price's own son reportedly called him "a bear to work with" and colleagues, including company co-founder Thomas Kidd, said he was aloof. Yet through his intuitive understanding of the market, along with a grueling work schedule, Price built his company into one of the leading investment management firms. In 1966, perhaps tired from the grind of nearly 30 years, Price sold his stake in the firm for a relatively small sum (published reports say he received less than $800,000) with the condition that control of the company remain with previously agreed upon successors. T. Rowe Price went public in 1986 and now has $149.8 billion in assets under management (as of June 30, 2002).

Higher highs, lower lows

Through the mid-1990s, the firm instituted an investment strategy that many analysts felt was more conservative than even Price's personal philosophy. For example, Price's funds never got swept up in the tech and Internet mania of the late 1990s. Though the firm had a healthy dose of tech stocks in its funds, the company's risk-averse style precluded it from getting on board the New Economy bandwagon. That strategy led to short-term results that were slightly below the market. (The T. Rowe Price Science and Technology fund, for example, grew 101 percent in 1999. While this growth was impressive, it was still lower than the 134.8 percent average for all tech funds in the same time period.) Management maintained that its focus on value was much more prudent and echoed what many investment gurus had been saying for quite some time: that tech and Internet stocks had been highly overvalued. Those principles have been proven true, as most of Price's funds haven't experienced the dramatic downturns typical among tech-heavy investors such as Janus Capital.

In November 2001, *The Wall Street Journal* reported that T. Rowe Group cut 180 jobs, or about five percent of its U.S. staff, mainly in its telephone-operations and technology areas. The 2001 job cuts are the first in decades at T. Rowe Price.

GETTING HIRED

T. Rowe Price recruits for analysts and associates at a number of colleges, mostly on the East Coast. Additionally, the firm scouts out marketing and IT talent during its campus visits. There is also a summer program for associates, analysts and IT specialists. Check out the company's career web site at www.trowepricecareers.com for a complete listing of available openings and schedule of campus visits.

For detailed 40- to 50-page insider reports on top finance employers like Goldman, Morgan Stanley, Merrill, Salomon Smith Barney, Lehman Brothers and more, get Vault Employer Profiles. Go to http://finance.vault.com.

T. Rowe Price recruits for analysts and associates at a number of colleges, mostly on the East Coast.

PricewaterhouseCoopers

1177 Avenue of the Americas
New York, NY 10036
Phone: (646) 471-4000
www.pwcglobal.com

DEPARTMENTS

Assurance and Business Advisory •
Business Process Outsourcing •
Financial Advisory Services • Tax
Services

THE STATS

CEO: Samuel A. DiPiazza, Jr.
Employer Type: Private Company
2001 Revenues: $22.3 billion
No. of Employees: 160,000

KEY COMPETITORS

Deloitte & Touche
Ernst & Young
KPMG

UPPERS

• Excellent benefits for working mothers
• Relaxed work environment

DOWNERS

• High turnover typical of Big Five firms

EMPLOYMENT CONTACT

PricewaterhouseCoopers
Human Resources
1177 Avenue of the Americas
New York, NY 10036
Phone: (646) 471-4000
Fax: (646) 471-4100
www.pwcglobal.com

THE BUZZ
WHAT EMPLOYEES AT OTHER FIRMS ARE SAYING

• "Gold standard accounting firm"
• "Big, bureaucratic"
• "Thorough, professional, incisive"
• "Inept and arrogant"

THE SCOOP

Big time Big Five

In the late 1990s, four of the "Big Six" firms — Price Waterhouse/Coopers & Lybrand and KPMG/Ernst & Young — were considering mergers that would consolidate the field. The KPMG/Ernst & Young union never materialized, but the Price Waterhouse and Coopers & Lybrand marriage did, becoming capital "P," lower case "w," capital "C," space-less PricewaterhouseCoopers (PwC) in 1998. The firm now has approximately 160,000 employees (including 10,000 partners) in 150 countries and, with $22.3 billion in revenue in 2001, is by far the largest of the Big Five.

PwC traces its history to 1849 when Samuel Lowell Price opened his practice in London. Five years later, William Cooper opened a practice of his own in London that would soon become known as Cooper Brothers. Price's firm joined with London's Holyland and Waterhouse in 1865, and the partnership was renamed Price, Waterhouse & Co. in 1874. It wasn't until 1957 that the Coopers & Lybrand partnership was formed. Both firms expanded internationally until the July 1998 union of Price, Waterhouse and Coopers & Lybrand, which created PricewaterhouseCooper, the world's largest professional services organization.

Long arm of the SEC

PricewaterhouseCoopers was the first casualty of an industry-wide crackdown on the practice of accountants owning stock in companies they audited. The Securities and Exchange Commission found in January 2000 that 1,885 PwC employees had ownership stakes in corporations audited by the firm. All told, 8,064 violations were uncovered; 45 percent of those violations were by partners in the firm. While neither admitting nor denying guilt, then-CEO James Schiro and Chairman Nicholas Moore wrote in a letter to the firm's partners that the report was "embarrassing to our firm and to all of us as partners" and that "equally important, it may also raise questions and concerns among our clients."

While the SEC investigation dealt with equity investments, questions about auditor independence have been a concern at professional services firms because of the revenues the companies can get from audit clients for consulting work. Some have suggested that firms will be reluctant to issue critical auditor's reports that might jeopardize a lucrative consulting relationship. The firms, recognizing the inherent conflicts, have looked at ways to separate their consulting units. KPMG spun off its consulting unit in a public offering; Ernst & Young sold its consulting arm to Cap Gemini of France. PwC thought it had a similar deal with computer maker Hewlett-Packard in September 2000. That deal fell through two months later after Hewlett-Packard's stock price plummeted, dropping the value of H-P's offer from $17-$18 billion to $15 billion.

PwC's new boss

In July 2001, CEO Schiro announced his intention to step down as soon as a successor was named and a transition could be executed. Though there was speculation that Schiro's departure was related to the failed HP deal (and, to a lesser extent, the SEC auditing probe), the firm and Schiro insisted his departure was amicable. Schiro, whose biggest accomplishment was overseeing the Price Waterhouse/Coopers & Lybrand merger, was named CEO at Swiss insurer Zurich Financial Services in May 2002.

In November 2001, PwC's board elected Samuel DiPiazza as the new CEO. DiPiazza joined Coopers & Lybrand in 1973 and served as head of PwC's North American tax-services operation and head of PwC's U.S. operations. DiPiazza's reign officially began in early 2002. Dennis Nally, a managing partner of PwC's U.S. business and a 28-year veteran of the firm, succeeded DiPiazza as senior partner of U.S. operations in March 2002.

Big blue consulting

PwC continued to wrestle with the future of its consulting arm and the events of late 2001 only added to the controversy. PwC competitor Arthur Andersen was nailed for its faulty audits of Houston, Texas-based Enron. Critics said one factor in Andersen's work was conflicts of interest stemming from the firm's consulting work for Enron. The fallout increased pressure on other professional services firms to separate their audit and consulting practices. In January 2002, PwC announced a spin off of PwC Consulting. PwC consulting soon decided to rename itself Monday, a much-mocked decision that further emphasized its independence from PricewaterhouseCoopers.

Not long after the re-branding announcement, PricewaterhouseCoopers had a sudden change of heart. The firm sold PwC Consulting/Monday to International Business Machines (IBM). The July 2001 deal, worth $3.5 billion, added PwC Consulting to

IBM's already formidable consulting operations. IBM Global Services had 150,000 employees and 2001 revenues of $35 billion.

PwC sheds staff

Hurt by a sagging economy, PricewaterhouseCoopers reportedly cut staff in some areas during 2001. The firm laid off 1,000 employees in its U.S. consulting unit in April 2001. In August 2001, PwC's U.K. consulting arm rescinded offers to approximately 80 people who were slated to start work at the firm in September. The firm then cut an additional 330 U.K. consulting employees in October 2001. In addition, many consultants in North America and India were forced to take a 5 percent to 10 percent pay cut.

Andersen's loss is PwC's gain

With Arthur Andersen's U.S. operations facing obstruction of justice charges for its role in Enron's bankruptcy, Andersen's innocent overseas affiliates attempted to salvage what they could of a business severely tarnished by their American partners. In March 2002, PwC snapped up a couple of those affiliates, merging with Arthur Andersen's Hong Kong and China units. According to a PwC spokeswoman, the merged firm will have 3,000 employees in Hong Kong and 3,000 in mainland China. Silas Yang, the chairman and senior partner of PricewaterhouseCoopers in Hong Kong, praised the "practice and professionalism of our new colleagues," and predicted the combined firm would be a leader in Hong Kong and China.

Additionally, as a result of the Enron scandal Andersen's clients began dropping the troubled firm as its auditor. There to pick up where Andersen was forced to leave off was PwC. By early March 2002, even before the criminal indictment against the firm was announced, three of the five largest clients to drop Andersen as its auditor — Merck, Freddie Mac and SunTrust Banks — hired PwC to take over.

And the Oscar goes to...

Not PricewaterhouseCoopers, though the firm does know before anyone who else who the little shiny men will go to. For 67 years PricewaterhouseCoopers has tallied the votes cast by the members of the Academy of Motion Picture Arts and Sciences, which annually doles out the coveted Oscar statues to honor film's best performances. In 2002 PwC partner and seven-year veteran ballot counter Greg Garrison, along with first time counter and fellow PwC partner Rick Rosas, oversaw the tallying. Before envelopes were opened and teary thank yous acted out, Garrison and Rosas were the only two people who knew which stars would take home the hardware. On Oscar night 2002, as is done each year, the PwC partners each carried briefcases with the golden envelopes and were driven to the show in separate cars under armed guard. Aside from counting votes, Garrison and Rosas also proofed the nominations announcement press release to confirm that the list of nominees was in order. Additionally, PwC representatives must make sure that ballots arrive safely at the post office from Academy headquarters. Apparently, that's not as easy as it sounds. In 2000 ballots for California members of the Academy got lost in the mail. As a result, the Academy was forced to send out new ballots and extend the voting deadline date. Eventually, the missing ballots did turn up — at a postal center in a Los Angeles suburb, where they had been accidentally mixed in with bulk mail shipments.

GETTING HIRED

PricewaterhouseCoopers' web site, www.pwcglobal.com, has a detailed career section that lists openings, contacts and recruiting schedules for experienced, undergraduate and MBA candidates. In the past, PwC has offered current employees incentives for connecting qualified recruits to the firm, so it pays to try to get to know someone on the inside.

OUR SURVEY SAYS

Party people

PwC insiders say they have a good time at work. Explains one source, "The people here are young — between 24 and 35. It's a relaxed atmosphere, and people feel very comfortable going out for a drink together after work. It's a very social place if that's what you choose, but you are never made to feel guilty for not participating in any activities or parties." Speaking of parties, "there are usually lots of them going on — mostly going-away parties. Big Five firms are notorious for high turnover. That's not a reflection on the company, just the nature of the beast." According to another insider, "The people here are friendly and fun. There is always lots of work to do, and you also have lots of freedom to do whatever you have to in your personal life outside of work — and even during work hours."

Different and nearly equal

Most insiders think "you can expect to be working for a diverse set of people with a diverse set of colleagues" at PwC. In terms of numbers, says one insider, "gender-wise, it's commensurate with the local region. Not 50-50, but for every three men, there are at least two women. Culturally, it varies by region," but basically it's reflective of the makeup of the local area, concludes that source. *Working Mother* recognized PwC's commitment to diversity; the firm became the first professional services firm to land in the top 10 of the magazines annual list of the "Best Companies for Working Mothers." PwC made the top 10 in 2001 in its sixth appearance on *Working Mother*'s top 100.

For detailed 40- to 50-page insider reports on top finance employers like Goldman, Morgan Stanley, Merrill, Salomon Smith Barney, Lehman Brothers and more, get Vault Employer Profiles. Go to http://finance.vault.com.

Gabelli Asset Management

One Corporate Center
Rye, NY 10580
Phone: (914) 921-5100
www.gabelli.com

DEPARTMENTS

Alternative Investments • Global
Research • Mutual Funds • Private
Asset Management

THE STATS

**Chairman, CEO and Chief
Investment Officer:** Mario Gabelli
Employer Type: Public Company
Ticker Symbol: GBL (NYSE)
2001 Revenues: $224 million
2001 Net Income: $61 million
No. of Employees: 130
No. of Offices: 6

KEY COMPETITORS

Alliance Capital Management
Franklin Resources
Vanguard Group

EMPLOYMENT CONTACT

Human Resources
Gabelli Asset Management, Inc.
One Corporate Center
Rye, NY 10580
Fax: (914) 921-5392
hr@gabelli.com

THE BUZZ
WHAT EMPLOYEES AT OTHER FIRMS ARE SAYING

- "Very strong firm"
- "Mario is a tough cookie"
- "Best value shop"
- "Going, going, ..."

THE SCOOP

Starting at the bottom

Self-taught stock picker Mario Gabelli founded Gabelli Asset Management (GAM) in 1977. In an interview with *Investor's Business Daily*, Gabelli detailed his humble roots. Gabelli told *IBD* that he learned about the stock market at age 16 while working as a caddie at a golf course in Scarsdale, N.Y. Armed with that experience — and an MBA from Columbia — Gabelli spent several years working as an analyst in the industry. He then went on to found GAM at a time when money managers and research firms were struggling due to changes in the industry. Gabelli credits his company's success to meticulous research techniques that he claims are better able to identify value investments. The firm says it seeks to "identify undervalued companies with dominant industry positions." Investors have apparently been convinced of Gabelli's purported bargain-hunting prowess: The firm's assets under management have grown from $8 billion in 1994 to over $24 billion in 2002. GAM now manages 28 mutual funds and more than 1,000 pension, trust and individual accounts.

Control freak

After more than 20 years as an independent firm, GAM went public in February 1999, raising $105 million. The terms of the IPO stipulated that Gabelli would retain control of 97.6 percent of GAM's voting shares after the offering. Some saw Gabelli's control as a drawback to the offering. *Barron's* called the company a "one-man show" and reported that some potential investors were uneasy with the prospect of buying into such a tightly controlled firm. *Barron's* also reported that Goldman Sachs pulled out as an underwriter of the offering because it believed Gabelli's compensation was too high. He reportedly receives 10 percent of the pre-tax profits, plus portfolio management fees. Additionally, Gabelli was slated to receive a deferred payment of $50 million in January 2002, plus interest.

Initially, the offering was a success. But the shares, which opened at $17, soon began trading at less than $15. Gabelli saw this as his chance to reclaim a chunk of his company. Less than two months after the IPO, the company announced a $3 million stock buyback program, which upset some investors. "It seems to me that Gabelli should have just sold fewer shares in the IPO in the first place," one institutional investor grumbled to the *New York Post* in October 1999. "He's buying back at 15 what I originally bought at 17. I am not a happy camper here." Through September 14, 2001, GAM repurchased 510,900 shares at an average cost of $17.38 per share.

And in January 2002, the firm's board authorized the repurchase of up to $10 million additional shares, including $3.1 million under the previous stock buyback program.

Microsoft dollars

In 2001 Microsoft chairman and co-founder Bill Gates decided to gamble on Gabelli. Gates's private investment firm, Cascade Investments LLC, which manages his personal fortune, bought $100 million in convertible notes from Gabelli Asset Management. If the notes are converted into stock, Cascade will own 6 percent of GAM. Mario Gabelli said the money will be used to expand his firm's European operations. This wasn't the first time that Gates and Gabelli hooked up. In 1999 Cascade invested $25 million in convertible notes in Lynch Interactive Corp., which operates rural independent telephone companies and whose chairman and CEO is Mario Gabelli.

GETTING HIRED

Introduce yourself

Check Gabelli's web site, www.gabelli.com, for a listing of full- and part-time openings. Resumes and cover letters can be submitted directly from the site, and must be sent as plain text files (no attachments). If an opening is not listed on the site for a desired position, interested parties can apply by sending a resume and cover letter directly to the Rye, N.Y., office.

Interested parties can apply by sending a resume and cover letter directly to [Gabelli's] Rye, N.Y., office.

Thomas Weisel Partners

One Montgomery Street
Suite 3700
San Francisco, CA 94104
Phone: (415) 364-2500
www.tweisel.com

DEPARTMENTS

Institutional Sales and Trading •
Investment Banking — M&A,
Corporate Finance and Private
Placements • Private Client • Private
Equity and Asset Management •
Research

THE STATS

Chairman and CEO: Thomas Weisel
Employer Type: Private Company
2001 Revenue: $346 million
No. of Employees: 675
No. of Offices: 5

KEY COMPETITORS

Credit Suisse First Boston
Morgan Stanley

UPPERS

- Entrepreneurial atmosphere
- Great peer relationships
- Junior bankers given lots of responsibility

DOWNERS

- Lots of office politics
- Poor training program
- Small size makes it tough to compete against bulge-bracket banks

EMPLOYMENT CONTACT

Human Resources
Thomas Weisel Partners
One Montgomery Street
Suite 3700
San Francisco, CA 94104
jobs@tweisel.com

THE BUZZ
WHAT EMPLOYEES AT OTHER FIRMS ARE SAYING

- "Rising small player"
- "Fallen angel"
- "Give it a few years"
- "It's not 1999 anymore"

THE SCOOP

Mighty merchants

Thomas Weisel Partners was founded in January 1999 by Thomas Weisel, Frank Dunlevy, J. Sanford Miller, Derek Lemke-Von Ammon and Alan Menkes. The firm bills itself as a merchant bank rather than an investment bank — a reference to the fact that the firm seeks to invest in private companies through several private equity funds, which total approximately $2 billion in assets under management. Thomas Weisel Partners' growth has been phenomenal; in its first year of operations the firm advised on 108 investment banking transactions worth $23 billion, including 54 IPOs (seven of which the firm lead-managed). In 2000 the firm advised on 140 deals, including 42 IPOs and 46 M&A transactions), for total revenues of $474 million. Additionally, according to *Investment Dealers' Digest*, Weisel Partners turned a profit after only four months in business.

Perhaps the firm's fast track to success lies in Weisel himself, who has a long history of founding firms. He was a founding partner of Robertson Coleman Siebel and Weisel. However, after a now-infamous falling out with partner Sandy Robertson, Weisel left to form Montgomery Securities. Robertson, on the other hand, went on to establish Montgomery's San Francisco rival, Robertson Stephens.

I'm outta here

Thomas Weisel founded Montgomery Securities in 1978. He sold Montgomery to NationsBank in 1997 for $1.3 billion. (Weisel himself reportedly netted between $100-$120 million from the deal.) Weisel originally planned to remain and run Montgomery after the sale. But his plan fell by the wayside when NationsBank merged with BankAmerica (now Bank of America).

Weisel clashed repeatedly with NationsBank CEO Hugh McColl after the union with BankAmerica. "At NationsBank, in effect, they were taking the entrepreneurial spirit away," Weisel would later tell *Forbes*. After the NationsBank/BankAmerica merger, Weisel felt the bank was trying to fold Montgomery into the combined firm. This, Weisel told *Red Herring*, constituted "a violation of the merger agreement and of my employment contract." (A little history: Montgomery narrowly escaped being merged with Robertson Stephens, because BankAmerica had purchased Robbie. Initially, NationsBank and BankAmerica discussed combining the two I-banks when the parents merged, but decided against it. BankAmerica then sold Robbie to

BankBoston and proceeded with its merger with NationsBank.) Weisel finally quit in September 1998. He told *Red Herring*: "It was very easy for me to say, 'Fine, see you later.' I had no interest in being around people who don't keep their promises." (It appears Weisel can enjoy the last laugh — McColl announced his resignation in January 2001 because of BofA's lackluster performance.)

You worked at BofA securities? Me too!

Shortly after splitting from Montgomery, Weisel started assembling a team with the intention of forming an investment bank of his own. Many observers felt Weisel — who was already well off financially and has numerous outside interests — took on the burden of forming an investment bank mainly out of a desire to stick it to his former colleagues at the new Banc of America Securities. This is a charge Weisel denies. "I wish them well," he told *The San Francisco Chronicle* of his former firm. "There's no animosity. I'd like to work with them."

Whatever his motives were, Weisel's actions certainly annoyed the new management of BofA. His new venture took approximately 150 former Montgomery employees, including 36 of the 70 partners currently at Weisel Partners. BofA struck back, though. The bank withheld bonuses from investment-banking analysts who left for Weisel in December 1998; three months later BofA filed a lawsuit against TWP, charging the firm with unfair hiring practices. BofA later restored most of the bonuses and the lawsuit was settled in late 2000 with Thomas Weisel Partners paying $20 million, according to *The San Francisco Chronicle*.

Renaissance man

Thomas Weisel is described by those around him as intense and driven. He holds an AB from Stanford and an MBA from Harvard and is an accomplished athlete. Weisel is a five-time speed skating champion who won his first title at the age of 14. (Rumor has it that Weisel just missed making the 1960 Olympic team.) Weisel has also served as chairman of the U.S. Ski Team. More recently, he sponsored Lance Armstrong and the U.S. Postal Service biking team in the Tour de France in 1999, 2000 and 2001. Weisel is a frequent financial contributor to the San Francisco Museum of Modern Art and a wing at the museum is named after him. His business prowess has also been recognized. He was named "Executive of the Year" in December 1999 by the *San Francisco Business Times* and won a 1999 "Banker of the Year" award from *Investment Dealers' Digest*.

Working with the system

Thomas Weisel must have brought in the new millennium with a smile. In January 2000, the California Public Employee Retirement System (CalPERS) invested $100 million for a 10 percent stake in the company. The investment valued the firm at approximately $1 billion after just a year in business. According to reports in *Investment Dealers' Digest*, CalPERS also agreed to invest $500 million in Thomas Weisel Partners' private equity funds and an additional $500 million "to support new business activity by the firm."

Rough seas ahead?

Despite a phenomenal year in 1999 and a great start in 2000, Thomas Weisel Partners wasn't immune to the fluctuations experienced throughout the industry in late 2000 and 2001. The downturn in the market for technology deals may have made the firm vulnerable. In January 2001, *Investment Dealers' Digest* published rumors that Thomas Weisel Partners might be up for sale and that the firm asked its partners to forgo compensation for the fourth quarter of 2000. The article went on to note that the firm "underwrote only one tech equity deal for $51.4 million versus six for $490.7 million in the fourth quarter of 1999, according to Thomson Financial Securities Data." A spokeswoman for the firm informed *IDD* that TWP is "definitely not for sale." Weisel himself sent a strongly worded letter to *IDD*, denying that the firm had seriously considered a sale or IPO. *IDD* stood by its assertion that the firm's partners were asked to go without pay in the fourth quarter but noted that the firm did pay up, though much less than it paid in the first half of the year.

Staying afloat

Although the firm's revenues dropped in 2001 to $346 million from $474 million, a 37 percent slide, the firm faired well despite the poor market conditions. Thomas Weisel Partners completed 59 M&A deals valued at $512 billion, which was good enough to rank the company 11th in total U.S. M&A transactions and third in U.S. technology M&A transactions, according to Thomson Financial. Notable deals during the year included advising Maxim on its $2.5 billion purchase of Dallas Semiconductor, advising JDS Uniphase on its $425 million purchase of IBM's Optical Transceiver Business, and co-lead managing Flextronics' $1 billion follow-on equity offering. Additionally, the firm's brokerage operations increased its average daily trading volume by 84 percent to 39.9 million shares per day, which, according the firm, ranked Thomas Weisel Partners 15th in trading volume at the end of the year.

What goes up, must come down

In early 2000, Thomas Weisel Partners had 400 employees. Just a few months later, the high-flying firm had increased its staff to 630. And by February 2001, when other firms on the Street were downsizing, Weisel further fattened its staff to 845, more than double the size a little over a year earlier. But the hiring stopped by mid-2001 — and turned into firing. Thomas Weisel Partners announced in August 2001 that 80 employees, mostly investment-banking professionals, would be let go. Chief Operating Officer Blake Jorgensen told *The San Francisco Chronicle*, "We're still dead set on building relationships and business," but added, "We're making some prudent moves to keep costs in line with market realities. The market has been slower to come back than earlier expectations." Previously, Jorgensen had told the *Chronicle* the firm was adding 45 employees in 2001, saying the personnel build-up was used "to smother clients with attention and build relationships" at a time when deals were scarce. Thomas Weisel Partners went through a second round of layoffs in November 2001, when 40 more employees were shown the door. Many of the cuts, a result of a near silent underwriting and merger market, came in the firm's San Francisco headquarters and, again, from its investment-banking operations.

The firm also lost three top executives bit by the entrepreneurial bug. In January 2002, founding partner Alan Menkes and two other partners announced they were striking out on their own. Menkes told *The Daily Deal* that the three wanted to focus on buyout opportunities while the firm's private equity operation was concentrating on growth investments. A firm spokesperson said the split was amicable but said it forced Thomas Weisel Partners to delay raising capital for its next private equity fund.

Japanese allies

In October 2001, Thomas Weisel Partners entered into an alliance with Nomura Holdings, Japan's largest brokerage firm. Nomura bought a 3.75 percent stake in Weisel Partners for $75 million, which valued the company at $2 billion, double the $1 billion valuation that the CalPERS' investment placed on Weisel less than two years earlier. Nomura also agreed to invest $125 million in private equity funds run by Weisel and, through its relationships with Japanese pension funds, promised to help raise a further $500 million for future Weisel private equity funds.

According to *The Wall Street Journal*, the alliance could help the two firms increase their cross-border M&A and other investment-banking deals between Japanese and American companies, an area that Goldman Sachs, Merrill Lynch, Morgan Stanley and other bulge bracket firms have historically dominated. CEO Thomas Weisel told the *Financial Times* that another rationale for the deal is for Nomura to market US private equity opportunities to Japanese investors. "Nomura has a huge footprint among Japanese institutions and retail investors, yet these investors have virtually no exposure to international private equity," Weisel said upon the announcement of the alliance.

Weisel Partners might also be setting its sights across the other ocean for additional partnerships. Dow Jones reported that the firm is considering similar private-equity and M&A alliances with European firms. Thomas Weisel confirmed the report, but denied that his company is "actively" looking for deals. Even so, word is the firm has discussed possible hook-ups with UK's HSBC Holdings and ABN Amro of the Netherlands. "We talk with them from time to time," Weisel admitted, "but I wouldn't consider those discussions being talks."

GETTING HIRED

Mission: tough, but not impossible

Insiders say the young and small Weisel Partners has toughened up its hiring standards in the past year. "Back in 2000, we would hire anybody. Now, we're doing a better job," says one source. A research analyst agrees. "The firm's motto used to be 'the best and the brightest,' but that definitely seemed to wane in 2000. Over the past year, though, the firm has become more selective." One banker says it's the firm's "small size and selectivity of the partners" that makes it difficult to land a job at TWP. However, the firm's small size can also work to a potential recruit's advantage. "The number of interviews is extensive, but getting in is not all that difficult as long as you find one ardent proponent internally," says one banker. Another source says, "Being small, the firm has the opportunity to make fast decisions. While Goldman requires 20 to 30 interviews over many separate days, we can make a decision after a recruit meets [a handful of] people," usually eight to 10. One employee admits that landing a position at the firm is "challenging," but says, "it's an entirely possible place to find a job. We hire a wide variety of people and really focus on fit, not just on being number one in your class."

That said, the firm mostly looks for new hires at top-notch undergrad and graduate programs, but does have "an open screening process for campuses we don't go to," says one contact. The interview process is "typical of the Street, with three to four rounds of interviews," say several insiders. Interview questions "focus on energy, drive, enthusiasm, as well as abilities and experience," says one source. Another contact remarks that recruits can also expect "very technical banking skill questions."

OUR SURVEY SAYS

Playing nice

Like its founder, TWP is an "entrepreneurial," "aggressive" and "competitive" place to work, say most insiders. Common catch phrases such as "non-hierarchical," "results-driven" and "team-oriented" are also frequently used in describing the firm's culture. TWP has a "hungry atmosphere with bulge-bracket experienced professionals," says one employee. "It's highly competitive, but not overbearing." Another contact says at TWP "one's individual efforts and achievements can really make a difference — and will be recognized." However, some employees say slack managers create a less than ideal environment. One source says, "It seems as if many partners came to Weisel hoping for a payday, with most having done well during last decade's bull market. So it's frustrating for lower rank colleagues who are generating far greater revenues to the firm." Another employee gripes, "Upper management's lack of skills, sophistication and market savvy creates an odd air of apathy among employees." At least one employee says that the firm's young age (it's only three years old) might have something to do with the negative opinions. "We're still moving a lot of pieces in an effort to develop a sustainable business, and the people side of our firm has lagged in its development."

For the most part, employees report good working relationships with their managers — and even better relationships with their peers or subordinates. "In general, top managers don't beat on lower level people like I've seen at other firms," says one research analyst. "That really doesn't fly here." Another employee calls managers' treatment of subordinates "excellent, unlike any other platform I've seen." Yet another contact observes that relationships are "very close between all members of the team, and we often socialize together after-hours." Some, though, call relationships with managers merely average. "It's adequate," says one employee, who adds, "But my relationships with subordinates are excellent."

Gotta have art

CEO Thom Weisel is not only an athlete, he's also an aesthete. Nearly all insiders agree that the firm's offices are impressive, crowned by the chief executive's own "fabulous" and "incredible" art collection. "Weisel has always splurged on pricy digs. All the offices double as a display for his art collection," says one employee. "The office environment is a personal focus of Thom," remarks one insider. It's "very comfortable with a great collection of modern art and an excellent infrastructure," says another source. However, Thom's sense of aesthetic has its weak points. According to one contact, "Amenities are excellent, but non-partner professionals must share offices — which is a complete hassle."

Close, but no cigars

TWP tries to pay its employees "middle of the Street" salaries, but, according to insiders, the firm doesn't always succeed. TWP's compensation has "generally been in line with industry averages, if not above," says one source, who adds, "The firm is very conscious of making salaries and bonuses competitive with the rest of the Street." Another contact remarks that TWP "strives to pay in Street ranges — not at the top of the range, but fairly in the range by class." Some contacts, however, strongly disagree. TWP "has acquired a reputation of paying below the Street," says one source. The firm "notoriously pays lower salaries with the promise of larger bonuses, but that's in a good year, which we didn't have in 2001," says another contact. One source gives the possible reason for the difference. TWP is a "smaller firm, so compensation is more volatile than larger firms. It's better in the good times, but worse in the bad times."

There's not much disagreement when it comes to benefits. As a result of the recent market downturn, TWP cut back on extras. "Perks are lame," gripes one employee. "Meals and travel allowances are a pittance, down enormously from 2000 levels." Another says, "Other than the gym membership, there's fewer perks than at the big bulge bracket firms." One insider even says it's now become "expensive as a professional to travel, because you must pick up the difference between firm policy and actual expenditures." At least one New York employee doesn't find it a hassle. "Meal allowance is reasonable, but transportation is weaker than that of my peer group. However, it's generally not a problem. It essentially means cabs, instead of car service, in the City."

Independent study

Although employees consistently give Weisel Partners' training program low marks, they report that the once non-existent program is showing improvement. "Training is very much needed. I was amazed that there was absolutely nothing in terms of training here when I joined two and a half years ago," says one insider. "For the first one and a half years the firm had little time to develop a training program," says another contact, who adds, "Gradually, though, they're improving in this area." Although the firm now has "a formal four-week training program, equivalent to the bulge bracket firms," sources still admit, "there's not tons of formal training."

"It's highly competitive, but not overbearing."

— Thomas Weisel Partners insider

THE VAULT 50:
26-50

Alliance Capital Management

1345 Avenue of the Americas
New York, NY 10105
Phone: (212) 969-1000
www.alliancecapital.com

DEPARTMENTS

Equity Management • Fixed Income
Management • Research

THE STATS

Chairman and CEO:
Bruce W. Calvert
Employer Type: Public Company
Stock Symbol: AC (NYSE)
2001 Revenue: $3.0 billion
2001 Net Income: $615 million
No. of Employees: 4,400
No. of Offices: 37

KEY COMPETITORS

Fidelity Investments
T. Rowe Price
Vanguard Group

UPPERS

• Excellent pay
• Reasonable hours

DOWNERS

• Bureaucracy
• Tough vacation policy

EMPLOYMENT CONTACT

Human Resources
Alliance Capital
1345 Avenue of the Americas
New York, NY 10105

THE BUZZ
WHAT EMPLOYEES AT OTHER FIRMS ARE SAYING

• "Blue chip buy side"
• "Average"
• "Big-time investor"
• "Hack shop"

THE SCOOP

With $433 billion in assets under management, Alliance is one of the world's largest investment managers. The firm offers institutional account management for corporate and public employee pension funds, and serves money market funds and deposit accounts. Alliance handles the employee benefit plans for 56 of the Fortune 100 companies in the U.S., and manages retirement funds for public employees in 36 of the 50 states.

The firm began in 1962 as the investment management department of Donaldson, Lufkin & Jenrette (DLJ). The department grew, and in 1971 was spun off into a full-fledged subsidiary of DLJ. In 1985 The Equitable Life Assurance Society of the United States (now called AXA Financial) acquired Alliance from DLJ. AXA Financial currently owns 53 percent of Alliance Capital.

GETTING HIRED

Many of the firm's equity, fixed-income analyst and portfolio manager positions are in its New York offices. Alliance says it looks for "knowledgeable and hardworking" applicants. The extent and type of knowledge required varies by position. The "Careers" link on the company's homepage takes potential applicants to a site hosted by HotJobs.com listing open positions at the company. Candidates can also submit a resume and cover letter directly to the company if interested in a position that's not listed as open.

OUR SURVEY SAYS

Some employees say "co-workers are generally okay," but criticize "upper-level bureaucracy" for "slow decision making." Other criticisms include a bad vacation policy and a year-end bonus that is reportedly great, though some complain it's based "more on corporate politics than merit." However, not all insiders agree with these assessments. Says one source, "The people are extremely open, kind and fun to work with." Earning "competitive pay," employees are generally expected to work 60-hour weeks, though "hours vary by department." Still, as one insider puts it, "The hours are reasonable, although overtime is expected without pay."

KPMG

345 Park Avenue
New York, NY 10154
Phone: (212) 758-9700
www.kpmg.com

DEPARTMENTS

Assurance • Consulting • Financial
Advisory • Tax and Legal

THE STATS

Chairman and CEO:
Eugene D. O'Kelly
Employer Type: Private Company
2001 Revenue: $11.7 billion
No. of Employees: 103,000
No. of Offices: 103

KEY COMPETITORS

Deloitte & Touche
Ernst & Young
PricewaterhouseCoopers

UPPERS

- Civic-minded firm
- Flexible hours

DOWNERS

- Low pay in accounting relative to other finance industries
- Turnover and travel typical of big accounting firm

EMPLOYMENT CONTACT

www.kpmgcareers.com

THE BUZZ
WHAT EMPLOYEES AT OTHER FIRMS ARE SAYING

- "Top accountant"
- "Boring"
- "Highly respectable, well-known"
- "Stodgy"

THE SCOOP

Formed by the 1987 merger of Peat Marwick International (PMI) and Klynveld Main Goerdeler (KMG), KPMG is the second-largest (in terms of revenue) of the Big Five firms, pulling in $11.7 billion in 2001 to PricewaterhouseCoopers' $22.3 billion. KPMG provides auditing, tax, legal and financial advisory services from its 750-plus locations in 152 countries. In February 2001, KPMG International spun off its consulting unit in an IPO, but kept (and still has) a 20 percent stake in the publicly traded KPMG Consulting. Late 2001 and early 2002 was a tough time for KPMG's corporate image. The firm faced several lawsuits and investigations, including one centering on the charge that Securities and Exchange Commission Chairman Harvey Pitt met privately with KPMG's CEO while the firm was being investigated for its work on Xerox's audit.

GETTING HIRED

Insiders report the firm stresses laid-back interviews, so don't expect a grilling. Rather, be prepared to talk about past experiences, computer skills, ability to work independently, why accounting and why KPMG. The firm's web site, www.kpmg.com, has a career section that lists openings all over the world. KPMG also maintains a separate web site, www.kpmgcampus.com, for school recruiting. The site allows candidates to submit resumes online, and offers interviewing tips and sample interview questions, including, "How do you define success?"

OUR SURVEY SAYS

It's not surprising that at a firm as large as KPMG, employees have many different takes on the corporate culture. One employee praised the "open-door" atmosphere, where "managers are able to answer questions and provide guidance." One tax consultant reports that the firm offers considerable flexibility in work schedules: "Some offices have flex time. For example, I work 10 to 7 to avoid rush hour traffic." At KPMG, "community involvement is encouraged and you are paid for four workday hours per month to perform volunteer work, provided that you match these hours with volunteer hours on your own time."

CIBC World Markets

622 Third Avenue
New York, NY 10017
www.cibcwm.com

DEPARTMENTS

Asset Management • Asset
Securitization • Equities •
Investment Banking • Merchant
Banking

THE STATS

Chairman and CEO: David Kassie
Employer Type: Subsidiary of
Canadian Imperial Bank of
Commerce
2001 Revenues: $2.6 billion
2001 Net Income: $526 million
No. of Employees: 4,900
No. of Offices: 25

KEY COMPETITORS

Bear Stearns
Lehman Brothers
TD Securities

UPPERS

• Generous compensation
• Lean deal teams mean early
  responsibility

DOWNERS

• Competitive culture
• Little known outside its niche

EMPLOYMENT CONTACT

Campus Recruiting
CIBC World Markets USA
622 Third Avenue
35th Floor
New York, NY 10017
campus_recruiting@us.cibc.com

THE BUZZ
WHAT EMPLOYEES AT OTHER FIRMS ARE SAYING

• "Improving all the time"
• "Not committed to U.S."
• "Strongest in Canada"
• "Trying to get big and not
  making it"

THE SCOOP

CIBC World Markets is the investment-banking and brokerage arm of the Canadian Imperial Bank of Commerce, Canada's second-largest bank. Like most investment banks with a commercial banking parent, CIBC provides a one-stop shopping experience for corporations, allowing clients access to debt and equity markets, asset securitization, leveraged lending and mergers and acquisitions advice. While many growing investment banks aspire to become bulge-bracket firms, CIBC has a different approach. Rather than pursuing the big clients that have existing relationships with banking behemoths, CIBC has set its sights on mid-sized corporations.

GETTING HIRED

Like most investment banks, CIBC World Markets is toughening standards for new hires. "Right now you could have all the top credentials and still not get a job due to the slump in I-banking," reports one source. The firm's method doesn't deviate from the typical hiring process. "A person will have a first round interview at their college," reports one source. "If they are selected for a final round interview, they will come to the New York office where they will have four interviews with senior bankers." "Overall, [expect] more than 15 individual interviews with mostly junior and senior bankers," says another employee. One contact reports getting questions about financial statements and discounted cash flows.

OUR SURVEY SAYS

While most assert that CIBC is a "meritocracy" with an "entrepreneurial" feel and a flat management structure, the firm can be "very competitive" and is often a "harsh working environment." "CIBC has a firmly entrenched face time culture," says one contact. "Even if you have absolutely nothing to do, you are expected to sit there and pretend that you are doing something useful." "Compensation at CIBC has tended to be on the high range for the Street," reports one well-paid analyst. The firm also has a 401(k) on par with its competitors and a private equity fund.

VAULT
29
PRESTIGE RANKING

Allen & Company

711 Fifth Avenue
9th Floor
New York, NY 10022
Phone: (212) 832-8000
Fax: (212) 832-8023

DEPARTMENTS

Asset Management • Investment Banking • Sales and Trading • Venture Capital

THE STATS

CEO: Herbert Allen, Jr.
Employer Type: Private Company
No. of Employees: 200
No. of Offices: 1

KEY COMPETITORS

Goldman Sachs
Lazard
Morgan Stanley

UPPERS

- Lucrative profit sharing
- Schmooze with the stars

DOWNERS

- Bad deals can savage salaries
- Extraordinarily competitive and difficult hiring process

EMPLOYMENT CONTACT

Human Resources
Allen & Company
711 Fifth Avenue
9th Floor
New York, NY 10022

THE BUZZ
WHAT EMPLOYEES AT OTHER FIRMS ARE SAYING

- "Entertainment powerhouse"
- "Narrow focus"
- "Very sexy"
- "Elite, clubby"

THE SCOOP

Brothers Charles and Herbert Allen founded Allen & Co. as a partnership in 1922. The company provides a mix of investment banking (including securities underwriting and mergers and acquisitions), private equity and venture capital and investment management services. Allen & Co. really took off when Herbert Allen, Jr., took over the reins of the firm in 1966 when he was 26 years old. Under Allen, the firm has established itself as the preeminent entertainment boutique bank. "Deals just don't get done in Hollywood unless [Allen & Co.] are involved," Barry Diller, then the chairman and CEO at USA Networks, told *Forbes*. Recent clients include Jim Henson Co. and Primedia. The firm is famous for its annual media industry conference in Sun Valley, Idaho.

GETTING HIRED

Allen & Co.'s personnel department does not accept outside calls, does not maintain a job hotline, and does not publicize job openings. The firm does, however, accept resumes mailed to its headquarters. Allen hires only MBAs as bankers and typically requires at least two to three years of experience. Insiders say getting a job directly out of business school is rare, and getting hired right out of college is "next to impossible."

OUR SURVEY SAYS

Bankers say working at Allen & Co. makes them feel like members of "a very special, secret society." Employees describe their offices as "classy," with "lots of dark mahogany on walls and desks" and "original Norman Rockwell paintings." Dress at Allen is "sharp but conservative" even though employees often work with "flashy media clients." In addition to "above-average" bonuses, sources adore the opportunity to "invest in Allen & Co. deals and share in profits." One banker says, "You must have a significant portion of your net worth at risk if you want to work here, and you must be a fee generator soon after arriving." Confides another contact: "There's salary plus a percentage of the fees from deals that you work on. You get paid when a fee comes in — no waiting for year-end bonus."

SG Cowen

1221 Avenue of the Americas
New York, NY 10020
Phone: (212) 278-6000
www.sgcowen.com

DEPARTMENTS

Corporate Bond Brokerage •
Corporate Finance • Fixed Income •
Institutional Sales and Trading •
Mergers and Acquisitions • Private
Equity • Research

THE STATS

President and CEO:
Kim Fennebresque
Employer Type: Subsidiary of
Société Général Group
No. of Employees: 1,500
No. of Offices: 13

KEY COMPETITORS

Banc of America Securities
Deutsche Bank

THE BUZZ
WHAT EMPLOYEES AT OTHER FIRMS ARE SAYING

- "Niche players"
- "Mid-tier firm, used to be tops"
- "Highly competitive"
- "Small-time"

UPPERS

- Contact with seniors
- Friendly culture

DOWNERS

- Narrow industry specialization for
  junior bankers
- Sparse support staff

EMPLOYMENT CONTACT

**Investment Banking (New York,
Boston, San Francisco)**

Analyst Recruiting
Jennifer Munoz
SG Cowen
1221 Avenue of the Americas
New York, NY 10020
Analyst.US-IB@us.socgen.com

Associate Recruiting
Alexa Vieira
SG Cowen
1221 Avenue of the Americas
New York, NY 10020
Associate.US-IB@us.socgen.com

Research (Boston)

Associate Recruiting
Colleen Finn
SG Cowen
Two International Place
Boston, MA 02110
Phone: (617) 946-3950
Fax: (617) 428-4658

THE SCOOP

SG Cowen was formed in 1998 when French bank Société Général acquired Cowen & Co., a New York investment-banking boutique specializing in the health care, technology and communications industries. Société Général paid $540 million for Cowen, which was founded in 1919. Société Général expanded Cowen's focus beyond its three core industries and the new firm began working in the gaming and leisure (including a respected sports advisory group) and power and utilities areas. In September 2001, the firm laid off 72 U.S. employees, or 11 percent of its staff in the country. The firm added investment banking and research staff in the consumer growth sector in June 2002. In January 2002, SG Cowen was named as a co-defendant in a $1 billion lawsuit stemming from the actions of a former broker who allegedly cheated clients out of as much as $125 million over 15 years.

GETTING HIRED

SG Cowen says it looks for accomplished and motivated individuals with strong academic backgrounds, and analytical, computer and communication skills. SG Cowen's web site has a separate section for investment banking, www.sginvestmentbanking.com, which contains job descriptions and contact information. The firm gives presentations to undergraduates and graduates at several schools, including NYU, Columbia, Cornell, Emory, Georgetown and UCLA. An associate explains her interview process: "I did a two-on-one for the first round. The second round was a round robin of one-on-ones. I interviewed with four people, and each interview was 30 to 45 minutes."

OUR SURVEY SAYS

With a small- to medium-size company atmosphere, insiders note that each department and office at SG Cowen has its own distinct culture. However, insiders agree that bankers are in general closer to each other at SG Cowen than at bulge-bracket firms. One source praises relationships with the company brass, saying upper management is interested in developing the abilities of its staff and are "even willing to make themselves available to anyone who needs them."

FleetBoston Financial

100 Federal Street
Boston, MA 02110
Phone: (617) 346-4000
www.fleet.com

DEPARTMENTS

Asset Management • Brokerage •
Commercial Banking • Investment
Banking • Retail Banking • Venture
Capital

THE STATS

Chairman: Terrence Murray
President and CEO:
Charles (Chad) K. Gifford
Employer Type: Public Company
Ticker Symbol: FBF (NYSE)
2001 Revenues: $19.1 billion
2001 Net Income: $931 million
No. of Employees: 56,000
No. of Offices: 250

KEY COMPETITORS

Bank of America
Citibank
J.P. Morgan Chase
Wachovia

UPPERS

• Job training
• Paid volunteer days
• Tuition reimbursement

DOWNERS

• Excessive bureaucracy
• Long work days

EMPLOYMENT CONTACT

Fleet, Employment Shared Services
111 Westminster Street
Mailcode: RI DE 03314G
Providence, RI 02903
college_recruiting@fleet.com

THE BUZZ
WHAT EMPLOYEES AT OTHER FIRMS ARE SAYING

• "Respectable"
• "Confused"
• "More commercial in focus"
• "Past its prime"

THE SCOOP

FleetBoston Financial is the holding company for one of the top 10 financial services firms in the U.S. and is one of the largest banks in the Northeast, where it has 1,500 branches. FleetBoston was formed by the merger of Fleet Financial and BankBoston in October 1999. FleetBoston offers the typical range of commercial and retail banking services, including deposits and loans. FleetBoston announced a major shift in strategy in early 2002. The company said it would begin to exit non-core businesses and focus on its less risky core units, mainly personal financial services and wholesale banking. FleetBoston initially planned to sell its troubled investment-banking subsidiary Robertson Stephens and its AFSA student loan servicing business. Fleet later shuttered Robertson Stephens after no buyer could be found.

GETTING HIRED

Fleet maintains a large database of resumes at its Rhode Island resume center. Applicants must indicate the department code that corresponds to individual job openings listed on the company's job hotline and on its web site, www.fleet.com. The site also lists internship opportunities, which are offered on an "as-needed basis," and the universities and colleges (all Northeast schools) that Fleet visits to find recruits. Candidates who do not attend one of the schools on the list can send a resume and cover letter to the firm at college_recruiting@fleet.com.

OUR SURVEY SAYS

Fleet employees call the company "meritocratic" and say that "quality work is always recognized." While some say that the bank offers "substandard" pay for the banking industry in exchange for "long workweeks," others say that the "advancement opportunities" and "prestige of working for the region's leading bank" provide adequate compensation. "We have a 401(k) plan where Fleet matches, dollar for dollar, up to 6 percent of your salary," reports one insider. Also, know that "the medical, dental and insurance benefits are very good."

9 West 57th Street
New York, NY 10019
Phone: (212) 847-5000
www.bofasecurities.com

DEPARTMENTS

Capital Markets • Floating Rate
Debt • Global Derivatives • Global
Foreign Exchange • Mergers and
Acquisitions • Mortgage-Backed
Securities • Portfolio Management •
Research • Sales and Trading •
Structured Finance

THE STATS

**President, Corporate and Global
Investment Bank:** Edward J. Brown, III
**President, Banc of America
Securities:** Carter McClelland
Employer Type:
Subsidiary of Bank of America
2001 Revenue: $9.2 billion
2001 Net Income: $1.9 billion
No. of Employees: 7,300
No. of Offices: 54

KEY COMPETITORS

Citigroup
J.P. Morgan Chase
Lehman Brothers
Merrill Lynch

THE BUZZ
WHAT EMPLOYEES AT OTHER FIRMS ARE SAYING

- "Rising star"
- "Killed the Montgomery
  franchise"
- "Wanna-be investment bank"

UPPERS

- "Livable" hours
- Meaningful assignments for junior
  bankers

DOWNERS

- Return to formal dress
- Sometimes contentious
  relationships with senior bankers

EMPLOYMENT CONTACT

Banc of America Securities
Campus Recruiting
9 West 57th Street
New York, NY 10019
www.bofasecurities.com/campus

THE SCOOP

Born of a complicated merger history, Banc of America Securities is the investment-banking arm of the giant Bank of America Corp., the Charlotte, N.C.-based commercial bank. Banc of America Securities has focused on companies in eight primary industries: technology, consumer retail products, health care, real estate, financial services, media and telecommunications, natural resources, and diversified industries. In 2001 the firm went through several rounds of job cuts totalling approximately 700 and closed of some of its smaller U.S. offices. On the plus side, BofA Securities placed seventh in *The Wall Street Journal*'s 2002 "Best on the Street" Analyst Survey; the firm picked up eight awards for its stock-picking prowess.

GETTING HIRED

Insiders report that Banc of America Securities recruits from "Ivy League and larger regional schools." Candidates can expect "one or two on-campus interviews followed by a Super Saturday event" where you'll meet at least five people. One MBA candidate who went through two rounds of interviews says the questions covered a lot of ground: "The first round is more technical and more 'Why do you like us and why do you want to do banking?' The second round is definitely determining whether [the candidate] fits with employees at [the company]."

OUR SURVEY SAYS

Insiders report that the firm culture "is relatively collegial. Junior level people work directly with MDs and VPs and the structure is relatively flat." While that provides junior employees with a lot of responsibility, it also puts them at the mercy of their bosses. "MDs and VPs have no problem giving work to ruin an evening or weekend when it is not necessary," fumes one banker. The firm announced a switch back to formal business wear in early 2002, but allows casual Fridays during the summer.

In terms of diversity, most bankers report that BofA Securities is "fairly diverse for the industry," though at least one contact mentions the firm has "very few females" in the senior ranks. Hours are considered "livable" and one M&A associate estimates an average workweek as "ranging from 65 to 75 hours."

Houlihan Lokey Howard & Zukin

1930 Century Park West
Los Angeles, CA 90067
Phone: (310) 553-8871
www.hlhz.com

DEPARTMENTS

Corporate Alliances • Corporate Finance • Distressed Transactions • Financial Opinions and Advisory Services • Financial Restructuring • Merchant Banking • Mergers and Acquisitions

THE STATS

Chairman: O. Kit Lokey
CEO: Franklin W. "Fritz" Hobbs
Employer Type: Private Company
No. of Employees: 500
No. of Offices: 9

KEY COMPETITORS

Blackstone
Jefferies & Company
Lazard
Merrill Lynch

UPPERS

- Client exposure, even for junior employees
- Major player in booming restructuring market

DOWNERS

- Little-known outside restructuring practice
- Tough, tough hours

EMPLOYMENT CONTACT

Houlihan Lokey Howard & Zukin
1930 Century Park West
Los Angeles, CA 90067
Fax: (310) 553-2173
employment-LA@hlhz.com

THE BUZZ
WHAT EMPLOYEES AT OTHER FIRMS ARE SAYING

- "Small, but sharp firm"
- "Hot now, but overrated"
- "Emerging force in restructurings"
- "Great restructuring practice, pity about the rest of the firm"

THE SCOOP

Founded in Los Angeles in 1970, Houlihan Lokey Howard & Zukin focuses on specialized investment-banking services to privately held middle-market companies. For the past 10 years, Houlihan Lokey has ranked among the top 20 M&A advisors in the U.S., and its financial restructuring group is the world's largest. The recent economic slump has been a boon to Houlihan Lokey's bankruptcy and restructuring division. One of the firm's recent clients was Excite@Home, which filed for Chapter 11 bankruptcy in September 2001, the third-largest Internet bankruptcy to date. In addition to its respected M&A and restructuring practices, the firm advises its clients on management buyouts, tax and estate-related valuations, and private placements.

GETTING HIRED

Insiders say Houlihan Lokey is "looking for technical people that fit in with the firm's culture and have a finance background." At Houlihan Lokey, "pedigree on resume goes a long way," says one contact. The firm's interview process puts a heavy emphasis on finance and accounting knowledge, and includes a written test on those subjects. There are usually two or three rounds, with the last one being a "Super Friday" that consists of a handful of interviews with associates, VPs and MDs.

OUR SURVEY SAYS

Houlihan Lokey has a distinct West Coast feel, according to its bankers. "[The firm] is aggressive and fast paced, but a little more relaxed than other firms because of the LA influence," says one insider. Houlihan Lokey is "like the Wild West in some ways," reports one cowboy. While he says that leads to an "entrepreneurial" atmosphere with "aggressive growth," he concedes that "sometimes [the firm is] not as professional as I would want." The firm traditionally trails the industry in compensation, but has recently been offering better-than-average pay. "I have heard that our [pay] is significantly above average, in part because we are so heavily involved with financial restructuring, which is the most active it has been in a decade," says one source.

Charles Schwab

101 Montgomery Street
San Francisco, CA 94104
Phone: (415) 627-7000
www.schwab.com

DEPARTMENTS

Capital Markets • Electronic
Brokerage • Retail Services •
Retirement Plan Services

THE STATS

Chairman and Co-CEO:
Charles R. Schwab
President and Co-CEO:
David S. Pottruck
Employer Type: Public Company
Ticker Symbol: SCH (NYSE)
2001 Revenue: $4.4 billion
2001 Net Income: $199 million
No. of Employees: 18,600
No. of Offices: 434

KEY COMPETITORS

Alliance Capital Management
Fidelity Investments
T. Rowe Price

UPPERS

• Eye-popping perks
• Great diversity

DOWNERS

• Average base pay
• Some periods of intense work

EMPLOYMENT CONTACT

Charles Schwab
101 Montgomery Street
San Francisco, CA 94104

THE BUZZ
WHAT EMPLOYEES AT OTHER FIRMS ARE SAYING

• "Everybody's stockbroker"
• "Big, conservative, dull"
• "Great reputation"
• "Volumes and margins are falling"

THE SCOOP

Charles Schwab began his finance career in 1963 by founding an investment advisory newsletter with two partners. In the late 1960s, Schwab and friends started First Commander Corp., a brokerage firm based in San Francisco. Schwab bought out his partners' stake in 1973 (renaming First Commander after himself) and sold the firm to BankAmerica in 1983. Three years later, he organized a leveraged buyout of the firm, which he took public in 1987. Schwab (the company) currently provides brokerage and asset-management services and has a respected online brokerage.

GETTING HIRED

Insiders say that hiring at Schwab is getting tight. "With the economy hurting it is not that easy [to get hired]," reports one contact. Prospective employees can expect at least two interviews with "standard questions," including "How do you handle change?" and "How do you handle stress?" Know the firm's web site, www.schwab.com. "You're told to look at the firm's web site and get familiar with it because you're going to be asked questions about it," reports one source. You'll also find job listings and an online application center there.

OUR SURVEY SAYS

More than anything, Schwab is praised for its diversity. "Schwab prides itself on its diversity and having employees that appreciate how much that enhances a company's performance," says one insider. The firm also pushes teamwork. "You have to have a good work ethic," warns one contact. "Your performance contributes to the team performance, which affects bonuses."

Speaking of compensation, Schwab's base salaries are a little on the light side, but the firm makes up for it. "Starting salaries won't knock your socks off, but the company match on money put into one's 401(k) is generous. It won't seem like all that big a deal at first, but they keep giving us special grants of stock, which splits all the time, and quarterly bonuses, and lots of little extras and perks along the way." Another insider reports that "pay will always be low to start off with until you get your professional Series 7 license to trade securities."

Bank of America

100 North Tryon Street
Charlotte, NC 28255
Phone: (888) 279-3475
www.bankofamerica.com

DEPARTMENTS

Asset Management • Consumer and
Commercial Banking • Global
Corporate and Investment Banking •
Principal Investing

THE STATS

Chairman and CEO:
Kenneth D. Lewis
Employer Type: Public Company
Ticker Symbol: BAC (NYSE)
2001 Revenue: $35.0 billion
2001 Net Income: $8.0 billion
No. of Employees: 142,700
No. of Offices: 4,500

KEY COMPETITORS

Citigroup
First Union
FleetBoston Financial
J.P. Morgan Chase

UPPERS

- Entrepreneurial culture
- Growing in investment banking and asset management

DOWNERS

- Big bank equals big bureaucracy
- Lacks Wall Street image

EMPLOYMENT CONTACT

Bank of America
Scanning Operations
Attn: WWW
CA4-707-01-37
PO Box 37000
San Francisco, CA 94137
careers@bankofamerica.com

THE BUZZ
WHAT EMPLOYEES AT OTHER FIRMS ARE SAYING

- "On the move"
- "Is there a credit that didn't default?"
- "Solid, respectable"

THE SCOOP

Bank of America (BofA) is the nation's largest bank in terms of deposits, and the country's second largest in terms of assets. Formed by the $43 billion merger of BankAmerica and NationsBank in September 1998, the Charlotte, N.C.-based BofA has approximately 4,300 branches in 21 states and the District of Columbia. With 8 percent of all U.S. deposits and 29 million households as customers, BofA is also the country's largest bank in terms of accounts under management.

GETTING HIRED

At Bank of America, MBA-level associates are recruited directly by each department. "Here's a tip," whispers one former employee. "You can't always choose your city. [The firm] will try, but for example, if you want to work in high-yield bonds, you aren't going to be working in San Francisco." The firm recruits on the undergrad level at UC Berkeley, UC Davis, Stanford, the University of Wisconsin and the University of North Carolina at Charlotte. Candidates from other schools and working professionals can search the company's job listings and submit a resume online at www.bankofamerica.com.

OUR SURVEY SAYS

Like any company that's grown through merger, Bank of America's culture has gone through some changes. "This used to be an organization where we felt like family," says a manager. The company is now "an extremely large retail bank with an extremely large retail bank culture." This shift in the corporate atmosphere has nevertheless fostered an "entrepreneurial" environment in which new employees receive "immediate exposure to clients, upper management and other bank groups." While some feel that the changes have been detrimental to employee morale, others approve of "a new aggressive attitude with an emphasis on teamwork."

Many insiders rave about their bosses. "The exposure to top management is gratifying," says one associate. "The culture involves teamwork, working hard and playing hard. You will not find many jerks in the organization, as they get culled fast," comments one insider.

VAULT
36
PRESTIGE
RANKING

WR Hambrecht + Co.

539 Bryant Street
Suite 100
San Francisco, CA 94107
Phone: (415) 551-8600
www.wrhambrecht.com

DEPARTMENTS

Brokerage • Corporate Finance
(Advisory and Underwriting) •
Equity Research • Private Equity •
Sales and Trading

THE STATS

Chairman and CEO:
William R. Hambrecht
Employer Type: Private Company
No. of Offices: 4

KEY COMPETITORS

SoundView Technology Group
Thomas Weisel Partners

UPPERS

• Early responsibility
• Friendly atmosphere

DOWNERS

• Niche focus dangerous in down
  times
• Pay below market

EMPLOYMENT CONTACT

employment@wrhambrecht.com

THE BUZZ
WHAT EMPLOYEES AT OTHER FIRMS ARE SAYING

• "Interesting concept, ahead of its
  time"
• "Has been at an early age"
• "Rising star"
• "Smaller player"

THE SCOOP

William Hambrecht founded his eponymous investment bank in January 1998, shortly after leaving another self-named bank, Hambrecht & Quist (now a part of J.P. Morgan Chase). Hambrecht's new firm, which has financial backing from financial services heavy hitters like Fidelity Investments, American Century Investments and American Express, provides underwriting and advisory services, brokerage, equity research, private equity and sales and trading services. The firm is best known for its "Open IPO" process, a system that sells IPO shares in a Dutch auction, where prices are determined by online bids. The method was cited by *Fortune* as an alternative to the usual IPO system that has drawn complaints of favoritism and corruption. WR Hambrecht + Co. has similar processes for its bond and secondary equity offerings.

GETTING HIRED

In a market unforgiving to niche banks, WR Hambrecht + Co. has scaled back its recruiting while it waits for a revival. The firm's web site, www.wrhambrecht.com, has a small career section that posts job openings. "They run it like a boutique," says one source. "[There's] no structured process per se." The firm's on-campus presence is currently minimal to non-existent. WR Hambrecht + Co. is doing virtually no recruiting on-campus during the current downturn, and has rescinded offers in 2001.

OUR SURVEY SAYS

The firm's culture is called "boutiquey" though generally "friendly." Small firms do have their advantages. "If you're an analyst coming into the firm you get exposure you won't get at a bulge bracket," says one insider. "Responsibility is something you get up front." The pay is a source of complaint: the firm capped salaries for all revenue producers at $60,000 in September 2001, though it did increase the revenue sharing payout percentages. WR Hambrecht + Co. does have decent 401(k) and health care plans and offers incoming employees stock options, once a necessary perk but now a reminder of a bygone, irrational era. "We were going to retire as multi-millionaires when the firm went public or was acquired," says one contact, reminiscing about better times. "It was kind of like a dot-com."

37 TIAA-CREF

730 Third Avenue
New York, NY 10017-3206
Phone: (212) 490-9000
www.tiaa-cref.org

DEPARTMENTS

Accounting • Financial Services •
Insurance • Investment Operations •
Pension Consulting Services

THE STATS

Chairman, President and CEO:
John H. Biggs
Employer Type: Not-for-Profit
2001 Revenue: $24.2 billion
2001 Net Income: $585.2 million
No. of Employees: 6,500
No. of Offices: 26

KEY COMPETITORS

Charles Schwab
Fidelity Investments
Vanguard Group

UPPERS

• Reasonable hours
• Responsibility at an early level

DOWNERS

• Bureaucratic, conservative culture

EMPLOYMENT CONTACT

TIAA-CREF
HR Staffing
730 Third Avenue
New York, NY 10017
Fax: (212) 916-5883
staffing5@tiaa-cref.org

THE BUZZ
WHAT EMPLOYEES AT OTHER FIRMS ARE SAYING

• "Best benefits of all finance
  firms"
• "Never heard of them"
• "Respected investment firm"

THE SCOOP

The Teachers Insurance and Annuity Association and College Retirement Equities Fund (TIAA-CREF) is a nationwide retirement system that manages the pension plans of more than two million teachers and staff members at colleges, universities and other nonprofit educational and research institutions. The firm consists of TIAA, which was founded in 1918 by the Carnegie Foundation for the Advancement of Teaching to provide portable pension programs for educators, and CREF, which was established in 1952 to provide variable annuities. The firm began offering investment products like mutual funds, IRAs and insurance to the general public in 1998. In 2001 *Fortune* magazine ranked the firm 24th on its annual list of the best companies for minorities, citing TIAA-CREF's practice of "preparing minorities for executive jobs with rotations through various departments, including the chairman's office." In addition, the firm garnered high marks on *Fortune*'s 2002 list of the most admired companies.

GETTING HIRED

The firm's web site, www.tiaa-cref.org, has a searchable list of job openings grouped by state. Send or fax resumes to TIAA-CREF's human resources department at its New York headquarters. Experience matters; the firm hires virtually no one straight out of college or business school for positions in the investment management division.

OUR SURVEY SAYS

The organization's claims to support diversity are echoed by employees, who describe a "very diverse and women/minority friendly" environment, with "equal opportunity for everybody based on merit." Says one insider, "They are very good at honoring and respecting all people." TIAA "will give you a lot of responsibility fairly quickly, but will do it in such a way that you can't cause too much damage to the policyholders or yourself if you are wrong," reports one insider. That contact adds, "All investments go through a thorough screening process, so everyone has 'signed on' when the money goes out the door."

VAULT
38
PRESTIGE
RANKING

CalPERS

Lincoln Plaza
400 P Street
Sacramento, CA 95814
Phone: (916) 326-3892
www.calpers.ca.gov

DEPARTMENTS

Actuarial and Employer Services •
Asset Management • Benefit
Services • Fiscal Services • Health
Benefit Services

THE STATS

President: William D. Crist
Employer Type: Government
No. of Employees: 1,600
No. of Offices: 9

KEY COMPETITORS

TIAA-CREF

UPPERS

- A giant and leader in its industry
- Relaxed environment that comes with working in public sector

DOWNERS

- Limited compensation working in public sector
- State agency equals governmental bureaucracy

EMPLOYMENT CONTACT

Human Resources
CalPERS
Lincoln Plaza
400 P Street
Sacramento, CA 95814
Fax: (916) 326-3065

THE BUZZ
WHAT EMPLOYEES AT OTHER FIRMS ARE SAYING

- "Big-time investor"
- "Wouldn't want to work there"
- "Great firm"
- "Stodgy, but influential"

THE SCOOP

In 1932 a state law created CalPERS, the California Public Employees' Retirement System. CalPERS administers investment and health care plans for active and retired state employees. With more than $150 billion in assets, CalPERS is currently the largest public pension fund in the U.S. (and the third largest in the world). In May 2002, James Burton, CalPERS CEO for over seven years, announced that he would be leaving the firm in the fall of 2002 to pursue work in the private sector.

CalPERS is known for using its power as a shareholder to voice its opinions on how corporations that it invests in should be run. CalPERS' officials often use the term "shareowner" instead of "shareholder" to stress the long-term commitment to an investment. Each year CalPERS combs its domestic stock portfolio for the poorest long-term performers and publishes the losers in a "Focus List," which includes specific changes that CalPERS would like to see implemented.

GETTING HIRED

CalPERS is a state agency, so its employees are civil servants. Therefore, potential employees must take an exam. The State Personnel Board (SPB) administers the tests for most positions, but CalPERS does oversee the testing and hiring process for some of the investment, actuarial and IT openings. CalPERS offers continuous testing, while the SPB administers tests on an as-needed basis. With the state closely involved in the hiring, it's a "very structured process," says one source, who adds that employee selectivity is "limited by the state civil service system."

OUR SURVEY SAYS

CalPERS lists its core values as "quality, respect, openness, accountability and integrity." According to one insider, these values "do reflect the culture" of the firm. The employee goes on to say that senior managers are "open and communicative." One contact explains that although the civil service system is "limiting with respect to compensation, the State Personnel Board does have some flexibility for certain staff in compensation, including bonuses."

Legg Mason

100 Light Street
Baltimore, MD 21202
Phone: (877) 534-4627
www.leggmason.com

DEPARTMENTS

Asset Management • Capital
Markets • Private Client

THE STATS

Chairman, President and CEO:
Raymond A. Mason
Employer Type: Public Company
Ticker Symbol: LM (NYSE)
2001 Revenues: $1.6 billion
2001 Net Income: $153 million
No. of Employees: 5,380
No of Offices: 142

KEY COMPETITORS

Bear Stearns
Merrill Lynch
T. Rowe Price

UPPERS

• Mid-level work for junior-level
  bankers
• Shiny, happy culture

DOWNERS

• Pay less than New York, San
  Francisco
• Regional focus, reputation

EMPLOYMENT CONTACT

www.leggmason.com/careers

THE BUZZ
WHAT EMPLOYEES AT OTHER FIRMS ARE SAYING

• "Steady middle-market player"
• "Why in Baltimore?"
• "Great stock pickers"

THE SCOOP

Legg Mason traces its beginnings to 1899, when George Mackubin founded an eponymous brokerage firm in Baltimore. Mackubin soon hired 19-year-old John Legg, Jr., for a low-level position. Legg became a partner by 1904 and gained sole control of the firm 45 years later. Legg & Co. (the firm was renamed when Legg and Mackubin split and again after Legg's death in 1963) merged with Mason & Co., a brokerage founded by Raymond Mason, in 1970. Today's Legg Mason provides investment management services to institutions and individuals (including institutional asset management, wealth management and mutual funds) and capital markets services (including investment banking, merchant banking, sales and trading and equity research).

GETTING HIRED

"The firm has targeted the top 15-20 schools" for recruiting, reports one insider. That includes schools like Harvard, Wharton and the University of Virginia. Legg Mason puts in a little extra legwork. "They focus on regional schools that bulge brackets don't focus on," says another source, including the University of Maryland, Villanova and the College of William and Mary. The full recruiting schedule is available on Legg Mason's web site, www.leggmason.com. Expect the typical process: an on-campus interview, followed by a super weekend. Interviews are a mix of technical and fit questions.

OUR SURVEY SAYS

Legg Mason's culture is "great," say insiders. "It's one of the things that drew me here," beams one contact. That source cites "[t]he level of responsibility you get on deals" as one of the best things about Legg Mason. Another insider notes the competitiveness is toned down at Legg. "There isn't the cut-throat culture of bulge-bracket firms [here]." Pay is "on par with other regional investment banks" if less than big cities. Working in Baltimore softens that blow, as the cost of living is much less than cities like New York or San Francisco. Hours can vary, but 70-90 per week seems to be the average.

U.S. Bancorp Piper Jaffray

800 Nicollet Mall
Suite 800
Minneapolis, MN 55402
Phone: (612) 303-6000
www.piperjaffray.com

DEPARTMENTS

Equity Capital Markets • Fixed
Income Capital Markets • Private
Advisory Services • Venture Capital

THE STATS

President and CEO: Andrew S. Duff
Employer Type:
Subsidiary of U.S. Bancorp
No. of Employees: 2,900
No. of Offices: 125

KEY COMPETITORS

Banc of America Securities
CIBC World Markets
Thomas Weisel Partners

UPPERS

• High level of job responsibility
• Street-comparable pay for junior bankers

DOWNERS

• Lack of diversity
• Long hours

EMPLOYMENT CONTACT

ECM Employment Services
Representative
800 Nicollet Mall
Minneapolis, MN 55402-7020
Phone: (800) 333-6000
applicant@pjc.com

THE BUZZ
WHAT EMPLOYEES AT OTHER FIRMS ARE SAYING

• "Strong regional player"
• "Haven't seen them in awhile"
• "Great research"
• "Has been"

THE SCOOP

Minneapolis-based U.S. Bancorp Piper Jaffray is the investment-banking unit of U.S. Bancorp, the eighth-largest retail bank in the U.S. in terms of assets. In May 1998, U.S. Bancorp, also headquartered in Minneapolis, paid $730 million to acquire Piper Jaffray, a firm founded in 1913 by H.C. Piper, Sr. and C.P. Jaffray. U.S. Bancorp Piper Jaffray offers its clients, most of which are small to mid-size companies, a range of I-banking services, including underwriting, M&A, research, sales and trading. In addition, the firm has a venture capital arm and an asset management division that is known as U.S. Bancorp Asset Management. In February 2001, the firm was named "Middle Market Mergers and Acquisitions Bank of the Year" by *Mergers and Acquisitions* magazine in its annual "Best in M&A Awards." Still, the firm's strongest unit might be its fixed-income division, rather than its M&A group. The firm has long been the established leader in municipal underwriting in the Midwest, and the firm regularly dominates the U.S. small municipal offering market.

GETTING HIRED

U.S. Bancorp Piper Jaffray's web site, www.piperjaffray.com, provides a listing of current job opportunities and contact addresses. In investment banking, Piper's analyst recruiting covers about 50 major colleges and universities with actual campus visits at about six schools. Associate recruiting has been focused on the top 10 business schools for the past 15 years. The associate recruiting process includes on-campus presentations and interviews with dinners for pre-selected candidates.

OUR SURVEY SAYS

Piper Jaffray is unique because "associates don't do any modeling; analysts do all the modeling," reports one insider. "It's great for an analyst, because you do all the models, including the complex ones." The firm offers "healthy salaries" that tend to vary with the performance of the stock market and "some of the best employee benefits in the industry." According to one insider, "First-year associates can get paid close to what they get paid in New York. Where it gets skewed is after four or five years. Here, people make a million dollars but it's not the rule."

Broadview International

One Bridge Plaza
Fort Lee, NJ 07024
Phone: (201) 346-9000
www.broadview.com

DEPARTMENTS

Late-stage Private Equity • M&A
and Private Placement Advisory •
Venture Capital

THE STATS

CEO: Paul Deninger
Employer Type: Private Company
No. of Employees: 200
No. of Offices: 4

KEY COMPETITORS

Credit Suisse First Boston
Lazard
Morgan Stanley
Thomas Weisel Partners

UPPERS

- Hours aren't bad for I-banking
- Junior employees given a lot of responsibility

DOWNERS

- Tech focus was devastating to business
- Uncertainty surrounding possible sale

EMPLOYMENT CONTACT

René Kraenzlin
Managing Director and Chief
Administrative Officer
Broadview International
One Bridge Plaza
Fort Lee, NJ 07024
Fax: (201) 346-9191

M&A advisory
AssociateRecruiter@Broadview.com
AnalystRecruiter@Broadview.com

IT, HR, Marketing and Finance
Careers@Broadview.com

THE BUZZ
WHAT EMPLOYEES AT OTHER FIRMS ARE SAYING

- "Very good boutique"
- "For sale"
- "Small niche player"
- "Do they still exist?"

THE SCOOP

In 2000, at the height of the hi-tech boom, New Jersey-based investment-banking boutique Broadview International was flying high. Founded in 1973, Broadview had become a major player in the middle-market M&A arena. A specialist in technology and media deals, Broadview executed 105 M&A transactions with a total value of nearly $32 billion worldwide in 2000. But in 2001, the firm only completed 43 M&A transactions worth $3.2 billion. Fearful of the struggling tech sector, Broadview reportedly retained M&A specialist Lazard in late 2001 to find a willing acquirer. Possible suitors included bulge bracket star Goldman Sachs and European giant UBS Warburg, but both deals fizzled, leaving Broadview's future uncertain.

GETTING HIRED

Broadview recruits analysts and associates at top U.S. and European schools. Calendars for presentations and on-campus interviews can be found at www.broadview.com. The firm hires undergrads into a two-year analyst program that begins with three weeks of training in the firm's office in Foster City, Calif. Unlike some investment banks, Broadview prefers one-on-one interviews to two-on-ones. The process for analysts involves an on-campus interview (or one at the firm's headquarters) and then a "super day," with four to six interviews.

OUR SURVEY SAYS

Insiders note the firm provides a lifestyle that is characteristic of working for a smaller firm. "The hours [at Broadview] are maybe 60 to 65 a week — that's a week at Club Med compared to Wall Street." Another insider pegs the hours a little higher. "It's minimum 60 or 70. Still, it's not expected that you'll be there on the weekends."

"Because you're in a small environment, if you're talented, everyone will know," explains one insider. One former analyst recounts leading a six-hour meeting with the CEO of a client. "I'm not saying that's typical, but if you know your shit, you'll get to do some cool stuff," says another contact.

American Century Investments

4500 Main Street
Suite 1500
Kansas City, MO 64111
Phone: (816) 531-5575
www.americancentury.com

DEPARTMENTS

Finance/Accounting • Investment
Management • Market/Research
Analysis • Retirement Plan Services •
Sales • Trading

THE STATS

President and CEO: William M.
Lyons
Chairman: James E. Stowers, Jr.
Employer Type: Private Company
2001 Revenue: $952 million
No. of Employees: 2,900
No. of Offices: 5

KEY COMPETITORS

Fidelity Investments
Putnam Investments
T. Rowe Price
Vanguard Group

UPPERS

- One month paid sabbaticals for
  qualified employees
- Opportunity for advancement

DOWNERS

- Little known outside their industry

EMPLOYMENT CONTACT

www.americancentury.com/careers

THE BUZZ
WHAT EMPLOYEES AT OTHER FIRMS ARE SAYING

- "Respected"
- "Boring"
- "Mutual funds"

THE SCOOP

American Century Investments was founded in 1958 by James Stowers, Jr., in Kansas City, Mo. Though the company initially offered just two mutual funds, American Century now offers individuals and institutions a variety of investment management options, including IRAs, 401(k)s and 403(b)s, trusts, separate and subadvisory accounts and more than 70 mutual funds. American Century had approximately $85 billion in assets under management as of July 2002.

Although he's no longer responsible for day-to-day management, Stowers still has an active role in the company, serving as co-chairman along with his son, James Stowers, III. The Stowers family retains a controlling interest in the firm, but President and Chief Executive Officer William Lyons handles the day-to-day management. Financial services giant J.P. Morgan Chase owns a big chunk of American Century; the former J.P. Morgan purchased a 45 percent stake in 1998.

American Century was ranked 23rd on *Fortune* magazine's February 2002 list of the "100 Best Companies To Work For," the third straight year the firm made the list. *Fortune* commended American Century's ability to weather the storm during the miserable economic climate of 2001, specifically citing the firm's avoidance of mass layoffs. The firm did eliminate six positions and ask 200 more employees to take different jobs in November 2001. American Century laid off an additional 90 employees, mostly in the IT department, in January 2002.

GETTING HIRED

Check out American Century's web site, www.americancentury.com, to search a listing of the company's job openings and to apply for positions online. Prospective employees can also create a profile based on their area of interest and preferred location. American Century will then e-mail candidates jobs that match the information in their profiles.

The firm says it is committed to providing opportunities for advancement. According to the firm, 52 percent of its job openings in 2000 were filled by people already employed at the firm. Based on pre-set goals, each employee creates what the firm calls an "individual success plan." Employees can monitor their plans through the company's intranet, complete with links that connect the individual's goals to department objectives. The firm offers additional courses onsite and online.

Franklin Resources

One Franklin Parkway
San Mateo, CA 94404
Phone: (650) 312-2000
www.franklintempleton.com

DEPARTMENTS

Asset Management • Portfolio and
Trading • Research • Sales and
Marketing • Transfer Agency
Operations

THE STATS

Chairman and CEO:
Charles B. Johnson
Employer Type: Public Company
Ticker Symbol: BEN (NYSE)
2001 Revenue: $2.4 billion
2001 Net Income: $485 million
No of. Employees: 6,400
No. of Offices: 70

KEY COMPETITORS

Fidelity Investments
Janus Capital
Vanguard Group

UPPERS

• Excellent job training
• Tuition reimbursement

DOWNERS

• Bureaucracy

EMPLOYMENT CONTACT

Human Resources
Franklin Templeton Investments
One Franklin Parkway
Building 970
San Mateo, CA 94403
Careers@frk.com

THE BUZZ
WHAT EMPLOYEES AT OTHER FIRMS ARE SAYING

• "Fine firm"
• "Stodgy"

THE SCOOP

An admirer of Benjamin Franklin's business philosophy, "With money and financial planning, prudence comes first," Rupert S. Johnson, Sr., named the company he founded in New York in 1947 after the revered founding father. Today, Franklin Resources (which operates under the name Franklin Templeton Investments) is the largest publicly traded mutual fund concern in the world with $278.6 billion under management as of May 2002.

Franklin was hit hard by the September 11th terrorist attacks. The attacks destroyed the offices of Franklin's Fiduciary Trust money-management subsidiary, killing 87 employees. Faced with financial shortfalls, the firm decided to cut salaries temporarily rather than headcount. Employees (including the CEO) took a 5 to 10 percent cut, depending on their salary. The pay was reinstated for employees making less than $200,000 on May 1, 2002.

GETTING HIRED

Franklin maintains a careers section on its web site, www.franklintempleton.com. The page lists job opportunities and contact information for positions at various offices. For entry-level employees, Franklin offers a two-year development program called the Futures Program (formerly known as the Management Training Program). The program is designed to expose employees to different functions and offers training in a variety of areas, including customer services/operations, marketing, sales and portfolio management.

OUR SURVEY SAYS

"When I think of Franklin," says one insider, "a few words come to mind — absorbing, high stress, fun, hard work." Says another contact, "The people I work with are a great bunch of people." Franklin employees note the pay is competitive. According to one employee, the best route for recent college grads is through the Futures Program: "It's a two-year program in which you rotate through various departments every four months. During the last several months of the program you hope to find a department that you like and that will take you on permanently."

VAULT 44 PRESTIGE RANKING

The Capital Group Companies

333 South Hope Street
52nd Floor
Los Angeles, CA 90071
Phone: (213) 486-9200
www.capgroup.com

EMPLOYMENT CONTACT

333 South Hope Street
Los Angeles, CA 90071-1477
Fax: (213) 486-9035
www.capgroup.com/HR2/

DEPARTMENTS

Global Institutional Investment
Services • Global Private Equity •
Mutual Funds for Canadian
Investors • Personal Investment
Management • U.S. Mutual Funds

THE STATS

Chairman: R. Michael Shanahan
President: Larry Clemmensen
Employer Type: Private Company
No. of Employees: 5,000
No. of Offices: 19

KEY COMPETITORS

Charles Schwab
Fidelity Investments
Vanguard Group

THE BUZZ
WHAT EMPLOYEES AT OTHER FIRMS ARE SAYING

- "Lifetime employment"
- "Not well known"
- "People focused"

THE SCOOP

Although the Capital Group Companies might have a lot to crow about, it is one of the most low-key firms in the financial industry. The privately held Capital Group has more than $550 billion in assets under management and 19 offices around the world, but its executives choose to keep a low profile, rarely granting interviews. Established during a time when the reverberations of the stock market crash of 1929 were still being felt, Capital Group's philosophy of prudent, long-term investing — as opposed to investing in the latest hot sector — continues to serve it well today.

The firm was founded in 1931 by investment researcher Jonathan Bell Lovelace. Sensing an impending market slump, Lovelace had sold many of his personal investments and left his job at investment firm E.E. MacCrone & Co. in 1929. He started Capital Research and Managment two years later, and the firm offered its first open-end mutual fund three years later. The firm expanded across the U.S. and internationally, starting with Geneva in 1962. In November 2001, Capital Group announced that it would begin to market its own line of funds in Canada, which has a much smaller mutual fund market than the U.S.

GETTING HIRED

Capital Group management prefers to refer to everyone who works at the firm as "associates," rather than "employees." According to corporate literature, the use of "associate" indicates that everyone who works for the company plays an important role in its growth. It should come as no surprise, therefore, that job candidates undergo a thorough interview process. Applicants should be prepared to "meet many people with whom you may interact if you become an associate." Those interested in employment at Capital should search the listing of open positions on the firm's site, www.capgroup.com. Resumes can be submitted online; they can also be faxed or mailed to a specific office with an opening.

Capital is known in the industry for having low turnover among associates; the firm says the annual rate hovers near 5 percent. Benefits may account in part for the low turnover. In addition to the standard health and 401(k) benefits given by most companies, Capital associates receive reimbursements for approved educational programs and gym fees, same-sex partner health benefits and a retirement fund contribution equivalent to 15 percent of annual salary that vests over six years.

Jefferies & Company

520 Madison Avenue
12th Floor
New York, NY 10022
Phone: (212) 284-2550
www.jefco.com

DEPARTMENTS

Asset Management • Corporate
Finance • International • Research •
Sales and Trading (Equity, High
Yield and Convertibles)

THE STATS

Chairman and CEO:
Richard B. Handler
Employer Type: Public Company
Ticker Symbol: JEF (NYSE)
2001 Revenue: $785 million
2001 Net Income: $59.5 million
No. of Employees: 1,200
No. of Offices: 21

KEY COMPETITORS

Credit Suisse First Boston
J.P. Morgan Chase
Morgan Stanley

UPPERS

• Excellent perks
• Junior bankers receive a lot of
  responsibility

DOWNERS

• Lack of brand name recognition
• Long hours

EMPLOYMENT CONTACT

**Corporate Finance and Investment
Banking**

Dee Dee Bird
Recruiting Coordinator
Fax: (310) 575-5165
dbird@jefco.com

All Other Areas

Mel Locke
Director of People Services
Fax: (310) 914-1066
mlocke@jefco.com

THE BUZZ
WHAT EMPLOYEES AT OTHER FIRMS ARE SAYING

• "Nimble niche player"
• "Middle-of-the-pack"
• "Great research"
• "Swashbuckling cowboys"

THE SCOOP

Best known for its institutional sales and trading capabilities, Jefferies & Company also provides research to institutional investors and investment-banking services to small and mid-sized companies. Founded in 1962 by UCLA graduate and ex-cattle rancher Boyd Jefferies, the firm made its mark in the 1960s and 1970s as a third-market trader (trading listed stocks over the counter). Jefferies currently concentrates on trading in equity, high yield, convertible and international securities, but the firm is committed to growing its advisory services, which include capital raising, M&A and corporate restructuring. Unlike its competitors, Jefferies managed to boost earnings by 8 percent and employee count by 20 percent in 2001.

GETTING HIRED

Insiders say candidates generally go through two rounds of interviews. The first round takes place on campus with "one senior and one junior" banker. The second round is held at Jefferies offices, where candidates meet with several senior bankers. One source says recruits can expect "a mix of questions — quantitative, modeling, personality and opinion." A relatively small firm with few openings, Jefferies runs a "selective hiring process at a limited number of universities." Asked where the firm searches for talent, several insiders cite the same four universities: Wharton, UCLA, Michigan and the University of Texas at Austin.

OUR SURVEY SAYS

Insiders at Jefferies say the firm has a "friendly atmosphere and places a lot of responsibility on the junior bankers," says one New York banker. Another source says, "the slight lack of structure has its pros and cons," but says, "it's a great place for junior bankers to get a broad experience." The firm's pay packages are "very competitive" with other firms, and a few insiders even say that "analysts are compensated near the top of the Street." "Hours are difficult, but better than most places. And senior people are usually flexible with the hours junior people work," says a New York employee.

Wachovia

301 South College Street
Charlotte, NC 28288
Phone: (704) 374-6161
www.wachovia.com

DEPARTMENTS

Capital Management • Corporate
and Investment Banking • General
Banking • Wealth Management

THE STATS

Chairman: Leslie M. (Bud) Baker, Jr.
CEO and President:
G. Kennedy (Ken) Thompson
Employer Type: Public Company
Ticker Symbol: WB (NYSE)
2001 Revenues: $22.4 billion
2001 Net Income: $1.6 million
No. of Employees: 84,000
No. of Offices: 3,400

KEY COMPETITORS

Bank of America
Citigroup
FleetBoston Financial

UPPERS

• Excellent benefits
• Fast growing company

DOWNERS

• Can be political
• Large cuts due to huge merger

EMPLOYMENT CONTACT

Wachovia Corporation
ATTN: Resume Processing
1525 West W.T. Harris Boulevard
Charlotte, NC 28288-0970
www.wachovia.com/careers

THE BUZZ
WHAT EMPLOYEES AT OTHER FIRMS ARE SAYING

• "Well respected southern player"
• "Want to be something they're
   not"
• "Rising"
• "In terrible shape"

THE SCOOP

Wachovia is the fourth largest bank in the U.S. in terms of assets. Created by the September 2001 merger of First Union and Wachovia, the firm has $187 billion in deposits and operates 2,800 branches across the East Coast. In addition to depositing checks and loaning cash, the firm offers investment banking, retail brokerage, insurance, mutual fund and corporate finance services. Although First Union actually purchased the significantly smaller Wachovia, the Wachovia handle survived the $14 billion marriage because the name was thought to be more prestigious.

GETTING HIRED

For more information on working for the new Wachovia, visit their career center at www.wachovia.com. The site contains links to open positions, college recruiting and the benefits of working for the bank. Wachovia recruits aggressively on college campuses and at job fairs. Additionally, a large percentage of candidates come through headhunters and referrals, insiders say. The company also advertises open positions in newspapers, although those in the know say it is "highly unusual" for people to get in that way. Candidates generally have an interview with human resources, followed by "a full day of interviewing" with a number of people.

OUR SURVEY SAYS

Insiders have different takes on the corporate culture at Wachovia. Says one insider: "The atmosphere is very political, but for a bank, it isn't bad. Not bad for a bank, though, is a hell of a lot worse than anywhere else." Another disagrees, saying "from my perspective, the corporate culture is fairly easygoing with a lot of emphasis on teamwork. There is no need nor room for prima donnas or empire builders, hence, no jealousies, back-biting or in-house political control fights." Despite the office politics, employees say management at Wachovia is "better than average in trying to create a good working environment for its employees." Employees applaud the company's efforts to promote a balance between work and family life through flex-time options.

Peter J. Solomon Company

767 Fifth Avenue
New York, NY 10153
Phone: (212) 508-1600
www.pjsc.com

DEPARTMENTS

Financing/Strategic Advisory •
Mergers and Acquisitions • Principal
Investing • Restructurings

THE STATS

Chairman: Peter J. Solomon
President: Kenneth Berliner
Employer Type: Private Company
No. of Employees: 47
No. of Offices: 1

KEY COMPETITORS

Dresdner Kleinwort Wasserstein
Houlihan Lokey Howard & Zukin

UPPERS

• Small deal teams = big
responsibility

DOWNERS

• Long hours

EMPLOYMENT CONTACT

Diane M. Coffey
Managing Director
Peter J. Solomon Company
767 Fifth Avenue
New York, NY 10153
careers@pjsolomon.com

THE BUZZ
WHAT EMPLOYEES AT OTHER FIRMS ARE SAYING

• "Smart"
• "Lost a lot of talent over the last
four years"
• "Good"

THE SCOOP

Peter J. Solomon Company (PJ Solomon) was founded in 1989 by Peter Solomon, an accomplished banker who served as deputy mayor of New York City under Ed Koch and counselor to the U.S. Treasury under Jimmy Carter. The firm specializes in mergers and acquisitions, restructuring and financing advisory. Since its founding, PJ Solomon has completed over 250 financing assignments. The firm advised Land's End on its $1.9 billion sale to Sears Roebuck in May 2002 and meat processor IBP on its $3.2 billion sale to Tyson Foods. Bankruptcy and restructuring clients have included Barney's, Bradlees, Discovery Zone and R.H. Macy & Co.

GETTING HIRED

PJ Solomon's web site, www.pjsolomon.com, has a small career section that includes an FAQ page for analysts and associates discussing the career path, culture and compensation, among other things. The firm recruits at Ivy League and top 20 schools (one source ticked off names like Wharton, Harvard, Columbia and Michigan, but the firm looks at other schools as well). "There's an initial round on-campus, then we bring you back [to New York] for a Super Saturday," reports one insider. "They're looking to see if you can work with the team," notes a source. Expect mostly fit and personality questions, though finance majors may see a few technical questions. "We don't blow them away with complicated accounting questions," reports one insider.

OUR SURVEY SAYS

The firm's culture is "pretty intense" says a source. The firm is "very entrepreneurial," and "team-oriented" with "small deal teams" meaning junior people "need to step up." "The hours can be tough," warns an insider, but the compensation is "standard to above" market rates, especially after PJ Solomon closed the Land's End/Sears merger, meaning more dough to go around the small company. The firm's training program is praised. "Professors come in and teach the [accounting] classes" while firm professionals teach other subjects in the program, which lasts a few weeks for new analysts or associates.

420 Montgomery Street
San Francisco, CA 94163
Phone: (800) 411-4932
www.wellsfargo.com

DEPARTMENTS

Capital Markets • Commercial
Banking • Consumer Banking •
Insurance • Institutional Investment
Services • Private Client Services •
Real Estate

THE STATS

Chairman, President and CEO:
Richard M. Kovacevich
Employer Type: Public Company
Ticker Symbol: WFC (NYSE)
2001 Revenues: $26.9 billion
2001 Net Income: $3.4 billion
No. of Employees: 134,000
No. of Offices: 5,400

KEY COMPETITORS

Bank of America
Citigroup
Wachovia

UPPERS

• Excellent training for commercial
  bankers
• Free and discounted banking
  services

DOWNERS

• Commercial bankers' pay
• Long hours

EMPLOYMENT CONTACT

careers@wellsfargo.com
www.wfjobs.com

THE BUZZ
WHAT EMPLOYEES AT OTHER FIRMS ARE SAYING

• "Respected"
• "Not well known in the east"
• "Regional"
• "Not a player"

THE SCOOP

In 1850 Henry Wells and William Fargo were among the New York businessmen who founded American Express, a mail delivery service that was the precursor to today's financial services behemoth. According to legend, Wells and Fargo were excited about the prospect of expanding west but couldn't convince their partners at American Express. As a result, the two started their self-named firm in 1852, providing banking and stagecoach and pony express delivery services. Wells Fargo separated its banking business from its express service in 1905, and has remained with banking since. Wells Fargo offers a complete range of financial services, including consumer and corporate banking, brokerage, insurance and venture capital. The firm is the largest U.S. mortgage banker and one of the leaders in providing online brokerage and banking services.

GETTING HIRED

Insiders at Wells Fargo caution, "The firm recruits very little, so the best way to get hired is to know someone who can send your resume to a senior manager." However, the corporate banking group does have a standard recruiting process that tries to snag 40 to 50 college and MBA graduates a year. Candidates for those positions can expect three rounds of interviews, one on-campus and then two at Wells Fargo, including one with an executive-level interviewer.

OUR SURVEY SAYS

Many Wells Fargo employees stress that the firm's culture is "very entrepreneurial," exemplified by Wells' catchphrase, "run it like you own it." Says one contact, "The corporate culture requires that you can change on a dime." That source calls the firm "always progressive" and says, Wells Fargo "is not an old-boy static network." One research analyst begs to differ. Wells "is an extremely conservative bank — probably the most [conservative] of any top 10 commercial bank." The training program is industry-renowned. Says one former employee, "Once you've been trained by Wells, most banks are dying to hire you."

SoundView Technology Group

1700 East Putnam Avenue
Old Greenwich, CT 06870-1333
Phone: (203) 321-7000
www.soundview.com

DEPARTMENTS

Investment Banking • Research •
Sales and Trading • Venture Capital

THE STATS

CEO: Mark Loehr
Employer Type: Public Company
Ticker Symbol: SNDV (Nasdaq)
2001 Revenues: $163.8 million
2001 Net Income: -$332.7 million
No. of Employees: 240
No. of Offices: 3

KEY COMPETITORS

Broadview International
Thomas Weisel Partners

UPPERS

• Exposure to senior bankers and clients
• Relaxed culture

DOWNERS

• Tech focus has hurt deal flow
• Lack of reputation

EMPLOYMENT CONTACT

For investment-banking analyst and associate positions, contact campusrecruiting@soundview.com

For opportunities listed on the firm's website or general employment inquiries, contact recruiting@soundview.com

THE BUZZ
WHAT EMPLOYEES AT OTHER FIRMS ARE SAYING

• "Rising small player"
• "Tech, ouch"
• "Willing to compromise, desperate"

THE SCOOP

SoundView Technology Group is an investment banking boutique focused exclusively on the technology sector. SoundView's services include public offerings, M&A, private placements, venture capital, research and institutional sales and trading. Formerly known as Wit Soundview and, before that, Wit Capital, the firm was founded in 1996 as the first online investment bank by Andrew Klein, who had previously founded Spring Street Brewing Company. By mid-2000, after buying banking boutique SoundView Technology Group and E*Trade's underwriting group E*Offering, the firm had mostly abandoned its online investment bank model. The firm laid off 60 workers in 2001 and sacked another 60 in early 2002.

GETTING HIRED

According to insiders, SoundView recruits mostly from "Ivy League and top-20" schools though one banker admits, "Consistent with other firms, we haven't done a lot of hiring recently." The firm generally holds first round interviews for college and MBA recruits on campus. Candidates who pass the initial screening will visit SoundView offices for a Super Saturday in which they can expect to meet up to 10 people, from MDs to analysts. The interviews are described as informal with an "emphasis on experience, intelligence and cultural fit." "Questions vary," says a current banker, "but what everyone is interested in is the candidate's interest in technology, since that's our sole industry focus."

OUR SURVEY SAYS

SoundView's culture is a "bit looser" than most Wall Street firms. "It's one of the few places where everyone still knows each other," says one employee. Because of the firm's small size, junior bankers will gain "great access to senior people and their experience," reports a SoundView banker. The firm's small size also means "there's nowhere to hide, you don't get lost in the shuffle." says one source. "If you're smart and dedicated, people will know pretty quickly. But if you're not, we'll find out about that, too." Insiders concede the bank tries to pay near the industry average; for better or worse, compensation includes more stock options than at most I-banks.

The Bank of New York

One Wall Street
New York, NY 10286
Phone: (212) 495-1784
www.bankofny.com

DEPARTMENTS

Asset Management • Corporate
Banking • Global Market Services •
Private Client Services • Retail
Banking • Securities Servicing and
Global Payment Services

THE STATS

Chairman and CEO:
Thomas A. Renyi
Employer Type: Public Company
Ticker Symbol: BK (NYSE)
2001 Revenue: $7.2 billion
2001 Net Income: $1.3 billion
No. of Employees: 19,180
No. of Offices: 400

KEY COMPETITORS

Bank of America
Citigroup
J.P. Morgan Chase

UPPERS

• Job security
• Profit sharing

DOWNERS

• Bureaucracy
• Limited advancement possibilities

EMPLOYMENT CONTACT

The Bank of New York
Human Resources
One Wall Street
13th Floor
New York, NY 10286

THE BUZZ
WHAT EMPLOYEES AT OTHER FIRMS ARE SAYING

• "Solid but boring"
• "Old blood"
• "Okay for private wealth
   management"
• "Past its prime"

THE SCOOP

The Bank of New York (BNY) was founded in 1784 and is now the oldest bank operating under its original name in the U.S. Alexander Hamilton, founding father and the first Secretary of the Treasury, wrote the company's constitution. Today, the bank has approximately $76 billion in assets and provides a full range of corporate and individual services, including retail and commercial banking services and custodial and trust services (the handling of assets for individuals and businesses). BNY suffered a financial hit related to the terrorist attacks of September 11, 2001. The firm was forced to temporarily close its offices at 1 Wall Street and a data facility at Barclay Street, just one block north of the World Trade Center. Though no Bank of New York employees were hurt, the firm did experience some temporary service outages related to the disruption of power and telephone service in Lower Manhattan after the attacks.

GETTING HIRED

The Bank of New York's web site, www.bankofny.com, has a complete listing of job openings, qualifications, descriptions and recruiting schedules. The firm posts developmental positions for both MBAs and college grads, as well as for those in computer technology. Expect to interview with an HR representative, then several division managers including (in some cases) the division head. And be careful not to fib on your resume or in your interviews. "Be aware that HR will check up on the information you provide them — experience, education, salary, etc.," says one source.

OUR SURVEY SAYS

Bank of New York employees praise the "unwritten policy of permanent job security" and the "collegial" corporate atmosphere. "I think [BNY] has a very stodgy reputation, but the reality is a bit different," reports one contact.

The firm also gets good marks for diversity. According to one insider: "As I look around the firm, I recognize that the work force — on all levels — reflects the diversity one expects to see in a place like New York City."

Increase your T/NJ Ratio
(Time to New Job)

Use the Internet's most targeted job search tools for finance professionals.

Vault Finance Job Board

The most comprehensive and convenient job board for finance professionals. Target your search by area of finance, function, and experience level, and find the job openings that you want. No surfing required.

VaultMatch Resume Database

Vault takes match-making to the next level: post your resume and customize your search by area of finance, experience and more. We'll match job listings with your interests and criteria and e-mail them directly to your in-box.

WORTH
MENTIONING

Arthur Andersen

33 West Monroe Street
Chicago, IL 60603
Phone: (312) 580-0033
www.andersen.com

DEPARTMENTS

Audit and Assurance • Corporate
Finance • Tax Advisory and
Consulting

THE STATS

Managing Partner: Larry Gorrell
Employer Type: Subsidiary of
Andersen Worldwide
2001 Revenue: $9.3 billion
No. of Employees: 19,000
No. of Offices: 75

KEY COMPETITORS

Deloitte & Touche
Ernst & Young
KPMG
PricewaterhouseCoopers

UPPERS

• Still has international reach

DOWNERS

• Uncertainty after Enron debacle

EMPLOYMENT CONTACT

Arthur Andersen LLP
33 West Monroe Street
Chicago, Illinois 60603
Fax: (312) 507-6748

THE BUZZ
WHAT EMPLOYEES AT OTHER FIRMS ARE SAYING

• "Enron not indicative of firm
  ability"
• "Their name is mud"
• "Justice Department is WRONG!"
• "Oh you poor, poor souls..."

THE SCOOP

Arthur Andersen, a firm steeped in tradition, is also a firm on the edge. The firm traces its roots back to 1913 when Arthur Andersen (who became Illinois' youngest CPA in 1907) founded an accounting firm along with his friend, Clarence DeLany. DeLany left the firm five years later and Arthur Andersen & Co. became one the most influential accounting firms of the 20th century, expanding its tax, audit and consulting practices internationally.

The firm's international practice, and certainly its reputation, is in peril after questions surrounding the firm's audit of Houston-based energy company Enron. Andersen's audits approved Enron's practice of shifting debts and investments to subsidiaries that Enron claimed were off its balance sheet. When the government disallowed the partnerships, Enron had to restate its earnings; hundreds of millions in previously reported revenue was wiped out. Investigators focused on Andersen when it was revealed that its employees shredded documents related to the Enron audit, even after the firm was subpoenaed by investigators. Arthur Andersen went on trial for obstruction of justice in May 2002. The firm claimed the shredding was done by only a few employees without management's approval. In June 2002, a jury convicted Arthur Andersen of obstruction of justice. Though the firm will appeal, it will stop doing auditing work in the U.S. as of August 31, 2002. According to *Forbes*, as of July 2002, over 400 clients responsible for approximately $1.4 billion in billings in 2001 fired Arthur Andersen. Offices in the U.S. and abroad have been sold or left the firm to align themselves with competitors, and the firm cut 7,000 jobs.

GETTING HIRED

Despite its uncertain future, Andersen continues to maintain a minimal recruiting presence. The firm's web site, www.arthurandersen.com, has a career section that allows users to search for a job by location and function. Still, the turmoil surrounding the firm has made search for a job at Arthur Andersen akin to inserting yourself into employment limbo. In addition to the 7,000 layoffs, the firm rescinded job offers to approximately 2,000 college, MBA and other students in the most recent recruiting cycle, a spokesperson told *The Washington Post*. In short, prospective hires should be aware that the firm is going through a difficult time and plan accordingly.

Federated Investors

Federated Investors Tower
1001 Liberty Avenue
Pittsburgh, PA 15222-3779
Phone: (412) 288-1900
www.federatedinvestors.com

DEPARTMENTS

Clearing Services • Investment
Management • Investment Research •
Marketing • Sales

THE STATS

Chairman: John F. Donahue
President and CEO:
J. Christopher Donahue
Employer Type: Public Company
Ticker Symbol: FII (NYSE)
2001 Revenues: $715.8 million
2001 Net Income: $168.4 million
No. of Employees: 1,800
No. of Offices: 7

KEY COMPETITORS

Janus Capital
T. Rowe Price
Vanguard Group

EMPLOYMENT CONTACT

Employment Services
19th Floor
Federated Investors
Federated Investors Tower
Pittsburgh, PA 15222-3779
Fax: (412) 288-6446
resume@federatedinv.com

THE BUZZ
WHAT CONSULTANTS AT OTHER FIRMS ARE SAYING

- "Strong buy side"
- "Not well known"
- "Very respected"

THE SCOOP

John Donahue, Richard Fisher and Thomas Donnelly founded Federated Investors in 1955. The trio borrowed enough capital to set up shop in Pittsburgh, Pa., where they began selling savings plans and mutual funds door-to-door. The company went public in 1960 and was purchased by Aetna in 1982. The firm claims to have introduced government bond funds, municipal bond funds and high-yield bond funds, as well as the method for valuing money market fund shares at $1.

Federated's management, especially the Donahue family, was reportedly unhappy with Aetna's control; the Donahues bought 75 percent of the firm back from Aetna in 1989 and the rest in 1996. J. Christopher Donahue, the eldest son of founder John, now runs the company. Christopher joined the firm in 1972 and was appointed COO in 1993. He became CEO five years later and led the company through its 1998 IPO. (The Donahue family still owns approximately 20 percent of the company's shares.)

Federated is a lesser-known investment management firm, mainly because the company's 138 mutual funds are targeted to financial intermediaries, including banks, broker/dealers, insurance companies, corporations and government agencies. The firm has a reputation for aggressively marketing its services to institutional clients, including wooing decision makers at the firms. "Millions of shrimp have sacrificed themselves for Federated Investors," Christopher Donahue told *Money & Investments*, referring to the company's penchant for wining and dining potential clients. The strategy has been effective; Federated has approximately $178 billion in assets under management (as of March 31, 2002).

GETTING HIRED

Federated's web site, www.federatedinvestors.com, lists open positions in numerous departments, including investment research, investor services, sales and product development. The web site suggests applicants send resumes to Federated's Pittsburgh headquarters.

The site also details the company's benefits program. Federated offers comprehensive health insurance, profit sharing, 401(k) and employee stock purchase plans, and tuition assistance, among other benefits.

TD Securities

31 West 52nd Street
New York, NY 10019
Phone: (212) 827-7300
www.tdsecurities.com

DEPARTMENTS

Debt Capital Markets • Foreign
Exchange • Institutional Equities •
Investment Banking • Private Equity

THE STATS

Chairman and CEO:
Donald A. Wright
Employer Type: Subsidiary of TD
Bank Financial Group
2001 Revenues: $3.1 billion
2001 Net Income: $914 million
No. of Offices: 19

KEY COMPETITORS

Banc of America Securities
CIBC World Markets
Lehman Brothers

UPPERS

• Friendly, relaxed environment
• Excellent work/life balance

DOWNERS

• Pay below Street average
• Reputation not firmly established
  outside Canada

EMPLOYMENT CONTACT

U.S.
Human Resources — Recruitment
TD Securities (USA)
31 West 52nd Street
New York, New York 10019-6101
Phone: (212) 827-7300
Fax: (212) 827-7248
recruiter@tdusa.com

Canada
Human Resources — Recruitment
TD Securities
66 Wellington Street West
P.O. Box 1, TD Bank Tower
Toronto, Ontario M5K 1A2
Phone: (416) 308 7581
Fax: (416) 982 2766
recruitment@tdsecurities.com

THE BUZZ
WHAT CONSULTANTS AT OTHER FIRMS ARE SAYING

• "Good reputation"
• "Too Canadian"
• "Up and comer"
• "Undefined image"

THE SCOOP

TD Securities is the investment-banking unit of Toronto Dominion Bank Financial Group (TD Bank), which was formed in 1955 by the merger of the Bank of Toronto and Dominion Bank. TD Bank, which reported revenues of $13.1 billion in 2001, also consists of retail bank TD Canada Trust, TD Commercial Banking, TD Asset Management and TD Waterhouse. TD Securities is active in all areas of corporate finance, including M&A and debt and equity underwriting. According to *The Financial Post*, TD Securities was the top debt underwriter in Canada for 2001, advising on 175 deals worth $10.9 billion. The firm ranked first in 2001 in terms of profitability among the top five Canadian wholesale banks. In a move that CEO Donald Wright said is designed to cut costs and position the firm for the long term, TD Securities will cut its workforce by 7 percent by October 2002.

GETTING HIRED

One banker says that securing a position at TD is "much easier than landing a spot at a bulge bracket firm." But, as one insider notes, "The number of hires each year is limited due to the size of the firm, allowing TD to be reasonably selective." The interview process is pretty standard, with three to four rounds of several interviews each. "Fit and people skills," say insiders, are the keys to winning a position at TD.

OUR SURVEY SAYS

Nearly all insiders say working at TD is as close to a day at the beach as you'll get in the industry. TD " prides itself on work/life balance," says one insider. "It's very loose, intense, but respectful," says another contact. One banker says TD is "a meritocracy where people skills are as important as execution ability and industry expertise." One contact cautions "you never forget you're working in a cut-throat industry where you're competing with your peers for advancement." Unlike the firm's culture, TD's pay scale receives low marks. Even so, because hours worked are also low, most employees aren't complaining. "We're not the highest paid bankers in New York, but I'm not in the office 105 hours a week either," remarks one banker.

FINANCE
RECRUITERS
DIRECTORY

Ashworth Group, Inc.
2424 Madison Ave.
Safety Harbor, FL 34695
Work Phone: (727) 799-2100
http://www.theashworthgroup.com
Emily Lee
President
Phone: (727) 799-2100
Fax: (727) 723-0383
Emily@erpjobcenter.net

BLB Consulting Inc.
110 East 42nd Street
Suite 1309
New York, New York 10017
Phone: (212) 808-0578
Fax: (212) 338-9696
www.blbco.com
Barbara Bartell, CPC
President
Phone: (212) 808-0578
Fax: (212) 338-9696
hr@blbco.com

Career Advantage Personnel Services
1215 East Airport Drive
Suite 125
Ontario, CA 91761
Phone: (909) 466-9232
www. CareerAdvantage.net
Brynda Woods
President
Phone: (909) 466-9232
Info@CareerAdvantage.net

Cascade Associates, Inc.
653 Skippack Pike
Suite 25
Blue Bell, PA 19422
Work Phone: (215) 619-0819
www.cascadehr.com
Phyllis Shurn-Hannah
President
Phone: (215) 619-0819 ext. 223
Fax: (215) 619-0822
p.shurnhannah@cascadehr.com

Diamond Consultants
16 Yorkshire Drive
Suite 100
Mendham, NJ 07945
Phone: (973) 252-4124
www.diamondrecruiter.com
Mindy Diamond
President
Phone: (973) 476-8578
Fax: (973) 252-0631
mdiamond16@aol.com
Number of Recruiters/Consultants: 4
Date Founded: 1997
Notable clients: Morgan Stanley, Salomon Smith Barney, Banc of America
Firm Description: 100% of business is devoted to finance industry. Diamond Consultants is an executive search firm with 2 separate divisions. Our brokerage division exclusively places retail stockbrokers/financial advisors with wirehouse, regional, boutique and independent firms nationwide. Our accounting division focuses exclusively on the placement of accounting professionals from the junior level to the executive nationwide. We pride ourselves on confidentiality, prompt feedback, professionalism and competence. We are located in New Jersey, but most of our clients are national firms with offices throughout the country. We are as successful in our searches in the West as we are in the East.

Commonwealth Financial Corporation
8262 Lees Ridge Road
Warrenton, Virginia 20186
Phone: (540) 349-8888
Fax: (540) 349-8889
www.gostaffit.com
Michael Atkins
CEO
Phone: (540) 349-8888
Fax: (540) 349-8889
matkins@gostaffit.com

Core Staffing, Inc.
59 Maiden Lane
23rd floor
New York, NY 10038
Phone: (212) 766-1222
Fax: (212) 766-9024
www.employcore.com
Adam Connors
Managing Director, Financial Staffing
Phone: (212) 766-1222 ext 233
Finance@employcore.com

Corporate Search Consultants
600 First Ave.
Suite 337
Seattle, WA 98104
Phone: (206) 332-0233
Fax: (206) 332-0230
M.B. Barbour
Principal
Phone: (206) 332-0233
Fax: (206) 332-0230
Info@cssearch.com

ET Search, Inc.
1250 Prospect Street
Suite 101
La Jolla, CA 92037-3618
Phone: (858) 459-3443
www.etsearch.com
Kathleen Jennings
President
Phone: (858) 459-3443
Fax: (858) 459-4147
taxpros@etsearch.com

ExpatRepat Services, Inc.
3402 Kensington Drive
Abilene, TX 79605
Phone: (915) 676-2290
www.expat-repat.com
Dr. Robert E. Scott
President
Phone: (915) 676-2290
Fax: (915) 695-2355
ERS@expat-repat.com

Flex Execs Management Solutions
645 Executive Drive
Willowbrook, IL, 60527
Phone: (630) 655-0563
www.flexexecs.com
Karen Murphy
Managing Partner
Phone: (630) 655-0563
Fax: (630) 655-0564
kmurphy@flexexecs.com
Number of Recruiters/Consultants: 4
Domestic offices: 1
Date Founded: 1990
Percentage of business devoted to the finance industry: 40%
Firm Description: Flex Execs Management Solutions has been providing executive search services since 1990. We have built our reputation by getting to know our clients' business, cultures and what makes them successful! Clients like our friendly, responsive style, quality of candidates, and our attention to detail. Candidates appreciate our caring attitude and our range of opportunities with mid- to Fortune 50 clients. Flex Execs offers both full-time and contract consulting opportunities and is a Women's Business Enterprise.

The Ford Group, Inc.
485 Devon Park Drive
Suite 110
Wayne, PA 19087
Phone: (610) 975-9007
Fax: (610) 975-9008
www.thefordgroup.com
Sandra D. Ford
CEO & Managing Director
Phone: (610) 975-9007
Fax: (610) 975-9008
info@thefordgroup.com

Flowerson Holdings, Inc.
21-57 Hazen Street Suite #1
Flushing, NY 11370
Phone: (718) 267-6752
Fax: (718) 278-3455
Marijan Cvjeticanin
President
Phone: (718) 267-6752
Fax: (718) 278-3455
FlowInvest@aol.com

HR Advantage, Inc.
P.O. Box 10319
Burke, VA 22015
Phone: (703) 978-6028
Fax: (703) 832-8539
www.hradvantageinc.com
Julie Rana
President
Phone: (703) 978-6028
Fax: (703) 832-8539
julierana@prodigy.net

Jetter & Company
90 New Montgomery Street,
Suite 1001
San Francisco, CA 94105
Phone: (415) 543-5252
www.Jetterco.com
Susan Jetter
President
Phone: (415) 543-5252
Susan@Jetterco.com

Judy Thompson & Associates,
Financial Executive Search, Inc.
5080 Shoreham Place
Suite 204
San Diego, CA   92122
Phone: (858) 452-1200
www.jtaa.net
Dee Johnson
Research Director
Phone: (858) 452-1200
Fax: (858) 623-5910
info@jtaa.net

Michael Page International
The Chrysler Building
405 Lexington Ave. 28th Floor
New York, NY 10174
Phone: (212) 661-4800
Fax: (212) 661-6622
Firm Description: With 26 years of experience MPI has become an established market leader in executive recruitment across 9 sectors. MPI operates in 15 countries with over 100 offices worldwide and employs nearly 3,000 people globally. MPI focuses on the recruitment of finance and accounting professionals (both junior and senior) into the finance and operations functions of companies. MPI's practice group has become the preeminent recruitment firm in servicing the fields of expertise in Accounting, Finance, Taxation, Public Accounting, Internal Audit, and Treasury. Capabilities span Research, Sales & Trading, Asset Management, Private Banking and Investment Banking in the front office, as well as particular strength in Finance, Accounting, Operations, Credit and Compliance on the support side. MPI clients cover a multitude of industry sectors including Telecommunications, Media & Entertainment, Consumer Products, Retail, Pharmaceutical, Advertising and Manufacturing. Client focus ranges from the Fortune 500 to growth-oriented, development stage entities.

Lyons Pruitt International, Inc.
40 Wall Street
32nd Floor (Rosen Suite)
New York, 10005
Phone: (212) 797-8888
www.lyonspruitt.com
Scott Lyons
Managing Director
Phone: (212) 797-8888
slyons@lyonspruitt.com

Martha Sloane Consultants, Inc.
500 Fifth Ave.
Suite 1183
New York, NY 10110
Phone: (212) 269-7789
Fax: (212) 269-7793
Martha Sloane
President
Phone: 212-269-7789
Fax: 212-269-7793
Msloane@ucs.net

NCC Executive Search
1300 Santa Barbara St
Santa Barbara, CA 93101
Phone: (800) 622 0431
www.nccx.com
Gary Kravetz
CEO
Phone: (800) 622 0431 x218
Fax: (805) 730 1689
gkravetz@nccx.com

Olschwanger Partners, LLC
7522 Campbell Road
Suite 113-196
Dallas, Texas 75248
Phone: (972) 931-9144
Fax: (972) 931-9194
www.osearch.org
Paul F. Olschwanger
Managing Director
Phone: (972) 931-9144
Fax: (972) 931-9194
pfo@osearch.org

PMJ & Associates
15 Toronto Street
Ste 602
M5C 2E3, Toronto Canada
Phone: (416) 364-9997
www.pmjpersonnel.com
Allen Fink
Manager
Phone: (416) 364-9997
Fax: (416) 364-8735
allen@pmjpersonnel.com

Resume Resources and Co.
789 MacDonough St., 5C
Brooklyn, NY 11233
Work Phone: (718) 919-1113
www.resumeresources.org
Harold Greene
President
Phone: (718) 919-1113
Fax: (718) 919-1113
Resume.res@verizon.net

Search Pro, Inc.
#400 8206-1200 Providence Road
Charlotte, NC 28277
Phone: (704) 849-9092
Fax: (704) 849-9095
www.searchpro.com
Mary Mallett, CPC
President
Phone: (704) 849-9092
Fax: (704) 849-9095
Mary@searchpro.com

Spencer Stuart
695 East Main Street
Stamford, CT 06901
Phone: (203) 975-4700
www.spencerstuart.com
Steve Zales
Middle Management Practice Leader
Phone: (203) 975-4700
Fax: (203) 359-0894
szales@spencerstuart.com

Spherion Professional Recruiting Group
7887 Washington Village Drive
Suite 200
Dayton, OH 45459
Phone: (937) 439-5501
www.spherion.com/professional
recruiting
Eric J. Sedwick
Branch Director
Phone: (937) 439-5501
Fax: (937) 439-5520
ericsedwick@spherion.com

Steve Ellis and Associates
10100 Santa Monica Blvd.
Suite 950
Los Angeles, CA 90067
Phone: (310) 829-0611
Fax: (310) 829-2024
www.searchellis.com
Steve Ellis
President
Phone: (310) 829-0611
Fax: (310) 829-2024
steve@searchellis.com

Toyjobs
26 Park Street
Suite 2001
Montclair, New Jersey 07042
Phone: (973) 744-0818
www.toyjobs.com
Thomas M. Keoughan
President
Phone: (973) 744-0818
Fax: (973) 744-0775
tom@toyjobs.com

The Travillian Group
321 East Main Street
Charlottesville, VA 22902
Work Phone: (434) 951-7665
www.travilliangroup.com
Stephanie Baglio
Managing Director
Phone: (434) 951-7665
Fax: (434) 951-0701
sbaglio@travilliangroup.com

Tryon & Heideman, LLC
8301 State Line Road
Suite 204
Kansas City, Missouri 64114
Phone: (816) 822-1976
Fax: (816) 822-9333
www.tryonheideman.com
Katey Tryon and Mary Heideman
Partners
Phone: (816) 822-1976
Fax: (816) 822-9333
tryonheideman@sprintmail.com

VIP Staffing, LLC
1717 K Street, NW
Suite #600
Washington, DC 20036
Work Phone: (202) 973-0179
www.vipstaffing.com
Eva Jenkins
President
Phone: (202) 973-0179
Fax: (202) 331-3759
evaj@vipstaffing.com

Youngblood Executive Search, Inc.
445 East Ohio Street
Suite 440
Chicago, IL 60611
Work Phone: (773) 684-8754
www.ayoungbloodinc.com
Ava D. Youngblood
President and CEO
Phone: (773) 684-8754
Fax: (773) 684 - 8754
avayoungblood@ayoungbloodinc.com

APPENDIX

Alphabetical Listing of Companies

Index of Companies by Industry

VAULT CAREER LIBRARY

Finance Glossary

Accounting Principles Board (APB): The predecessor of the Financial Accounting Standards Board (FASB).

American Institute of Certified Public Accountants (AICPA): The leading organization of the auditors of corporate financial reports.

Annual report: A combination of financial statements, management discussion and analysis, and graphs and charts provided annually to investors; they're required for companies traded publicly in the U.S.

Asset management: Also known as investment management. Money managers at investment management firms and investment banks take money given to them by pension funds and individual investors and invest it. For wealthy individuals (private clients), the investment bank will set up an individual account and manage the account; for the less well-endowed, the bank will offer mutual funds. Asset managers are compensated primarily by taking a percentage each year from the total assets managed. (They may also charge an upfront load, or commission, of a few percent of the initial money invested.)

Audit: An examination of transactions and financial statements made in accordance with generally accepted auditing standards.

Auditor: A person who examines the information used by managers to prepare the financial statements and attests to the credibility of those statements.

Bond spreads: The difference between the yield of a corporate bond and a U.S. Treasury security of similar time to maturity.

Bulge bracket: The largest and most prestigious firms on Wall Street (including Goldman Sachs, Morgan Stanley, Merrill Lynch, Salomon Smith Barney and Credit Suisse First Boston).

Buy-side: The clients of investment banks (mutual funds, pension funds) who buy the stocks, bonds and securities sold by the banks. (The investment banks that sell these products to investors are known as the sell-side.)

Certified public accountant (CPA): In the United States, a person earns this designation through a combination of education, qualifying experience and by passing a national written examination.

Chartered Financial Analyst (CFA): A designation given to professionals who complete a multi-part exam designed to test accounting and investment knowledge and professional ethics.

Commercial bank: A bank that lends, rather than raises, money. For example, if a company wants $30 million to open a new production plant, it can approach a commercial bank for a loan.

Commercial paper: Short-term corporate debt, typically maturing in nine months or less.

Commitment letter: A document that outlines the terms of a loan a commercial bank gives a client.

Commodities: Assets (usually agricultural products or metals) that are generally interchangeable with one another and therefore share a common price. For example, corn, wheat and rubber generally trade at one price on commodity markets worldwide.

Common stock: Also called common equity, common stock represents an ownership interest in a company. (As opposed to preferred stock, see below.) The vast majority of stock traded in the markets today is common, as common stock enables investors to vote on company matters. An individual who owns at least 51 percent of a company's shares controls the company's decisions and can appoint anyone he/she wishes to the board of directors or to the management team.

Comparable company analysis (Comps): The primary tool of the corporate finance analyst. Comps include a list of financial data, valuation data and ratio data on a set of companies in an industry. Comps are used to value private companies or better understand a how the market values an industry or particular player in the industry.

Consumer Price Index (CPI): The CPI measures the percentage increase in a standard basket of goods and services. The CPI is a measure of inflation for consumers.

Convertible bonds: Bonds that can be converted into a specified number of shares of stock.

Derivatives: An asset whose value is derived from the price of another asset. Examples include call options, put options, futures and interest-rate swaps.

Discount rate: A widely followed short-term interest rate set by the Federal Reserve to cause market interest rates to rise or fall, thereby spurring the U.S. economy to grow more quickly or less quickly. More specifically, the discount rate is the rate at which federal banks lend money to each other on overnight loans. Today, the discount rate can be directly moved by the Fed, but largely maintains a symbolic role.

Dividend: A payment by a company to shareholders of its stock, usually as a way to distribute profits.

Equity: In short, stock. Equity means ownership in a company that is usually represented by stock.

ERISA: Employee Retirement Income Security Act of 1974. The federal law that sets most pension plan requirements.

The Fed: The Federal Reserve, which gently (or sometimes roughly), manages the country's economy by setting interest rates.

Federal funds rate: The rate domestic banks charge one another on overnight loans to meet Federal Reserve requirements. This rate tracks very closely to the discount rate, but is usually slightly higher.

Financial Accounting Standards Board (FASB): A private-sector body that determines generally accepted accounting principles in the United States.

Financial accounting: The field of accounting that serves external decision makers, such as stockholders, suppliers, banks and government agencies.

Fixed income: Bonds and other securities that earn a fixed rate of return. Bonds are typically issued by governments, corporations and municipalities.

Generally Accepted Accounting Principles (GAAP): The broad concepts or guidelines and detailed practices in accounting, including all conventions, rules and procedures that make up accepted accounting practices.

Glass-Steagall Act: Part of the legislation passed in 1933 during the Great Depression designed to help prevent future bank failure — the establishment of the F.D.I.C. was also part of this movement. The Glass-Steagall Act split America's investment-banking (issuing and trading securities) operations from commercial banking (lending). For example, J.P. Morgan was forced to spin off its securities unit as Morgan Stanley. The act was gradually weakened throughout the 1990s. In 1999 Glass-Steagall was effectively repealed by the Graham-Leach-Bliley Act.

Graham-Leach-Bliley Act: Also known as the Financial Services Modernization Act of 1999. Essentially repealed many of the restrictions of the Glass-Steagall Act and made possible the current trend of consolidation in the financial services industry. Allows commercial banks, investment banks and insurance companies to affiliate under a holding company structure.

Growth stock: Industry leaders that investors and analysts believe will continue to prosper and exceed expectations. These companies have above average revenue and earnings growth and their stocks trade at high price-to-earnings and price-to-book ratios. Technology and telecommunications companies such as Microsoft and Cisco are good examples of traditional growth stocks.

Hedge: To balance a position in the market in order to reduce risk. Hedges work like insurance: a small position pays off large amounts with a slight move in the market.

Hedge fund: An investment partnership, similar to a mutual fund, made up of wealthy investors. In comparison to most investment vehicles, hedge funds are loosely regulated, allowing them to take more risks with their investments.

High-grade corporate bond: A corporate bond with a rating above BB. Also called investment grade debt.

High yield debt (a.k.a. Junk bonds): Corporate bonds that pay high interest rates (to compensate investors for high risk of default). Credit rating agencies such as Standard & Poor's rate a company's (or a municipality's) bonds based on default risk. Junk bonds rate below BB.

Initial Public Offering (IPO): The dream of every entrepreneur, the IPO marks the first time a company issues stock to the public. Going public means more than raising money for the company: By agreeing to take on public shareholders, a company enters a whole world of required SEC filings and quarterly revenue and earnings reports, not to mention possible shareholder lawsuits.

Institutional clients or investors: Large investors, such as pension funds or municipalities (as opposed to retail investors or individual investors).

Lead manager: The primary investment bank managing a securities offering. (An investment bank may share this responsibility with one or more co-managers.)

League tables: Tables that rank investment banks based on underwriting volume in numerous categories, such as stocks, bonds, high yield debt, convertible debt, etc. High rankings in league tables are key selling points used by investment banks when trying to land a client.

Leveraged Buyout (LBO): The buyout of a company with borrowed money, often using that company's own assets as collateral. LBOs were the order of the day in the heady 1980s, when successful LBO firms such as Kohlberg Kravis Roberts made a practice of buying up companies, restructuring them and then reselling them or taking them public at a significant profit.

The Long Bond: The 30-year U.S. Treasury bond. Treasury bonds are used as the starting point for pricing many other bonds, because Treasury bonds are assumed to have zero credit risk taking into account factors such as inflation. For example, a company will issue a bond that trades "40 over Treasuries." The "40" refers to 40 basis points (100 basis points = 1 percentage point).

Making markets: A function performed by investment banks to provide liquidity for their clients in a particular security, often for a security that the investment bank has underwritten. (In others words, the investment bank stands willing to buy the security, if necessary, when the investor later decides to sell it.)

Management accounting: The field of accounting that serves internal decision makers, such as top executives, department heads, college deans, hospital administrators, and people at other levels of management within an organization.

Market capitalization (market cap): The total value of a company in the stock market (total shares outstanding multiplied by price per share).

Merchant banking: The department within an investment bank that invests the firm's own money in other companies. Analogous to a venture capital arm.

Money market securities: This term is generally used to represent the market for securities maturing within one year. These include short-term

CDs, repurchase agreements and commercial paper (low-risk corporate issues), among others. These are low risk, short-term securities that have yields similar to Treasuries.

Mortgage-backed bonds: Bonds collateralized by a pool of mortgages. Interest and principal payments are based on the individual homeowners making their mortgage payments. The more diverse the pool of mortgages backing the bond, the less risky they are.

Municipal bonds (Munis): Bonds issued by local and state governments, a.k.a. municipalities. Municipal bonds are structured as tax-free for the investor, which means investors in munis earn interest payments without having to pay federal taxes. Sometimes investors are exempt from state and local taxes, too. Consequently, municipalities can pay lower interest rates on muni bonds than other bonds of similar risk.

Mutual fund: An investment vehicle that collects funds from investors (both individual and institutional) and invests in a variety of securities, including stocks and bonds. Mutual funds make money by charging a percentage of assets in the fund.

P/E ratio: The price-to-earnings ratio. This is the ratio of a company's stock price to its earnings-per-share. The higher the P/E ratio, the more expensive a stock is (and the faster investors believe the company will grow). Stocks in fast-growing industries tend to have higher P/E ratios.

Passive investor: Relies on diversification to match the performance of a stock market index (e.g., the S&P 500 Index or the the Wilshire 4500 Completion Index). Because a passive portfolio strategy involves matching an index, this strategy is commonly referred to as indexing.

Pit traders: Traders who are positioned on the floor of stock and commodity exchanges (as opposed to floor traders, situated in investment bank offices).

Pitchbook: The book of exhibits, graphs and initial recommendations presented by bankers to prospective clients when trying to land an engagement.

Prime rate: The base rate U.S. banks use to price loans for their best customers.

Private accountants. Accountants who work for businesses, as well as government agencies, and other non-profit organizations.

Producer Price Index: The PPI measures the percentage increase in a standard basket of goods and services. PPI is a measure of inflation for producers and manufacturers.

Proprietary trading: Trading of the firm's own assets (as opposed to trading client assets).

Prospectus: A report issued by a company (filed with and approved by the SEC) that wishes to sell securities to investors. Distributed to prospective investors, the prospectus discloses the company's financial position, business description and risk factors.

Public accountants. Accountants who offer services to the general public on a fee basis including auditing, tax work and management consulting.

Request For Proposal (RFP): Statement issued by institutions (i.e., pension funds or corporate retirement plans) when they are looking to hire a new investment manager. They typical detail the style of money management required and the types of credentials needed.

Retail clients: Individual investors (as opposed to institutional clients).

Return on equity: The ratio of a firm's profits to the value of its equity. Return on equity, or ROE, is a commonly used measure of how well an investment bank is doing, because it measures how efficiently and profitably the firm is using its capital.

Roadshow: The series of presentations to investors that a company undergoing an IPO usually gives in the weeks preceding the offering. Here's how it works: The company and its investment bank will travel to major cities throughout the country. In each city, the company's top executives make a presentation to analysts, mutual fund managers and other attendees and also answer questions.

S-1: A type of legal document filed with the SEC for a private company aiming to go public. The S-1 is almost identical to the prospectus sent to potential investors. The SEC must approve the S-1 before the stock can be sold to investors.

S-2: A type of legal document filed with the SEC for a public company looking to sell additional shares in the market. The S-2 is almost identical to the prospectus sent to potential investors. The SEC must approve the S-2 before the stock is sold.

Sales memo: Short reports written by the corporate finance bankers and distributed to the bank's salespeople. The sales memo provides salespeople with points to emphasize when hawking the stocks and bonds the firm is underwriting.

Securities and Exchange Commission (SEC): A federal agency that, like the Glass-Steagall Act, was established as a result of the stock market crash of 1929 and the ensuing depression. The SEC monitors disclosure of financial information to stockholders and protects against fraud. Publicly traded securities must be approved by the SEC prior to trading.

Short-term debt: A bond that matures in nine months or less. Also called commercial paper.

Specialty firm: An investment management firm that focus on one type of style, product or client type.

Syndicate: A group of investment banks that together will underwrite a particular stock or debt offering. Usually the lead manager will underwrite the bulk of a deal, while other members of the syndicate will each underwrite a small portion.

T-Bill Yields: The yield or internal rate of return an investor would receive at any given moment on a 90-120 government treasury bill.

Tax-exempt bonds: Municipal bonds (also known as munis). Munis are free from federal taxes and, sometimes, state and local taxes.

10K: An annual report filed by a publicly traded company with the SEC. Includes financial information, company information, risk factors, etc.

10Q: Similar to a 10K, but filed quarterly.

Treasury Securities: Securities issued by the U.S. government. These are divided into Treasury Bills (maturity of up to two years), Treasury Notes (from two years to 10 years maturity), and Treasury Bonds (10 years to 30 years). As they are government guaranteed, treasuries are often considered risk-free. In fact, while U.S. Treasuries have no default risk, they do have interest rate risk; if rates increase, then the price of U.S. Treasuries will decrease.

Underwrite: The function performed by investment banks when they help companies issue securities to investors. Technically, the investment bank buys the securities from the company and immediately resells the securities to investors for a slightly higher price, making money on the spread.

Value stock: Well-established, high dividend paying companies with low price to earnings and price to book ratios. Essentially, they are "diamonds in the rough" that typically have undervalued assets and earnings potential. Classic value stocks include oil companies like ExxonMobil and banks such as BankAmerica or J.P. Morgan Chase.

Yield: The annual return on investment. A high yield bond, for example, pays a high rate of interest.

Recommended Reading

Suggested Texts

Burrough, Bryan and Helyar, John. *Barbarians at the Gate: The Fall of RJR Nabisco*. New York: Harper & Row, 1990.

Chernow, Ron, *The House of Morgan: An American Banking Dynasty and the Rise of Modern Finance*. New York: Atlantic Monthly Press, 1990.

Endlich, Lisa. *Goldman Sachs: The Culture of Success*. New York: Alfred A. Knopf, 1999.

Gordon, John Steele, *The Great Game: The Emergence of Wall Street As a World Power*. 1653-2000. New York: Scribner, 1999.

Josephson, Matthew, *The Robber Barons*. New York: Harcourt, Brace, and Company, 1962.

Lewis, Michael. *Liar's Poker*. New York: Norton, 1989.

Lewis, Michael. *The Money Culture*. New York: W. W. Norton, 1991.

Rolfe, John and Traub, Peter. *Monkey Business: Swinging Through the Wall Street Jungle*. New York: Warner Books, 2000.

Stewart, James Brewer. *Den of Thieves*. New York: Simon and Schuster, 1991.

Suggested Periodicals

- Accountancy Age
- American Banker
- Business Week
- The Daily Deal
- The Economist
- Forbes
- Fortune
- Institutional Investor
- Investment Dealers' Digest
- Investor's Business Daily
- The Wall Street Journal

About the Authors

Chris Prior is the finance editor at Vault. He graduated from Queens College of the City University of New York. Before joining Vault, Chris was a staff reporter at *Treasury and Risk Management Magazine*, a financial trade publication based in New York.

Derek Loosvelt is a graduate of the Wharton School at the University of Pennsylvania. He is a writer and editor and has worked for *Brill's Content*, Inside.com and *blue* magazine. Previously, he worked in investment banking at CIBC and Duff & Phelps.